HOUSEHOLD
Hints & Tips

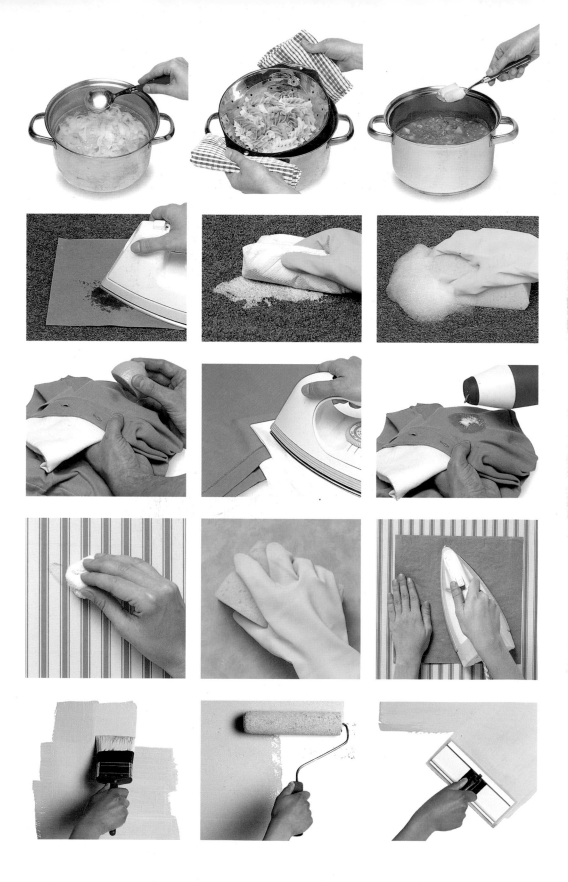

RAP 359 1346'

A DK PUBLISHING BOOK

Project Editor Victoria Sorzano
Project Art Editor Jayne Carter
Designer Darren Hill
Senior Editor Stephanie Jackson
Managing Art Editor Nigel Duffield
Senior Managing Editor Krystyna Mayer
Senior Managing Art Editor Lynne Brown
Production Sarah Coltman
US Editor Laaren Brown

First American Edition, 1996
2 4 6 8 10 9 7 5 3 1
First published in the United States by
DK Publishing, Inc.
95 Madison Avenue
New York, New York, 10016

Copyright © 1996
Dorling Kindersley Limited, London

Library of Congress
Cataloging-in-Publication Data

Kent, Cassandra
Household hints and tips / by Cassandra Kent
p.   cm.
Includes index.
ISBN 0-7894-0432-X
1. Home economics.   I. Title
TX159.K46 1996   95-30089
640—dc20   CIP

Color reproduced by Chroma Graphics, Singapore.
Printed and bound in Italy by Graphicom.

CONTENTS

INTRODUCTION 6

HOUSE CLEANING 10

STAIN REMOVAL 32

CLOTHES & LAUNDRY 56

HOUSEHOLD
Hints & Tips

Cassandra Kent

Introduction

THE KEY TO RUNNING A HOME well is organization. Keep clutter to a minimum, establish a cleaning routine that you can live with, and make time for regular repairs and maintenance. This book is filled with common-sense solutions, expert advice, and traditional tips that will help you do these things quickly and easily – so that you have more time to enjoy yourself at home.

USING THIS BOOK

KEEPING A CLEAN HOME

The first three chapters cover every aspect of keeping a home clean – from how to care for different types of floor surface, to how to remove red-wine stains. House Cleaning describes the correct procedures for cleaning the different surfaces and rooms in your home. Clothes and Laundry demystifies washing instructions and procedures, and offers useful advice on caring for clothes, shoes, and accessories. Stain Removal is a complete step-by-step full-color guide that shows you exactly how to remove even the most stubborn mark from every type of surface.

How to remove stains
To find out what to do (and what not to do) to remove stains from clothes, furniture, and carpets, see pages 32–55.

REPAIRS AND RESCUES

Most well-run homes require a little more attention than simple cleaning. Care and Repair describes how to care for various objects and how to repair them if they get broken. Home Improvements features tips on performing decorating tasks quickly and efficiently, and Home Maintenance guides you through the home, pinpointing all the areas where things could go wrong and detailing the appropriate action in case they do. Accidents and emergencies occur even in the best-run homes, and it is vital to know how to deal with them. Health and Safety features life-saving techniques and treatments for injuries and ailments of every description.

Perfect painting
For tips on painting walls, and ceilings, wallpapering rooms, and caring for tools, see pages 88–105.

HOMEMAKING MADE EASY

There is more to homemaking than cleaning and maintenance. For most people, cooking – whether it is a pleasure or a chore – is a major feature of home life. Food and Drink offers hundreds of tips on solving common kitchen problems, storing food, cooking meat and vegetables, and baking perfect cakes and pastry. Housekeeping provides short cuts and advice on specialized homemaking skills such as sewing, flower arranging, caring for plants and pets, and entertaining. Finally, the comprehensive index and chapter-by-chapter color coding make it easy to find tips throughout the book.

Flower care
Knowing how to care for cut flowers can prolong their life. See page 147 for the relevant details.

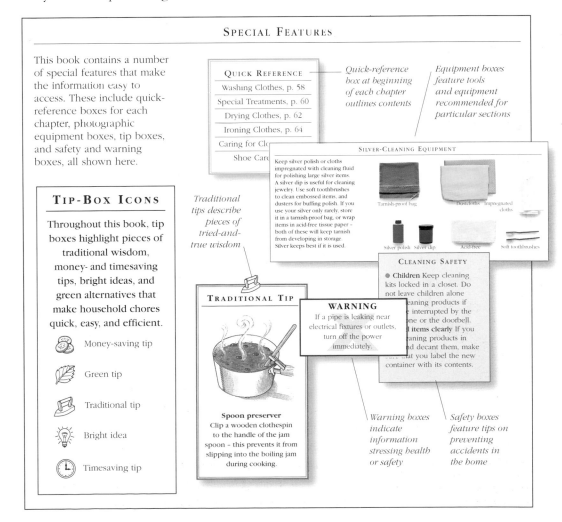

SPECIAL FEATURES

This book contains a number of special features that make the information easy to access. These include quick-reference boxes for each chapter, photographic equipment boxes, tip boxes, and safety and warning boxes, all shown here.

QUICK REFERENCE
Washing Clothes, p. 58
Special Treatments, p. 60
Drying Clothes, p. 62
Ironing Clothes, p. 64
Caring for Clo
Shoe Care

Quick-reference box at beginning of each chapter outlines contents

Equipment boxes feature tools and equipment recommended for particular sections

SILVER-CLEANING EQUIPMENT

Keep silver polish or cloths impregnated with cleaning fluid for polishing large silver items. A silver dip is useful for cleaning jewelry. Use soft toothbrushes to clean embossed items, and dusters for buffing polish. If you use your silver only rarely, store it in a tarnish-proof bag, or wrap items in acid-free tissue paper – both of these will keep tarnish from developing in storage. Silver keeps best if it is used.

Tarnish-proof bag
Dustcloths Impregnated cloths
Silver polish Silver dip Acid-free Soft toothbrushes

TIP-BOX ICONS

Throughout this book, tip boxes highlight pieces of traditional wisdom, money- and timesaving tips, bright ideas, and green alternatives that make household chores quick, easy, and efficient.

Money-saving tip

Green tip

Traditional tip

Bright idea

Timesaving tip

Traditional tips describe pieces of tried-and-true wisdom

TRADITIONAL TIP

Spoon preserver
Clip a wooden clothespin to the handle of the jam spoon – this prevents it from slipping into the boiling jam during cooking.

WARNING
If a pipe is leaking near electrical fixtures or outlets, turn off the power immediately.

CLEANING SAFETY

● **Children** Keep cleaning kits locked in a closet. Do not leave children alone [with] cleaning products if [you are] interrupted by the [teleph]one or the doorbell. [Labe]l items clearly If you [buy cl]eaning products in [bulk an]d decant them, make [sure th]at you label the new container with its contents.

Warning boxes indicate information stressing health or safety

Safety boxes feature tips on preventing accidents in the home

MAKING LISTS

Lists help you get things done efficiently, without wasting time through forgetfulness. Make a master list of food and household items that you shop for regularly, and add or delete entries before each shopping trip (see right). Keep the master in your home log book (see opposite) and make copies to be stuck on the refrigerator door. Every year, write down the dates of birthdays on a large calender and add social events, holidays, and appointments. Have the whole household use the calendar to communicate their plans. Lists can also be used to plan your tasks for the week, prepare for holidays, and organize parties.

Shopping lists
Keep a copy of your general shopping list stuck to your refrigerator door, and cross off items as they run out.

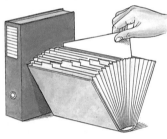

Home office
Set up a filing system for your important paperwork, so that you can access documents easily when you need them.

PLANNING YOUR TIME

If you have a busy household, approach managing it almost like running an office. Set aside a regular time each week to deal with correspondence and bills and to plan your chores and appointments for the week ahead. When scheduling tasks, allow yourself extra time for traveling, lines at checkout counters, and traffic delays. Be sure to leave some free time for yourself each day, either to relax and enjoy yourself or to deal with any unexpected problems – you never know when a child may need to talk or a friend may need your help.

ATTACKING HOUSEHOLD CLUTTER

Nothing makes a home seem as disorganized as unnecessary clutter. Go through your home periodically and dispose of things you do not need. These may include clothes you never wear, old magazines, and broken toys and gadgets. To dispose of undamaged items, hold a garage sale, or donate the items to a charity. Cut down on clutter by placing shelves near the front door, and by allocating a shelf to each family member. They can leave frequently used items here when they come in, and they will always be able to find them easily when they are about to go out again.

Personalized shelves
Family members can leave much-used items such as toys, umbrellas, and boots on their shelf near the door.

MAKING A HOME LOG BOOK

A home log book is useful for keeping all the information about your home in one easily accessible place. It is particularly handy for details that will slip away over a period of time – such as the telephone number of a certain repair service, or the solvents used to remove a particular stain. Use several notebooks, or a ring binder, to create a system to suit you. It helps if there is scope to add or remove pages, and also to include things like fabric or paint swatches. Dedicate a part of the log book to the items in your home: make a household inventory – this will prove invaluable if you have a fire or a theft. Keep a copy of all guarantees, instruction booklets, and the dates of purchase of major items in this section.

A master diary of important dates and events is another vital part of your home log book.

Making a log book
Ring binders make ideal log books because they allow you to add and remove pages easily. Alternatively, use notebooks, one for each different area of your home life.

ADDITIONAL INFORMATION

Most homes require regular maintenance, so keep a note of what repairs were done when, as well as any details about decoration (see p. 99). You may wish to dedicate a section to health, with a list of emergency telephone numbers (see p. 165) and a record of every visit made to a doctor by a family member. A section devoted to local services and information is also useful – consult it as a guide to cab companies, local takeouts, or library hours. Keep your log book in a sensible place where it is close at hand, and make sure that all members of the household know where it is.

HOME LOG BOOK CONTENTS

The sections below are a rough guide to what a home log book could contain.

HOUSEHOLD DIARY
● Keep a list of dates such as birthdays, school terms, inoculations, and dates when things like insurance have to be paid. Update it each year, and transfer it to a calendar.

HOUSEHOLD INVENTORY
● List all valuable household items, and serial numbers where applicable. Take photographs of valuable items (see p. 119).
● Keep copies of guarantees, instruction booklets, and records of dates of purchase. If instruction booklets prove too bulky, keep them in a separate folder.

HOME MAINTENANCE AND DECORATING
● See page 99 for what to include in a decorating log.
● Note the names, addresses, and telephone numbers of anyone you employed for repairs or decorating.
● Write down where there are electrical cables, central-heating pipes, and any other items that might cause problems when decorating.

OTHER INTERESTS
● If you entertain frequently, make a record of the guests you invited to each gathering and the food that was served.
● Gardeners can set up gardening logs that contain essential planting details.
● Set up a car log with details such as insurance policy numbers, dates of repairs, and tire pressures.
● Keep a cleaning file to record how you removed stains from items (see p. 11).

HOUSE CLEANING

CLEANING DOES NOT HAVE TO BE hard work if you follow a few basic rules. Invest in the right equipment, and take care of it. Dusting is the key to a clean home, so keep that task on your regular agenda. Sensible use of the vacuum cleaner and all its attachments makes light work of many chores, not just cleaning carpets. There is no need to be obsessive; a home need not be squeaky clean to look good.

HOUSE-CLEANING EQUIPMENT

These are the essential items you will need for keeping your home clean. Buy a plastic storage box with a handle, which you can use for carrying equipment around. If your home has lots of stairs, consider investing in two sets of cleaning tools to avoid carrying them. Clean all equipment after use.

Household dustcloths

Chamois leather

Dustpan and brush

Sponge mop

Rubber gloves

Acrylic dusting brush

Cloths for wet work

Scrubbing brush

Floor-cleaning cloth

Bucket

Long-handled broom

HOUSE-CLEANING MATERIALS

Nowadays, there is a product to clean almost everything in your home. Although manufacturers would like you to believe that their products are essential, all you need are some key items. A cleaning kit that contains dishwashing liquid, nonabrasive and abrasive household detergent, detergent with enzymes, furniture polish, and metal polish will maintain all the surfaces in your home.

Household bleach   Cream cleaner   Spray cleaner   Furniture polish   Ammonia

EXTRA ITEMS

- **For specific marks** Ammonia, household bleach, rubbing alcohol, laundry borax, washing soda, and turpentine are useful for cleaning particular surfaces, and for removing difficult stains. Keep them away from children.
- **From the kitchen** Salt, lemon juice, glycerin, white vinegar, and baking soda can be used as gentle, environmentally friendly household cleaners.
- **Specialized cleaners** Buy TSP for washing down very dirty walls. Keep a supply of leather food for feeding and protecting leather furniture.

Denatured alcohol (dyed)   Denatured alcohol   Liquid cleaner   Turpentine   Dishwashing liquid

Laundry borax   Floor and wall cleaner   Detergent with enzymes   Washing soda   Metal polish

MAKING RECORDS

- **A cleaning file** Make a record of how you cleaned special items, and what you used, to avoid trial and error the next time. Keep this file in your home log book (see p. 8–9).

Baking soda   Salt   Lemon juice   Glycerin   White vinegar

CLEANING AND SAFETY

- **Keep children safe** Keep your cleaning kit locked away in a closet. Do not leave children alone with cleaning products if you are interrupted by the telephone or the doorbell.
- **Label items clearly** If you buy products in bulk and decant them, make sure you label the new container clearly with its contents.

- **Protect your skin** Wear rubber gloves if you are using strong household cleaners. Avoid contact with skin, eyes, and clothes when using bleach or ammonia.
- **Beware of fumes** Open windows in the rooms you are cleaning (if possible) to provide ventilation. Avoid open flames, as they may cause chemicals to ignite.

- **Do not mix cleaners** Some chemicals react adversely when mixed. If a cleaning product has not worked on a surface, rinse it off before using another cleaner.
- **Watch your step** If you are cleaning hard-to-reach places, always stand on a ladder or stepstool. Standing on a chair or table is dangerous, and could cause an accident.

GENERAL CLEANING

Lᴵᴛᴛʟᴇ ᴀɴᴅ ᴏꜰᴛᴇɴ is the best way to keep your home clean. If you leave things for weeks, you will find yourself with a major chore on your hands. Clean living rooms once a week; sinks and kitchen surfaces should be cleaned daily.

MAINTAINING EQUIPMENT

Kᴇᴇᴘ your equipment in good condition; otherwise, you will have to spend extra time getting it back into shape. Always clean equipment before you put it away, and store items properly. Wash cleaning rags regularly, and discard any that are too dirty to reuse.

STORING EQUIPMENT

Tie plastic bag with string

Store used pads in soapy water

Use half a pad at a time

Broom care
Wash brooms in soapy water from time to time. Store upside down to prevent the bristles from bending – you can make a rack using two thread spools.

Sponge mops
Rinse floor mops thoroughly after use (they should not need any extra washing). Store the heads in plastic bags so that they do not dry out and warp.

Steel-wool pads
Keep steel-wool pads in soapy water to stop them from rusting, or wrap them in aluminum foil. Save money by cutting them in half so that they go twice as far.

CLOTHS AND SPONGES
● **Cleaning and storage** Shake dustcloths well in the yard or out of a window after you have used them. Soak slimy sponges in vinegar and water. Store dustcloths and polishing cloths in plastic bags.

CHAMOIS LEATHERS
● **General care** Chamois leathers are expensive, but will last for years if well cared for. Wash in warm, soapy water, and rinse thoroughly. Let dry away from direct heat to preserve the skin's natural oils.

BRUSHES
● **Using toothbrushes** Old toothbrushes are perfect tools for cleaning intricate metal-work, grouting, around taps, and awkward spaces. Save as many as you can, and keep them in your cleaning kit.

VACUUM CLEANERS

Use your vacuum cleaner for as many tasks as possible. The range of attachments can be used to clean curtains, furniture, and upholstery, as well as floors. Check the brushes and rollers before you start vacuuming – the machine will not work well if it is clogged up. A range of vacuum cleaners is available for carrying out different tasks. Handheld vacuum cleaners are ideal for cars and for cleaning up spills.

● **Upright vacuum cleaners**
These are best for covering large areas of floor, but they cannot always get under furniture or into awkward corners.
● **Cylinder vacuum cleaners**
These are good for cleaning awkward areas, such as stairs and under low furniture, but can be cumbersome to use.
● **Wet-and-dry vacuum cleaners**
These suck up water as well as doing routine cleaning.

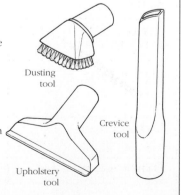
Dusting tool
Crevice tool
Upholstery tool

METHODS AND ROUTINES

Establish and maintain a cleaning routine so that all areas of your home receive regular attention and the work does not pile up. Use these tips to get around rooms ef make your home appear tidy – eve know it is not as clean as it could b

CLEANING METHODS

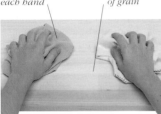

Grasp a clean dustcloth in each hand

Dust in direction of grain

Two-handed dusting
Using two dustcloths – one in each hand – will help you clean the surfaces in a room in half the time and with half the effort.

Two-bucket method
Wash floors and walls using two buckets: fill one with cleaning solution, and the other with water for rinsing the sponge or mop.

TIMESAVING TIP

Cleaning in a hurry
If visitors are coming and you are unprepared, make do with cleaning the hallway, tidying obvious clutter, and throwing away dead flowers. Straighten cushions, chairs, and rugs to create the impression of order. Spray room freshener and dim the lighting or use candlelight.

TIMESAVING DUSTCLOTH

Place dustcloth in kerosene and vinegar

Wear gloves to protect your hands

1 To create a dustcloth that leaves a shine, soak a dustcloth in oil with a few drops of lemon oil added.

2 Remove the dustcloth when it is fully saturated and squeeze dry. Store it in a screwtop jar. Buff to finish.

CLEANING ROUTINES
● **Daily cleaning** Kitchens and bathrooms should be cleaned daily (see p. 24–30).
● **Regular cleaning** Bedrooms and living rooms should be cleaned weekly. Begin by ventilating the room and tidying up. Starting at one side of a door, dust all items and surfaces, working around the whole room. Always dust higher surfaces first, since some dust may fall onto lower surfaces. Finally, vacuum or sweep the floor.
● **Occasional cleaning** Every few months, give all rooms a thorough going over. Take down curtains for cleaning, shampoo upholstery and carpets, and clean walls and windows. Tidy up closets, and dispose of any items that you no longer use.

ROOMS	CLEANING FREQUENCY
BATHROOMS AND KITCHENS	Clean these rooms daily to maintain good hygiene.
BEDROOMS	Air beds each morning, as we lose 1 cup (250 ml) of moisture every night. Clean rooms weekly.
LIVING ROOMS	Clean once a week. Vacuum floors twice a week if necessary.
OTHER AREAS	Vacuum halls twice a week. Clean little-used rooms monthly.

FLOORS

IRT IS TRANSMITTED TO FLOORS from outdoors, so lay a doormat inside all exterior doors to remove dirt from shoes. If you keep floors clean by sweeping or vacuuming regularly, you will cut down on heavy-duty cleaning.

CLEANING HARD FLOORS

Hard floors that are dusty look dirtier than unvacuumed carpets. Sweep, vacuum, or mop them regularly – particularly hallway, kitchen, and bathroom floors. Wood floors need polishing; marble, vinyl, and tile floors require heavy-duty cleaning from time to time.

SWEEPING FLOORS

Removing dust
Sweep or vacuum hard floors every few days, paying special attention to corners, where dirt collects and builds up.

MOPPING FLOORS

Effective mopping
Damp mop all sealed floors weekly, using the two-bucket method. Do not use soap when mopping slate or stone floors.

SCRUBBING FLOORS

Heavy-duty washing
Scrub stone, concrete, and tile floors with floor cleaner and a scrub brush occasionally to get rid of accumulated dirt.

POLISHING FLOORS

Give floors a good shine, and your home will look well cared for. Use the right type of polish for your floor, and remember that polish builds up and will need to be removed from time to time. Use floor cleaner, ammonia, or commercial wax remover to remove polish.

TYPES OF POLISH

SOLID PASTE POLISHES
These solvent-based polishes are suitable for vinyl, wood, and cork. Application is difficult and must be done by hand, but the shine lasts a long time.

LIQUID SOLVENT POLISHES
These are also suitable for vinyl, wood, and cork. They are easier to use than solid paste polish, but they are not as long lasting.

WATER-BASED EMULSION POLISHES
These usually contain silicone. They can be used on all floors except linoleum, unsealed wood, and cork. They are easy to apply and long lasting.

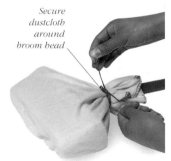

Secure dustcloth around broom head

Improvised polisher
Tie a dustcloth around a soft broom, and use this instead of an electric polisher to apply and buff wax polish. Always clean floors thoroughly before you apply polish for the first time.

TYPES OF FLOORING

Hard floors can take a lot of heavy wear, but different types of surface need varying amounts of attention. Sweep hard floors daily if necessary, and clean them according to their type. Do not let dirt build up so that cleaning becomes a hands-and-knees job.

TYPE	TREATMENT
VINYL An easy-care floor covering that lasts well if cared for correctly.	● Sweep regularly. When dirty, wash vinyl with a solution of household detergent and warm water. Rinse with clear water. Apply a water-based polish, but do not allow it to build up. ● Never use a solvent-based polish on vinyl; it can destroy the surface. Remove stubborn marks with a little emulsion polish on a damp cloth.
LINOLEUM A tough flooring, but take care not to overwet, because this can cause damage.	● Wipe linoleum floors with a mop dampened in a weak solution of water and household detergent. Use a water-based polish – which will not leave a watermark – on kitchen and bathroom floors, and a wax polish on floors elsewhere in the home. ● Remove scuff marks by rubbing with fine-grade steel wool dipped in turpentine.
WOOD Treatment depends on whether or not the wood is sealed.	● Sweep or dry mop unsealed floors regularly to remove dust and dirt. Clean sealed wood floors with a mop dampened and wrung out. To give the floor a shine, polish with wax or emulsion polish. ● Use a damp cloth to remove sticky marks on unsealed floors. Remove wax polish from sealed wood floors with a cloth and turpentine.
CORK Needs regular sweeping. Make sure you do not overwet cork while mopping or it will crack.	● Mop regularly with a solution of warm water and household detergent, and apply wax polish occasionally. Try to avoid a buildup of polish around the edges of the room as this eventually results in a sticky deposit that attracts dirt. ● When laying cork tiles, ensure that the edges are sealed to stop water seeping in from the sides.
CERAMIC TILES This surface is as hard as nails, so anything dropped on it will break. Be careful.	● Clean with a solution of dishwashing liquid applied with a sponge mop or a cloth, then wipe over with a chamois leather. Mop up spills immediately – wet floors are dangerously slippery. ● Do not polish ceramic tiles, since this will make them slippery. Clean grouting with a soft-bristled brush dipped in a strong solution of detergent.
QUARRY TILES Pretty, but porous unless sealed. Rub faded tiles with steel wool and turpentine, then apply colored solid paste polish.	● Glazed quarry tiles need mopping regularly with water and a little general-purpose cleaner. Scrub unglazed quarry tiles with this solution to remove dirt. Rinse thoroughly. Polish with liquid or solid paste polish, preferably nonskid. ● Treat newly laid tiles with linseed oil. Do not wash them for at least two weeks afterward.

SPECIAL FLOOR TREATMENTS

Avoid scuffing or scratching hard floors, because these marks can be difficult to remove. Polish the rockers on rocking chairs to prevent them from scratching floors, and slip small mats underneath furniture when moving heavy pieces across a room.

REMOVING STAINS FROM WOOD FLOORS

● **Ink stains** Treat ink stains by dabbing them with household bleach, applied on a cotton swab. Blot quickly with paper towels, and repeat if necessary.

● **Candle wax** Harden spilled candle wax with an ice cube, then ease off the wax with a blunt knife. Rub in a little liquid floor polish, then buff well, using a soft cloth.

REMOVING SCRATCHES FROM WOOD FLOORS

Rub scratch gently

1 Rub the scratch with fine steel wool. Be careful not to spread the rubbed area any farther than necessary. Wear gloves when using steel wool.

2 Mix a little brown shoe polish with floor wax, and apply the mixture to the area. Rub in well, so that it blends with the rest of the floor.

REPAIRS TO FLOORS

● **Vinyl and cork** Remove burn marks by rubbing with fine sandpaper. If a burn is very noticeable, cut out the damaged part with a craft knife and insert a new piece.

● **Linoleum** These floors tend to crack with age. Cover any cracks with clear packing tape, then apply a coat of clear polyurethane varnish.

● **Broken tiles** Repair holes in tiles with wall or wood filler. Apply the filler slightly higher than the floor, and sand down when dry. Apply color (shoe polish or artist's oils), then finish with clear floor seal.

● **Wood floors** Where a wet basement is causing rising dampness, a fairly easy solution is to lift the flooring and paint the concrete subfloor with a special waterproof coating.

QUARRY TILES

● **Restoring color** If color has faded, remove any old polish with steel wool and turpentine. Wash, rinse, and apply pigmented wax polish when dry. Buff well to make sure that the polish is not picked up on shoes.

Treating white patches
These are caused by lime in the subfloor and will disappear eventually. Hasten the processs by washing with a solution of 4 tbsp (60 ml) vinegar to 5 quarts (5 liters) water. Do not rinse.

VINYL AND LINOLEUM

● **Paint stains** Remove fresh latex by rubbing with a damp cloth. Rub fresh oil-based paint stains with steel wool dipped in solid paste polish. Saturate dried paint stains with boiled linseed oil. Let stand, then wipe off.

Wear gloves when using strong chemicals

Scuff marks on vinyl
Remove scuff marks on vinyl floors with turpentine applied on a cloth. A pencil eraser may also do the trick, or try rubbing the mark with a cloth dipped in water-based polish.

FLOOR COVERINGS

Carpets and rugs are among the most expensive items of room decoration, so take care of them to make them last. Always follow care instructions given by the carpet manufacturer to ensure that your carpet stays in good condition for as long as possible.

CLEANING CARPETS

● **Vacuuming** Vacuum regularly to remove dust and dirt, and keep the pile in good condition. Ideally, go over each area eight times – but fewer will do if you are in a hurry. Take advantage of all the attachments to clean around the edges of each room and under low furniture.

● **Shampooing** Apply carpet shampoo by hand to dirty patches. If the whole carpet is dirty, shampoo it using a machine, or call a professional cleaner. Shampoo wall-to-wall carpets in place – they may shrink if you take them up and wet them, and you will have to pay for relaying the carpet.

GREEN TIP

Dry shampoo
To freshen your carpet cheaply and ecologically, liberally sprinkle baking soda all over it. Leave for 15 minutes, then vacuum thoroughly. Not only will your carpet be clean, you will have discouraged pests and neutralized odors.

FURNITURE MARKS ON CARPETS

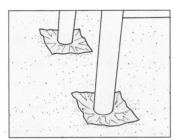

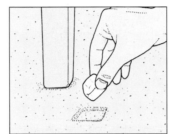

Damp carpets
If you need to replace furniture before a recently shampooed carpet is fully dry, place squares of foil beneath the furniture legs to prevent the furniture from marking the carpet.

Raising crushed pile
To raise indentations in carpets caused by the weight of heavy furniture, place an ice cube in the dent, and let the ice cube melt. Let the area dry naturally, then vacuum.

RUGS AND MATS

● **Cleaning** Take rugs outside and beat with a carpet beater or an old tennis racket. Vacuum natural floor coverings (rush, sisal, coconut matting); when dirty, scrub with salty water, rinse, then let dry away from direct heat.

HOUSEHOLD PESTS AND SMELLS

Carpets and rugs are susceptible to pests such as carpet beetles, and they also pick up and hold smells from cigarette smoke, frying food, and pets.

● **Carpet beetles** A telltale sign of carpet beetles is their shed skins, usually around carpet edges. These pests are difficult to eradicate because they get into well-hidden places. Kill as many as you can by sprinkling laundry borax around the carpet edges, and also over the padding before a new carpet is laid.

● **Cigarette smoke** The smell of smoke lingers in carpets and upholstery. Put a bowl of water in a discreet place if you are expecting smoking visitors. Lighting candles also helps. Cover the bottoms of ashtrays with baking soda to prevent butts from smoldering.
● **Vinegar air freshener** A small container of vinegar left in any room of the house keeps the room smelling fresh, even if the house is closed for a while. Add vinegar to the water in humidifiers occasionally – it will keep the air fresher.

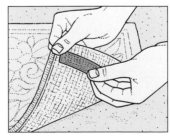

Creeping rugs
Prevent rugs from sliding around on hard floor surfaces by sticking pieces of heavy-duty double-sided tape around the edges. Use pieces of Velcro to prevent rugs from creeping on carpet.

WALLS AND CEILINGS

Unless you live in a heavily polluted area or have a houseful of smokers, you do not need to clean your walls and ceilings more than once a year. Do not tackle more than a room at a time – this task is physically demanding.

WALL COVERINGS

Dust nonwashable wallpaper regularly to prevent dirt from building up. Never use water because it will loosen the paper from the wall. Sponge washable wall coverings with a dishwashing liquid solution, working from bottom to top. Rinse clean with warm water.

CLEANING NONWASHABLE WALLPAPER

Removing marks
Rub marks with a scrunched up piece of crustless white bread, or an eraser. Rub gently to avoid damaging the wall covering – it may take several attempts before the marks begin to disappear.

Removing grease marks
Apply a warm (not hot) iron over brown paper to absorb grease marks. Repeat using clean parts of the brown paper until all the grease is absorbed, then apply an aerosol grease solvent.

CLEANING VINYL

General care
Wash vinyl wall coverings occasionally, using a detergent solution applied on a sponge. Start from the bottom and work your way up, and rub gently so as not to damage the surface.

PATCHING WALLPAPER

1 Badly marked wallpaper may need to be patched rather than cleaned. Tear a matching piece, pulling away from you as you tear to create an uneven edge (which will show up less obviously than a cut edge).

2 Stick the new patch into position with wallpaper paste, making sure that the pattern matches. If you are patching old wallpaper, leave the new piece in the sun to fade for a few days before patching.

SPECIALTY WALL COVERINGS

● **Grasscloth** Clean carefully, since the grasses can come loose very easily. Simply dusting is sufficient – use a soft-brush vacuum-cleaner attachment on low suction. Be careful not to place furniture against grasscloth; it may rub the grasses loose and leave unsightly marks.
● **Burlap paper** Dust regularly, using a vacuum-cleaner attachment. Dyes in burlap paper tend to run, so do not wet. Remove marks by rubbing with a piece of crustless white bread.

PAINTED SURFACES

Painted walls and ceilings can be kept in good condition for a long time with regular cleaning. But marks such as heavy tobacco stains can be difficult to eradicate. If this is a problem, redecorating may be a better solution than trying to scrub off the stains.

CEILINGS

● **Cleaning** Do not wash ceilings – a fresh coat of paint is more effective. Dust with the improvised duster shown below, a long-handled brush, or the upholstery attachment on your vacuum cleaner.

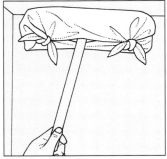

Making a ceiling duster
Tie a clean dustcloth loosely around a broom head, and use to dust ceilings thoroughly from time to time. Remember to give the broom a shake at intervals.

WALLS, DOORS, AND TRIMMINGS

● **Cleaning walls** Use a warm solution of dishwashing liquid to clean walls. Do not stop in the middle of cleaning – you will create a tidemark that is difficult to remove. Wash one wall at a time completely.

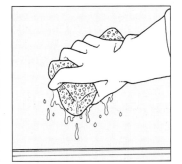

Wall-washing method
Always start at the bottom of a wall and work upward. This may sound like extra work, but it is easier to wipe dirty trickles off a clean surface than off a dirty one.

● **Very dirty walls** Clean with a solution of TSP (follow the manufacturer's instructions for strength of dilution) before using other cleaners.
● **Doors and baseboards** Wash with a solution of dishwashing liquid (not detergent, which can affect paint color). Rinse with clear water, and pat dry.

MARKS ON WALLS

● **Tackling stains** Most marks come off painted walls, but treat them gently to avoid damaging the paintwork. Rub fingerprints and pencil marks gently with an eraser. Wash food stains off with undiluted nonabrasive household cleaner. Where furniture has bumped into a wall and left a mark, try rubbing it out with an eraser first, then apply household cleaner as above.

OTHER WALL TYPES

Ceramic tiles often show dirt in the grouting between the tiles. Wood-paneled walls need frequent dusting (you can use your vacuum cleaner for this) and polishing once a year. Marks on bare brickwork are difficult to remove, so dust these walls frequently.

CERAMIC TILE WALLS

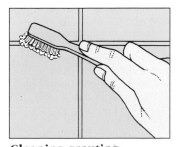

Cleaning grouting
Use an old, clean toothbrush dipped in a bleach solution to clean grouting between tiles. If the grout is filthy, it may be easier to apply new grouting.

WOOD PANELING

Removing polish
When the polish on wood walls builds up, remove it using fine steel wool and turpentine. Rub gently but firmly, following the direction of the grain.

BRICKWORK

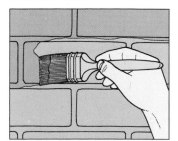

Sealing brick walls
Apply a sealer to bare brickwork so that the brickwork will just require dusting and damp wiping. Use a soft paintbrush, and make sure the wall is clean.

WINDOWS

Dirty windows spoil the look of a home. Clean the outsides as often as necessary, depending on the area in which you live, and wash the insides two or three times a year. Do not forget to dust windows when you clean each room. Use a soft acrylic brush.

WASHING WINDOWS

Homemade cleaner
Make your own solution for washing windows by adding vinegar to water in a plant-spray bottle. Vinegar cuts grease, and brings out the good shine.

WIPING WINDOWS

Using newspaper
Wipe newly washed windows clean with crumpled newspaper. This is a cheap alternative to a chamois leather, and the ink will give the glass an extra shine.

TIMESAVING TIP

Protecting curtains
To avoid removing curtains when cleaning windows, loop them over a hanger.

SMEAR-FREE WINDOW CLEANING

● **Window-washing weather**
Wash windows on cloudy days, when they are damp and every fingerprint and mark shows up. Sunny days are less ideal for window washing, since the windows dry too quickly, leaving smeary marks.

● **Smear finder** When cleaning the outside and inside of a window, use horizontal strokes on one side and vertical strokes on the other. This way you can easily tell which side of the window still has the odd smear left.

MIRRORS

When cleaning mirrors, avoid using water, which can trickle down behind the glass and damage the silvering. Instead, use a commercial glass cleaner, then buff the mirror well.

ELECTRIC FIXTURES

Clean plastic wall outlets and light switches by wiping them with denatured alcohol on a clean cloth. Metal fixtures need the appropriate metal polish. Lightbulbs should be dusted and cleaned regularly – dirty bulbs can reduce lighting efficiency by up to 50 percent.

CLEANING FIXTURES

● **Using templates** To avoid getting cleaner or polish on walls when cleaning fixtures, make a template that fits around the fixture, and hold it in place during cleaning.

WARNING

Turn off electricity before cleaning electrical fixtures. Do not clean lightbulbs while they are in their sockets.

CLEANING LIGHTS

● **Lightbulbs** Before removing a lightbulb for cleaning, switch off the electricity. If the light has been on, wait for the bulb to cool down. Dry it thoroughly before replacing. Never use water on a bulb that is still in its socket.
● **Scented bulbs** Wipe a little vanilla extract on the tops of lightbulbs with a soft cloth. When you turn on the lights, the scent will be released.

Swivel the bulb in the cloth

Cleaning lightbulbs
Hold lightbulbs by the base and carefully wipe over with a wrung-out damp cloth.

RADIATORS AND HEATERS

Clean radiators once a week in winter and less often when not in use. Wipe with a dishwashing liquid solution, and clean behind them with a vacuum-cleaner attachment or a radiator brush. Wipe heaters with a dishwashing liquid solution.

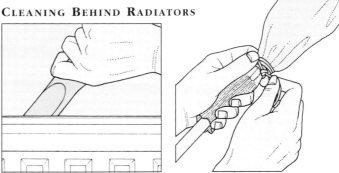

CARE AND UPKEEP
● **Heating and air vents** These attract dust, so make sure that you catch them before they become clogged up. A bottle brush is the best way to remove grime as it builds up.
● **Protecting flooring** Place a drop cloth under radiators during cleaning so dust and liquid do not fall on the floor.
● **Marks above radiators** Rising hot air creates marks on walls above radiators. Installing shelves above radiators will help prevent this and will also direct heat into the room.

CLEANING BEHIND RADIATORS

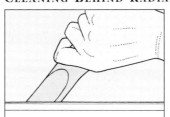

Vacuum cleaning
Use the crevice tool of your vacuum cleaner to either suck or blow accumulated dust from behind radiators.

Improvised brush
Cover a broom handle with a sponge, then an old sock. Use to clean behind radiators; change the sock when it gets dirty.

FIREPLACES

An open fire is very cheerful, but fireplaces will grow dirty with a buildup of soot unless you act before the soot becomes ingrained. (See page 54 for treatment of soot marks.) Clean the fire surround thoroughly as soon as the fireplace season is over.

CLEANING CHIMNEYS
● **Wood burning chimneys** Have chimneys that are used to burn wood swept twice as year, as residue resin from the wood may catch fire.

METAL PARTS
● **Polishing** To clean the metal on fireplaces, use blacking or a commercial cleaner.

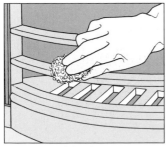

Applying blacking
Wearing gloves, apply blacking on a piece of steel wool. Polish the blacking with a soft cloth.

CLEARING GRATES
● **Removing ashes** Remove coal ashes weekly, but leave wood ashes in the grate – they will act as a good base for your fire all winter.

CLEANING SURROUNDS
● **Brick** Scrub well with a hard scrub brush and clean water. Sponge burn marks with vinegar, and rinse.
● **Ceramic tile** Wash with a solution of dishwashing liquid or household detergent, and rinse. Use a nonabrasive household cleaner on soot marks (see also p. 54).
● **Marble** Sponge with a soap flake solution, then rinse and dry with an old towel. If polished, use a product specially designed for marble. Products are also available for repairing damaged marble; see page 81 for treating stains.

DISPOSING OF ASHES
● **Hot embers** Always use a metal container when carrying ashes to the garbage bin, as any undetected hot embers will burn through plastic.

TRADITIONAL TIP

Making a scented fire
Throw pieces of dried citrus peel onto a fire to scent a room pleasantly. Pinecones have the same effect.

FURNISHINGS

T HE UBIQUITOUS VACUUM cleaner and its attachments are useful for keeping most furniture, upholstery, and window coverings free from dust. Always remove stains when they occur; save the deep cleaning for an annual event.

WOODEN FURNITURE

W ooden furniture can last for years, even centuries. Dust wood frequently, always working along the direction of the grain.

Be careful not to get unsealed wood wet; water will cause swelling. See pages 71–73 for special treatments for wooden furniture.

DUSTING WOOD

Carved wood
Dust with a synthetic fluffy duster. Rub the duster first to increase static collection. A soft paintbrush also works well.

EVERYDAY PIECES
● **Basic care** Clean wooden furniture with a detergent solution applied on a damp cloth. Rinse and buff to a shine. Occasionally, use an aerosol or pump polish.
● **Teak furniture** Modern teak furniture only needs dusting. Polish these items with teak oil or cream, used sparingly, once or twice a year.
● **Painted wood** Wipe with a solution of dishwashing liquid (unless fragile), then rinse with clear water, and dry. Use undiluted dishwashing liquid to remove marks.

VALUABLE PIECES
● **Antique furniture** Keep away from direct heat and sunlight, which cause damage. Dust regularly. Remove sticky marks with a little vinegar and water. Use a beeswax polish on antique furniture once or twice a year (see p. 71).
● **French-polished wood** Buff in the direction of the grain, using a soft dustcloth. Occasionally, use a wax polish and rub in well. Use a little turpentine to remove sticky marks and fingerprints. If the French polish is damaged, call a professional.

OTHER HARD FURNITURE

W icker and cane furniture require regular dusting with a brush or vacuum-cleaner attachment. Marble and metal furniture need

a little more care. Plastic furniture is easy to keep clean – just wipe with detergent solution occasionally, then rinse with clear water.

MARBLE FURNITURE
● **General care** Marble just needs dusting with a cloth or soft brush. Occasionally, wipe with soapy water, and rinse before buffing the surface. Do not use polish on white marble. See page 81 for removing stains on marble.

WICKER FURNITURE
● **Cleaning** Use a vacuum cleaner on blow to push out dust. Scrub wicker furniture occasionally with a nail brush dipped in dishwashing liquid solution. Rinse, and dry.

CANE FURNITURE

Apply salty water with a sponge

Thorough cleaning
Scrub cane furniture from time to time with a soap flake solution. Rinse with salty water to keep the cane stiff.

METAL FURNITURE

Removing rust
Use a stiff wire brush to remove rust on metal furniture. Coat metal furniture that is kept outdoors with rustproof paint.

UPHOLSTERY

Dust upholstered furniture with the dusting tool attachment of the vacuum cleaner. Feel down the backs and sides of chairs and sofas to retrieve items such as coins before using the crevice tool to remove dust. To remove stains on upholstery, see pages 32–55.

REGULAR CARE
● **Slipcovers** Remove covers when dirty, and wash them according to fabric. While the covers are still damp, put them back on the furniture, and press with a cool iron. Glazed chintz covers can be washed, but the glaze may be removed.
● **Upholstery** Clean this yourself using upholstery shampoo (always follow the manufacturer's instructions), or call in a professional firm. When removing marks, be careful not to overwet.

REMOVING LINT

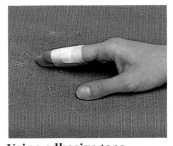

Using adhesive tape
To remove lint and pet hair from upholstery, wind adhesive tape around your fingers (sticky side out) and brush it over the fabric.

LEATHER AND VINYL
● **Leather care** Dust leather frequently. Apply hide food occasionally. Rub it in well so it does not stain clothes.
● **Dirty leather** Wipe with a damp cloth wrung out in a soap flake solution (take care not to overwet). Do not rinse. Allow to dry naturally, then polish as usual.
● **Vinyl upholstery** Dust and wipe with a damp cloth regularly. Use a soap flake solution to clean dirty vinyl.

CURTAINS AND BLINDS

These are an important part of the effect of a room. Expensive curtains and blinds should be dry cleaned by a professional: an expert will measure them before taking them down and ensure that they are returned fitting as well as they did originally.

CURTAINS
● **Washing** Always have lined curtains professionally dry cleaned, even if they are washable – the different fabrics may shrink at varying rates if you wash them yourself. Wash large curtains in your bathtub, since they are too heavy for a machine and could cause damage.

General care
Dust curtains frequently, using the upholstery attachment of your vacuum cleaner. Stand on a stepstool to reach the top.

BLINDS
● **Roller blinds** Vacuum with the upholstery attachment or dusting tool. If the blinds are spongeable, wipe them with a solution of dishwashing liquid, then rinse with a damp cloth. An application of aerosol blind stiffener will help keep them clean. (It is best to apply this outdoors.)

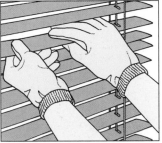

Venetian blinds
Dust by running hands encased in cotton gloves along the slats. Wash blinds in the bathtub (keep the roller mechanism dry).

● **Balloon shades** Vacuum folds regularly. Unfold shades occasionally, and wash or dry clean according to the fabric.

BRIGHT IDEA

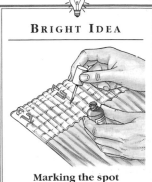

Marking the spot
When removing curtain hooks, mark their spaces with nail polish. This way you will not have to spend time guessing the correct spacing when replacing the hooks.

BATHROOMS

THESE ROOMS NEED daily cleaning. Encourage members of your household to clean sinks and bathtubs after they have used them. Dirty bathrooms are unattractive and unsanitary. They are also more difficult to clean if left dirty.

BATHROOM-CLEANING KIT

Store your bathroom-cleaning kit in the bathroom ready for everyone to use after they have finished. Rinse sponges, cloths, and toilet brushes after each use. If bathroom sponges become slimy from a buildup of soap, soak them in white vinegar and water, and wash them in the washing machine. Flush toilet cleaner away before using the toilet; otherwise, splashes might damage the skin.

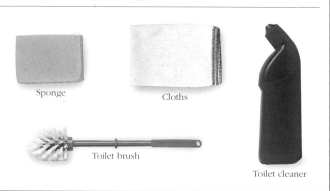

Sponge

Cloths

Toilet brush

Toilet cleaner

BATHS, SHOWERS, AND SINKS

Dishwashing liquid is fine for cleaning baths, showers, and sinks; you do not need special cleaners. Wipe around immediately after use to keep these areas clean. Prevent condensation in bathrooms by running cold water into baths before running the hot water.

ACRYLIC BATHS

Removing scratches
Rub with metal polish. For deep scratches, rub with ultrafine wet-and-dry sandpaper, then finish off with metal polish.

BATHROOM SINKS
● **Drains** Pay special attention to sink drain holes and overflows. Clean with a bottle brush, and pour a little bleach down them once a week.

OTHER BATH TYPES
● **Enamel and porcelain** Clean with a nonabrasive cleaner – harsh abrasives will dull the bath's surface. Rub stubborn marks with turpentine. Rinse with a solution of hot water and dishwashing liquid.
● **Fiberglass** Treat carefully, as the color is in the surface coating only. Use dishwashing liquid – avoid abrasives, metal polish, and harsh cleaners.

SHOWERS
● **Shower doors** Remove hard-water deposits by wiping with white vinegar. Leave for 30 minutes, then rinse.
● **Shower curtains** These tend to develop mildew, which can be removed by soaking in a bleach solution, rinsing, and hand or machine washing. Remove soap buildup by soaking in warm water with a little fabric softener.

STAINS ON BATHS AND SINKS

● **Blue-green marks** These are caused by the minerals in water from dripping faucets. Use a vitreous enamel cleaner to clean enameled surfaces.
● **Rust marks** Remove using a commercial bath-stain remover that contains scale remover.

● **Hard-water marks** Use a vitreous enamel cleaner on enameled surfaces, and cream cleaner on acrylic surfaces.
● **Tidemarks** Rub bad marks on enamel and acrylic with turpentine, then rinse with a dishwashing liquid solution.

FIXTURES

Clean taps regularly so that dirt does not build up. For chrome taps, remove greasy marks with dishwashing liquid, and serious marks with metal polish; restore dulled old chrome with special chrome cleaner for cars. Clean rubber plugs with turpentine.

CLEANING BATHROOM TAPS

● **Removing scale** Where scale builds up on chrome taps, rub well with half a lemon until the scale disappears. Rinse thoroughly, then buff dry.

● **Gold-plated taps** Wipe with a barely damp cloth after each use. Do not rub. Never use metal polish, because it will damage the finish.

SHOWERHEADS

● **Cleaning** Unscrew showerheads from time to time and rinse out hard-water scale. Rub deposits with white vinegar.

Submerge shower-head completely

Descaling faucets
Tie a plastic bag or a yogurt cup containing vinegar or descaler over the faucet. Leave until the scale is dissolved, then rinse.

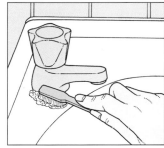

Cleaning tap bases
Use an old, clean toothbrush dipped in cream cleaner to get rid of the deposit and grime that builds up behind taps.

Clogged showerhead
Soak in a bowl of warm, undiluted vinegar or descaler. Use a toothbrush or darning needle to clean blocked holes.

TOILETS

Brush toilets thoroughly each day. Wipe the seat, tank, and outside of the bowl once a week, and clean the bowl with a commercial toilet cleaner. Do not regularly use bleach to clean a toilet; if left for any length of time it may cause crazing or cracking in the glaze.

HEAVY-DUTY CLEANING

● **Dirty toilets** Use a toilet brush with a rag tied firmly over the head to push the water out of the bowl. Bale out the last bit, then clean the bowl thoroughly with bleach. Flush immediately.

● **Damaged surfaces** Treat hard-water deposits with a paste of laundry borax and white vinegar. Leave for a few hours, then rinse. Cracked and crazed bowls harbor germs and should be replaced.

TRADITIONAL TIP

Bathroom smells
A clever method of getting rid of bathroom odors is to strike a match or light a candle. The flame burns away noxious gases.

OTHER BATHROOM TIPS

Slip soap into a sponge

● **Leftover soap** To use up ends of soap, cut a slit in a sponge, and place the soap pieces into it. This creates a delightful soapy sponge for the bath.
● **Bath plugs** If rubber plugs are difficult to remove, slip a curtain ring onto the top – the plug will pull out easily.

KITCHENS

L IKE BATHROOMS, kitchens need daily cleaning, since dirty food-preparation surfaces or equipment can cause food poisoning. Keep pets away from surfaces where food is prepared – or work strictly on cutting boards.

KITCHEN-CLEANING EQUIPMENT

Keep these items by your kitchen sink. Do not use dirty kitchen-cleaning equipment. Wash steel wool and scouring pads after each use, and get rid of cleaning cloths when they become worn or dirty. A dishwashing brush is more effective than a sponge, and it can be useful for getting into corners of pans and dishes.

Steel-wool pads

Scouring pads

Dishwashing brush

Cleaning cloth

Dishwashing liquid

SINKS AND SURFACES

Keep sinks and surfaces in the kitchen squeaky clean for sanitary reasons. Clean laminate countertops with a damp cloth dipped in baking soda or cream cleaner. Avoid harsh abrasives and any household cleaners containing bleaches, which can be poisonous.

PORCELAIN SINKS
● **Easy clean** Fill your sink with hot water and a few drops of household bleach. Wearing a rubber glove, reach in and adjust the drain so that the water drains out very slowly, giving everything a good cleaning. Rinse well.

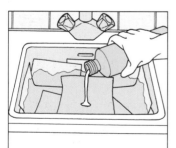

Sparkling white sinks
Place a layer of paper towels around the bowl of the sink, and saturate with household bleach. Leave for 30 minutes, then remove towels (wearing gloves). Rinse well before use.

STAINLESS STEEL SINKS
● **Restoring shine** Clean sinks daily with dishwashing liquid. Use denatured alcohol or white vinegar to remove water spots. Give the sink a good shine by rubbing with soda water or using stainless-steel polish. Rinse thoroughly.

Removing lime scale
Lime scale tends to build up around drains in hard water areas. Cut a lemon in half and rub the deposit vigorously with the cut surface. Alternatively, use a commercial scale remover.

KITCHEN SURFACES

● **Kitchen cabinets** Empty cabinets several times a year, discarding anything that is no longer fresh. Wash interiors with a mild solution of detergent, then rinse. Wipe the base of each item before replacing in the cabinet.
● **Wooden kitchen tables** Scrub unsealed wood tables that are used for meals or food preparation regularly to keep grease and germs at bay. Sealed wood tables just need frequent wiping.

STOVES

Wipe stove exteriors from time to time with a damp cloth. Clean off spills with dishwashing liquid or household cleaner. If you are cooking food that may bubble over in the oven, place the dish on a baking tray; the tray is easier to clean than the oven floor.

CLEANING OVENS

● **Basic care** Keep ovens clean by wiping them out – while still warm – with a damp cloth dipped in baking soda. Use abrasive household detergent to remove stains on ovenproof glass, but wait until the glass is completely cold.

● **Dirty ovens** Clean with a commercial oven cleaner (this does not apply to self-cleaning ovens). Clean up any spills on oven floors to prevent them from becoming encrusted.

MICROWAVES

● **Basic cleaning** Wipe out after each use. If the cavity smells, microwave a bowl of water with a little added lemon juice on high for one minute, then wipe out.

HOBS

● **Cleaning** Wipe hobs after cooking. Where food has burned around burners, cover with a cloth wrung out in dishwashing liquid solution. Leave for a couple of hours before wiping clean.

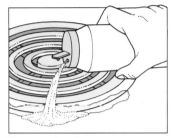

Preventing burns
Pouring salt onto food spills that occur during cooking will prevent the spills from burning; this works inside ovens as well.

REMOVABLE PARTS

● **Shelves and grills** Oven shelves can be cleaned in the dishwasher. Or, place dirty shelves and grills in the tub, and soak in a solution of enzymatic detergent and hot water. Use old towels to protect the tub surface.

● **Grill pans** Wash after each use; otherwise, the buildup of fat may become a fire hazard.

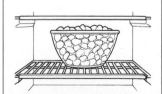

Lining grill pans
Place foil inside grill pans so that you can simply discard the foil when it becomes dirty, rather than having to wash the pan.

REFRIGERATORS AND FREEZERS

Use baking soda and warm water to wipe the insides of refrigerators and freezers – soap or dishwashing liquid will leave a smell and can taint food. If you need to defrost your freezer, store food in coolers, or ask friendly neighbors to borrow space in their freezers.

CLEANING AND DEFROSTING

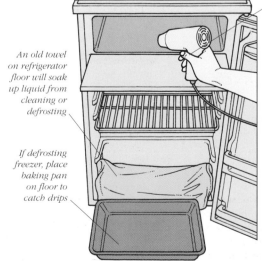

An old towel on refrigerator floor will soak up liquid from cleaning or defrosting

If defrosting freezer, place baking pan on floor to catch drips

Use a hair dryer to speed up defrosting – keep it away from plastic

Cleaning refrigerators
Once every few months, remove all the food, switch off the refrigerator, and wipe down all the surfaces. Defrost the freezer at the same time if necessary.

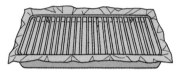

REFRIGERATOR SMELLS

● **Deodorizing refrigerators** Leave a bowl filled with cat litter or charcoal to absorb smells in refrigerators that are going to be switched off.

● **Persistent smells** Wipe all nonmetal parts of the refrigerator with a solution of 2 tbs (30 g) baking soda in 1 quart (1 liter) of water to remove persistent smells.

WASHING DISHES

Do it right away! That is the golden rule if you wash your dishes by hand (people with dishwashers have a little more leeway). If you cannot wash dishes at once, remember to soak everything you can. Change dishwater as soon as it starts to look dirty or greasy.

GENERAL TIPS

● **Smells on hands** Immersing hands that smell from food preparation in hot water will set the smell. Prevent this by rubbing vinegar over hands before doing the dishes.

● **Stained china** Remove tea and coffee stains on cups and cigarette burns on china by rubbing with a damp cloth and baking soda.

DISHWASHING SEQUENCE

● **Glassware** Wash first. Rinse glasses used for milk or alcohol in cold water before washing. Place a rubber splash guard on your tap to reduce the risk of glasses being chipped.

● **Cutlery** Wash after glassware. Do not leave items with wood, bone, china, or plastic handles in water for any length of time.

● **Crockery** Wash after cutlery. Scrape or rinse off all food debris. Do not use hot water on egg-, milk-, or starch-based foods, or they will set.

● **Pots and pans** Wash last. Let soak while washing other items. Use the methods described opposite to clean discolored or burned pots and pans.

WASHING GLASSWARE BY HAND

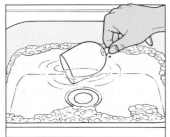

Preventing cracks
To ensure that glasses do not crack when you place them in hot water, slip them in sideways instead of bottom first. Always be sure to check the water temperature *before* you put on rubber gloves.

Crystal and fine china
Place a towel on the bottom of the sink to act as a cushion when washing crystal and fine china. Alternatively, use a plastic bin to prevent items from bumping against the hard surface of the sink.

GREEN TIP

Cut through grease
Add a little vinegar to the rinse water. It cuts through grease and leaves dishes sparkling clean.

DISHWASHERS

These are the ultimate kitchen tools. Always use the recommended type and amount of detergent – too much detergent makes too many suds and prevents the machine from cleaning properly. Check the dishwasher's inlet and outlet hoses periodically for blockages.

BASIC CARE

● **Cleaning** Wipe dishwasher exteriors regularly, and clean the inside with household detergent. Run the dishwasher empty occasionally, using a special interior cleaner.

● **Choosing cycles** Try out all the cycles on a dishwasher; a shorter cycle may clean just as well as a longer one.

WASHING ITEMS

● **Not dishwasher safe** Wash valuable glassware, china and glassware decorated with a metal strip, delicate china, and antique china by hand – never wash them in a dishwasher.

● **Cutlery** Never put stainless steel with silver or silver-plated cutlery – the silver may become pitted or stained.

WASHING PROBLEMS

● **Dishes not clean** If food specks remain on dishes after washing, you may have overloaded the dishwasher, not used enough detergent, or used the wrong cycle.

● **Cloudy glasses** This is the result of hard-water deposits. Use more detergent and – if suitable – rinse aid and salt.

POTS AND PANS

Soaking pots and pans after use makes them easier to clean. Some nonstick surfaces just need to be wiped over with paper towels. To remove persistent smells from a pan, fill the pan with water and 2 tbsp (30 ml) of white vinegar, and bring this mixture to a boil.

ALUMINUM

Use apple skins only

Removing discoloration
Boil natural acid – try an onion, lemon juice, rhubarb, or apple peel – in discolored aluminum pans. Do not soak aluminum (or stainless steel) pans for long or leave food in them because they will discolor and pit.

COPPER

Dip lemon in salt to make it mildly abrasive

Removing tarnish
Rub the exteriors of copper pots with the cut side of half a lemon dipped in salt to remove tarnish. Or fill a spray bottle with vinegar and 3 tbsp (45 g) salt, and spray onto the copper. Let sit, then rub clean.

CAST IRON
● **Cleaning** Dry cast iron thoroughly after washing to prevent rusting. Rub a little oil around the inside to keep it seasoned. Clean the outside with commercial oven cleaner.

BURNED POTS AND PANS
● **Soaking burns** Fill a badly burned pan with a solution of enzymatic detergent. Leave for a couple of hours, then bring to the boil and remove as much deposit as possible. This treatment may need to be repeated several times before the burn disappears.
● **Thick burns** Allow the burn to dry, pick off as much of the deposit as possible, then use the treatment above.

EQUIPMENT AND APPLIANCES

Take care of your kitchen equipment, and it will last for years. Do not put pots, pans, or other pieces of equipment away with any specks of food still adhering to them. Wash and dry wooden items immediately after use. Always disconnect appliances before cleaning.

HARD-TO-CLEAN ITEMS

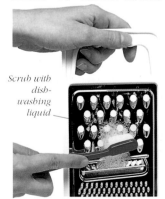

Scrub with dish-washing liquid

Cleaning graters
Get debris out of graters and sieves with an old toothbrush. Boil a few old toothbrushes to sterilize them, and keep them in your kitchen-cleaning kit.

SMALL APPLIANCES
● **Blenders** Rinse the jar as soon as you have used it. Pour in a little dishwashing liquid and warm water, and blend thoroughly to clean. Repeat with water to rinse.
● **Food processors** These usually have several parts, some of which can be washed in a dishwasher. Check the manufacturer's instructions; some plastic parts should be washed only on the top rack.
● **Coffeemakers** Keep the internal parts clean by running undiluted vinegar through them, as if making coffee. Run clean water through the cycle twice afterward to rinse away any remaining vinegar.

WOODEN ITEMS

Rub with cut lemon

● **Cutting boards** After cutting foods such as fish or garlic, remove smells by rubbing cutting boards with half a lemon.
● **Rolling pins** Sprinkle with salt, and rub with your hand to loosen particles of pastry. Then wash, rinse, and dry.
● **Wooden bread bins** To stop mildew from developing, wipe bread bins with white vinegar on a cloth. Dry open.

KITCHEN WASTE

Keeping your kitchen free from waste is important for health as well as for aesthetics. If garbage is left around, particularly in hot weather, odors are produced, creating new problems. To discard fat, freeze it in an old can, then throw the can out.

DISPOSAL UNITS

Cleaning and care

Stop electric waste-disposal units from becoming smelly by grinding citrus peels in them. Clear food debris by pouring a bucket of hot water with a handful of washing soda down them from time to time.

RECYCLING WASTE

● **Plastic containers** Keep plastic margarine and cottage cheese containers – they can be used for freezing food, and come in handy around the house when mixing glue or cleaning paintbrushes.
● **Plastic bags** After shopping, save and reuse plastic grocery bags as garbage can liners.

Clean foil with a damp cloth

Reusing kitchen foil

Recycle kitchen foil, which is rarely worn out after just one use. Wipe with a damp cloth, or – if it is very dirty – soak it in a hot solution of dishwashing liquid. When clean, rinse, and smooth out with a cloth.

SINK DRAINS

● **Weekly cleaning** Put a capful of washing soda down the drain once a week, and follow it with a potful of boiling water. This keeps the sink clean and removes blockages that have built up.
● **Grease and fat** If you pour fat down the sink by accident, follow it immediately with a potful of boiling water. Repeat the treatment until it clears. You can pour used fat down an outdoor drain, but follow it with some washing soda and boiling water.
● **Sink plugs** If your rubber plug tends to come out during washing up, roughen the plug edges with steel wool.

SCENTED KITCHEN

Cinnamon sticks

● **Baking scent** Cook brown sugar and cinnamon on very low heat on a pan on the stove – this will make your kitchen smell as if you have been baking all day.
● **Simmering cloves** To create a delicious smell around the house and increase humidity, simmer some cloves in water.

DEALING WITH PESTS AND SMELLS

ANT DETERRENTS

● **Ant-free cabinets** Hang sprigs of dried pennyroyal, rue, or tansy in kitchen cabinets to keep ants away from your foods and dishes.
● **Keeping ants out** If you know where ants are coming in, sprinkle dried mint, chili powder, or laundry borax across their trail. Plant mint near windows and doors.

● **Ants' nests** Mix one part laundry borax with one part confectioners' sugar. Scatter the mixture over a piece of wood near the site of the nest. The ants will be attracted by the sweet sugar and will then be poisoned by the laundry borax.

OTHER PESTS

● **Cockroaches** Leave a mixture of equal parts of flour, cocoa powder, and laundry borax; or a mixture of equal parts of baking soda and confectioner's sugar in shallow dishes. Keep away from children and pets.

FOOD SMELLS

● **Burned food** Boil a few slices of lemon in a saucepan to clear the air of burned food smells.
● **Fried food** Place a small bowl of white vinegar next to the stove whenever you are frying foods. This helps prevent unpleasant fat smells.

CLEANING CHECKLIST

THIS CHART CONTAINS brief guidelines for cleaning the different surfaces found in the home. For more detailed instructions on caring for various household items and surfaces, and undertaking minor repairs, see pages 70–87.

SURFACE	BASIC CLEANING METHOD	SPECIAL NOTES
TILES	Wipe with household detergent, and rinse to remove residual traces. Clean dirty grouting with a household bleach solution.	Remove soap splashes with a solution of one part white vinegar to four parts water. Rinse.
BRICK	Scrub with a solution of dishwashing liquid, taking care not to overwet since bricks are porous. Rinse and dry.	Sponge burn marks with vinegar, and rinse. See p. 54 for removing soot marks from brick.
CONCRETE	Dissolve a cup of washing soda in a bucket of warm water, and wash. Sweep concrete floors regularly.	See p. 158 for removing oil stains from concrete garage floors.
LEATHER	Wipe with a damp cloth rubbed on a bar of glycerin soap. Apply a thin coat of hide food occasionally.	See p. 23 and 82 for cleaning and caring for leather furniture.
GLASS	Use a window-cleaning product on glass surfaces. Do not get it on carpets; it will stain.	Try to avoid touching glass, as it shows fingerprints. Use vinegar to remove greasy marks on glass.
MARBLE	Sponge with a soap flake solution, and rinse. Use specialized products for any further treatments needed.	See p. 22 for caring for marble furniture, and p. 81 for removing unsightly stains on marble.
SLATE	Clean with a dishwashing liquid solution. Rinse with a damp cloth, then buff to a shine.	Use marble polish on smooth slate. Scrub textured slate with a brush and dishwashing liquid solution.
PLASTIC	Wipe over with dishwashing liquid. Use an aerosol cleaner to protect plastic from dust.	Soak smelly plastic containers overnight in a baking soda and warm water solution.
STAINLESS STEEL	Wash and dry immediately after use. Polish occasionally. See p. 26 and 76 for additional care advice.	Tends to discolor and pit, so immerse it in water for as short a time as possible.
SILVER	Polish regularly. If stored, keep items in tarnishproof paper or bags. See also p. 74–75.	Never mix silver and stainless steel in a dishwasher's cutlery basket. Egg will stain silver cutlery.
WOOD	Dust, sweep, and mop regularly, and polish only occasionally. Do not wet unsealed wood.	See p. 14–16 for wood floors, p. 22 for wooden furniture, and p. 71–73 for caring for wood.

STAIN REMOVAL

THE SECRET OF REMOVING STAINS is to treat them at once – or as soon as possible after they occur. Stains that are left to soak in and dry are more difficult to remove and may, in some cases, be impossible to get out. Keep a kit with stain-removal equipment, cleaners, and solvents handy, so you can act quickly when accidents happen. Here you will find essential information on stain-removal equipment and methods, as well as specific treatments for the most common stains.

STAIN-REMOVAL EQUIPMENT

These are the items that you will need for your stain-removal kit. Together with the cleaners and solvents on the opposite page, they will enable you to tackle stains effectively. Keep your kit in a separate box, and replace items as necessary.

● **To absorb grease** Use brown or blotting paper, together with an iron, to remove grease.
● **To blot stains** Use anything that is disposable, such as paper towels. Never use anything that is dyed.
● **To apply solvents** Use cotton balls or a white rag. Never use colored cloth, which may transfer dye to stained items.
● **To dilute stains** Use a sponge to apply clean water to stains, or use a soda syphon, which will flush stains out of carpets.
● **To scrape up deposits** Use an old spoon or a metal ruler to lift off stain deposits.
● **For protective covering** Rubber gloves protect your hands when you use harsh cleaners or toxic solvents. Always wear gloves when using ammonia and bleach.

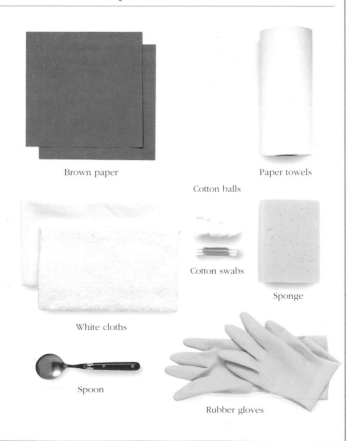

Brown paper

Paper towels

Cotton balls

Cotton swabs

Sponge

White cloths

Spoon

Rubber gloves

CLEANERS AND SOLVENTS

The cleaners and solvents shown here will remove most household stains. Keep the items that you use most in your stain-removal kit. Ammonia, denatured alcohol, laundry borax, hydrogen peroxide, turpentine, and acetone are toxic. Lemon, eucalyptus oil, glycerin, and vinegar are all natural stain remedies. Carpet shampoo, biological detergent with enzymes, and talcum powder are helpful for treating stains on carpets, clothes, and furniture, respectively.

Denatured alcohol (dyed in some areas)

Denatured alcohol

Carpet shampoo

Ammonia

DILUTION FORMULAS
● **Ammonia** Add 1 tsp (5 ml) to 2 cups (500 ml) of cold water.
● **Laundry borax** Add 1 tbsp (15 g) to 2 cups (500 ml) of warm water.
● **Hydrogen peroxide** Dilute one part to six parts cold water.
● **Glycerin** Dilute with equal parts warm water.

Laundry borax

Detergent with enzymes

Talcum powder

Lemon

Eucalyptus oil

Hydrogen peroxide

Glycerin

Turpentine

Dishwashing liquid

Acetone

White vinegar

COMMERCIAL CLEANERS

Specialized laundry products (for example, prewash sticks and sprays), commercial stain removers, and stain solvents are ideal for removing marks on fabric and carpets. You can also buy grease solvents for grease and oil marks, and commercial upholstery- and carpet-spotting kits, which contain small bottles of different chemicals that you mix together to treat stains.

Prewash stick

Foam stain remover

Aerosol stain remover

Prewash spray

Stain solvents

TACKLING STAINS

Treat stains at once, but test the method on a hidden part of the item first. To avoid spreading a stain, dab at it instead of rubbing it, and always work from the outside to the center. Never use hot water, which will set stains.

TYPES OF STAIN

Stains can be divided into two main types: built-up stains and absorbed stains. Some substances, such as blood and egg, produce a stain that is a combination of the two. Always treat these "combination stains" as built-up stains first, then treat them for absorption.

BUILT-UP STAINS

Removing deposits
Built-up stains are made by thick substances that need to be scraped off before treatment. Scoop them up quickly so that they do not penetrate far.

ABSORBED STAINS

Blotting liquid
Thin liquids will sink quickly into a surface. Blot the area with paper towels or a white cloth immediately. Launder or sponge to remove the rest of the stain.

OTHER STAINS

● **Mystery stains** If you do not know the cause of a stain, proceed with caution. Soak washable items, then launder them according to fabric. Sponge nonwashables with clear warm water. If staining persists, apply a hydrogen peroxide solution (see p. 33).
● **Dried stains** To loosen dried stains, use a glycerin solution (see p. 33). Sponge off this initial treatment before using another chemical that may react with the glycerin.

DIFFERENT SURFACES

Stains should be treated not only according to type, but also according to the surface on which they fall. The three methods below outline the basic treatments that can be used for stains on carpets, stains on nonwashable fabrics or upholstery, and stains on clothes.

CARPETS

Apply shampoo on a sponge

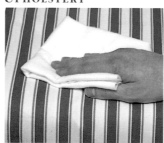

Shampooing carpets
After removing any deposit, treat the remaining mark with a solution of carpet shampoo. If this leaves a startlingly clean spot, you will need to shampoo the entire carpet using either a manual or an electric machine.

UPHOLSTERY

Absorbing stains
Scrape up any deposit, and blot the stain well. Apply talcum powder, and leave until it appears discolored, having absorbed the stain. Wipe away with a cloth. Apply more talcum powder if the mark persists.

CLOTHES

Dab mark, rather than rubbing it

Dabbing away stains
Treat stains on washable clothes as soon as they occur, and always before you launder the item. Use lukewarm or cold water and a cloth to dab the mark. Alternatively, soak the garment if recommended.

STAINS ON WASHABLE FABRICS

Laundering a stained garment can set the stain, making it very difficult to remove. Always treat stains before laundering, using one of the three methods below. Observe the guidelines for different fabrics, and invest in any laundry aids you think might be useful.

GENERAL TREATMENT

Rinsing off stains
Rinse stains in cold or lukewarm water as soon as possible after they occur. Alternatively, sponge with clear water until the stain fades. Never use hot water on stains; it will cause them to set.

LAUNDRY AIDS
● **Detergents** These come in varying strengths, and many contain additives to remove stains. Some stains require extra treatment with one of the substances below.
● **Detergent with enzymes** This works well on stains that contain proteins, such as egg yolk, blood, and sweat. It is often a constituent of ordinary detergents, but is best used separately for stain removal.
● **Bleach** This has a whitening effect, so it should be used with care on colors. Avoid contact with your skin and clothes. (See also p. 58.)
● **Laundry borax** This old-fashioned laundry aid is an excellent stain remover. Dilute for sponging or soaking (see p. 33), or sprinkle directly onto stains (see p. 41).
● **Other aids** Stain solvents and prewash sticks and sprays help remove marks on clothes (see p. 33). Ink stains are best treated by soap flakes.

PROTEIN STAINS

Soaking items
Stains made from substances such as milk and blood respond best to soaking in enzymatic detergent. Do not soak items longer than recommended; always immerse the whole item.

PERSISTENT STAINS

Applying a solvent
If stains persist after rinsing or soaking, use a stain or grease solvent before laundering. Place a white cloth under the stain to avoid transferring the stain to another layer, then dab.

FABRICS	TREATMENT NOTES
COLORS	Treat stains with care to avoid producing bleached patches. Soak the whole item when using a bleaching treatment such as laundry borax.
WHITES	Natural fabrics can usually be bleached. Synthetics and mixtures can yellow with this treatment and may respond better to the correct detergent.
NATURAL FABRICS	Because these can be washed at high temperatures, rinsing or presoaking items before laundering is usually enough to remove most stains.
SYNTHETIC FABRICS	These are easily damaged by some chemicals, so test any treatment on a hidden part before tackling the stain.
DELICATES	These fabrics should always be treated cautiously. Avoid using strong chemical treatments on delicate fabrics.

FOOD STAINS

Most food stains can be removed using the basic methods shown on pages 34–35, provided you act quickly. The worst culprits are those featured here – stains from greasy foods, egg, and foods containing strong colorings.

OIL, FAT, AND GREASE STAINS

Grease stains are straightforward to remove from fabric, but they may cause more of a problem on carpets and furniture. Ties and scarves are susceptible to grease spots; use fabric-protection spray on nonwashable items when they are new or newly dry cleaned.

ON CARPETS

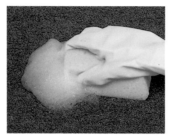

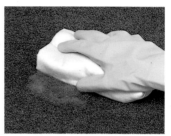

1 Place a piece of brown paper over the grease mark. Apply the tip of a warm iron until the grease is absorbed into the brown paper.

2 Apply a solution of carpet shampoo to the remaining mark, using a sponge. Rub into the carpet gently but firmly for a few minutes.

3 Wipe off the foam with a clean sponge or cloth. Inspect the mark; if it remains or reappears later, repeat the treatment from the beginning.

ON FURNITURE

Cover stain with talcum powder

Brush off talcum powder with dry, fluffy cloth

1 Sprinkle talcum powder thickly over the grease mark. Let stand until the grease begins to be absorbed.

2 After 10 minutes, brush off the talcum powder. If the mark still appears to be greasy, repeat the treatment.

ON CLOTHES

● **General treatment** Blot excess grease, using paper towels. Dab gently, taking care not to spread the stain. For nondelicate fabrics, which can be washed at reasonably high temperatures, laundering will remove residual marks.

● **Delicate fabrics** Dab delicate fabrics with a little eucalyptus oil, then either hand wash them, or machine wash at a low temperature. If the fabric is to be dry cleaned only, sponge the eucalyptus oil off with clear, warm water.

GREASE ON SHOES

Repair adhesive

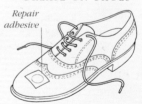

● **Leather shoes** Apply a little bicycle puncture repair adhesive to grease spots. Leave overnight, then peel off. Use shoe polish or hide food to finish up. Well-cleaned leather shoes will resist grease – just wipe over with a paper towel.
● **Suede shoes** Blot well, then rub with a block suede cleaner. Treat bad stains with a pad of white cotton dampened with lighter fluid. Check first on a test area to make sure that the color is not adversely affected.

OTHER GREASY STAINS

Foods such as avocado, peanut butter, and those listed below contain oil or fat, and may leave behind a grease patch. Tackle the grease stain before dealing with any remaining color. Substances such as car oil, ointments, and lotions should also be treated as grease.

MAYONNAISE
- **On washable fabrics** Sponge with warm water, then soak in a solution of enzymatic detergent before laundering.
- **On nonwashable fabrics** Wipe with a damp cloth, then use an aerosol grease solvent.

ICE CREAM
- **On washable fabrics** Wipe with a damp cloth, then soak in a detergent solution.
- **On nonwashable fabrics** Blot, then wipe with a damp cloth wrung out in warm water. Use a grease solvent.

GRAVY
- **On washable fabrics** Soak overnight in tepid water, then launder according to the fabric. Soak dried marks in enzymatic detergent if the fabric permits.
- **On nonwashable fabrics** Use an aerosol stain remover.

Mayonnaise on carpets
Scrape up as much as possible, then blot. Use a general stain remover for light marks, and the carpet treatment opposite to remove heavier stains.

Ice cream on carpets
Scrape up the deposit, and wipe the area with a damp cloth. Clean with a solution of carpet shampoo. Use a stain remover or grease solvent if marks remain.

Gravy on carpets
Scoop up what you can with a spoon, or blot the area dry with paper towels. Treat with a liquid stain remover followed by an application of carpet shampoo.

EGG STAINS

Egg is a tricky stain. The merest drop of hot water causes it to set and form a crusty deposit that is much harder to remove than a fresh stain. If you cannot treat an egg stain immediately, cover it with a damp cloth to keep it moist and prevent it from setting.

ON FURNITURE

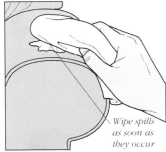

Wipe spills as soon as they occur

Remove the deposit
Use a damp white cloth to remove the spilled egg. If only egg white has been spilled, sponge the stain with cold, salty water. For yolk alone, dab repeatedly with lather from dishwashing liquid solution.

ON CARPETS
- **Basic treatment** Scrape up the deposit, then use a liquid stain remover to tackle what remains. If a mark is still visible when dry, apply a carpet-shampoo solution.

ON CLOTHES
- **Washable fabric** Sponge with cold, salty water. Rinse off when the stain has disappeared. Soak in an enzymatic detergent solution if necessary (and appropriate).
- **Nonwashable fabric** Sponge with salt water, then sponge off with clear water, and blot dry. Use an aerosol stain remover on remaining marks.

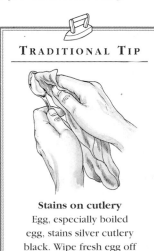

TRADITIONAL TIP

Stains on cutlery
Egg, especially boiled egg, stains silver cutlery black. Wipe fresh egg off cutlery after use. Rub black stains with salt.

COLORED FOOD STAINS

Color is the last thing you treat when dealing with a food stain. Get rid of the deposit first, then treat any grease element. Finally, tackle the color, which may require several attempts. Specific treatments for well-known "difficult" food stains appear below.

FOOD TYPE	ON WASHABLE FABRICS	ON OTHER SURFACES
TOMATO SAUCE Treat tomato sauce and other thick bottled sauces in the same way.	Hold fresh stains under cold running water, and rub between your fingers. Apply a prewash treatment, then launder according to fabric.	On carpets, remove deposit, and sponge with warm water. Blot dry, apply carpet shampoo, and wipe off. When dry, use a spray stain remover. Follow these steps for nonwashable fabrics, omitting the shampoo.
MUSTARD Mustard powder can be brushed off. Prepared mustard produces a stain that is difficult to remove.	Rub fresh stains between your fingers in a mild detergent solution, then sponge with an ammonia solution (see p. 33). Soften dried stains at first with a glycerin solution (see p. 33), and let stand for at least an hour.	Sponge carpets and furniture with a mild detergent solution, then an ammonia solution (see p. 33). Avoid overwetting, and finish by sponging with clean water. Stubborn stains require professional cleaning.
JAM AND PRESERVES These leave sticky residues that should be scooped up and wiped with a damp cloth.	Laundering should remove stains. Soak dried marks for half an hour in a laundry borax solution (see p. 33).	Sponge furniture with a warm dishwashing liquid solution. Sprinkle laundry borax on the mark, and sponge off after 15 minutes. On carpets, use carpet shampoo, then denatured alcohol (try on a test area first).
CURRY AND TURMERIC These are two of the worst stains. Do not get them on wall coverings, where the only solution is a patch.	Rinse stains in tepid water. Rub in a glycerin solution (see p. 33), leave for half an hour, and rinse. Launder in enzymatic detergent, if suitable. Use a hydrogen peroxide solution (see p. 33) on persistent stains.	Sponge carpets and furniture with a laundry borax solution (see p. 33). If this does not work on furniture, have the covers dry cleaned (if possible). A laundry prewash stick may also be effective on carpets.
BEETS This stain is difficult to remove because the color is deep and persistent.	Rinse under cold, running water until as much color as possible has come out. Soak colored fabrics in a laundry borax solution (see p. 33). For whites, use the treatment for dried tea stains shown on p. 41.	Do not attempt to remove stains on nonwashable fabrics or furniture yourself. Have both slipcovers and upholstery professionally cleaned.
CHOCOLATE Dropped pieces of chocolate are a problem once they get warm or if someone sits on them.	Allow to set, then scrape the dry deposit with a blunt knife. Soak, then launder in enzymatic detergent if suitable; otherwise launder as usual. For persistent stains, use the treatment for dried tea stains shown on p. 41.	Allow to set, then scrape up with a blunt knife. Apply a lather of carpet shampoo (for both furniture and carpets), rubbing in gently. Wipe off with a damp cloth, and use a liquid stain remover when dry.

SPILLED BEVERAGES

Start by blotting stains caused by spilled drinks, then go on to more intensive measures. Always use white cloth, tissues, or paper towels. Never use colored paper towels, which may bleed dye into the stain and worsen it.

RED WINE STAINS

Red wine is one of the most common carpet stains. Salt is effective for preventing stains on table linen from spreading, but on carpets it creates a permanent damp patch that attracts dirt to the area. Use the three-step treatment below or pour white wine over the area.

ON CARPETS

1 Blot the spill immediately, then sponge repeatedly with warm water. If you have a soda syphon, use it to flush the stain – the soda water plus the spraying action will lift the stain effectively.

2 Blot dry, then apply the foam from carpet shampoo on a sponge, working it in well. Sponge again with clear water, and repeat the treatment as often as necessary until clear.

3 Cover any remaining stain with a glycerin solution (see p. 33), and leave for up to an hour. Sponge off with clear water, and blot well. Apply a little denatured alcohol on a sponge to reduce old stains. Use the tip at right for a quick rescue when you cannot treat stains properly.

DRIED STAINS ON FURNITURE

1 Apply a glycerin solution (see p. 33) to loosen the stain. Leave the solution on for at least 30 minutes.

2 Sponge off with a weak, warm solution of dish-washing liquid. Wipe with a cloth wrung out in clear water.

FRESH STAINS ON FURNITURE

1 Blot, sponge with warm water, and blot again. Repeat if necessary. Cover persistent marks with talcum powder while still damp.

2 Brush the talcum powder off after a few minutes, using a soft brush or cloth. Continue the treatment until the mark disappears.

QUICK ACTION

Pour white wine onto red wine spill immediately

Pour some white wine over a red wine spill as soon as it occurs. Blot both liquids well, sponge with clear, warm water, then pat the area dry.

ON CLOTHES

● **General treatment** Rinse fresh wine stains in warm water. If the stain persists, soak the garment in a laundry borax solution (see p. 33) or a heavy-duty detergent, then launder according to fabric type.

● **Delicate fabrics** Bleach stains on white wool or silk with a hydrogen peroxide solution (see p. 33). Rinse, then hand wash.

ON TABLE LINEN

● **Fresh stains** Bleach white cotton and linen items. Soak colored items in a heavy-duty detergent solution, then launder as usual. Alternatively, use the treatment for dried tea stains shown on page 41.

Beer and Alcohol Stains

Beer and alcohol stains are fairly easy to remove from most surfaces (unless they are brightly colored or sticky liqueur stains). Old beer and alcohol stains are another matter, however, and require more drastic treatment if they are to come out satisfactorily.

On Clothes
● **Beer and alcohol** Rinse or soak in tepid water, then launder according to fabric type. On whites, use a hydrogen peroxide solution (see p. 33) to bleach any remaining marks. On colors, sponge with a white vinegar solution – 2 tbsp (30 ml) vinegar to 2 cups (500 ml) of water – until stains disappear.

On Furniture
● **Beer** Blot thoroughly, then sponge with a cloth wrung out in clean, warm water. Treat remaining marks with a spray-on stain remover.
● **Spirits** Sponge with clean, warm water until all traces of stickiness are removed, then use an upholstery-spotting kit. Have delicate fabrics that might watermark professionally dry cleaned.

On Carpets
● **Beer stains** Sponge with clean, warm water, or flush with a soda syphon, then blot. If marks remain, use a solution of carpet shampoo.
● **Alcohol stains** Treat as above, acting quickly to prevent color from soaking in. If colored marks remain, sponge with denatured alcohol on a damp cloth.

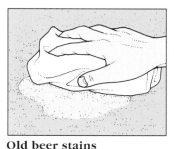

Old beer stains
Gently wipe old beer stains on carpets with denatured alcohol until the mark begins to fade.

Liqueur Stains

These tend to be stickier than other spilled alcohol drinks. If any stains from highly colored liqueurs remain after treatment, use a stain remover or denatured alcohol on the mark, testing first on an inconspicuous area.

● **Carpets** Flush stain with a soda syphon to dissipate stickiness, and blot the residue with paper towels. Apply carpet shampoo.
● **Upholstery** Sponge with warm water until all traces of stickiness are gone. Take care not to overwet. Apply carpet shampoo; use an upholstery-spotting kit on any remaining marks. Professionally dry clean any slipcovers that might watermark.
● **Clothes** Rinse the mark in warm water, then wash or dry clean the item as usual.

Fruit Juice Stains

Fruit juices cause problem stains because of the color residue they leave – especially dark-colored fruits such as red berries and black grapes. If they are allowed to dry they can be difficult to remove and – unless treated carefully – will leave a permanent mark.

Fresh Stains
● **Clothes** Rinse under cold running water until as much of the mark as possible is removed. Treat any remaining color with denatured alcohol or a stain remover.
● **Carpets** Blot with paper towels. Rub the area with a laundry prewash stick, and let stand for a few minutes. Rinse off, blot, and shampoo. Treat any remaining color with denatured alcohol.
● **Furniture** Sponge with cold water, and blot dry. Use a liquid stain remover.

Dried Stains

Loosen stain with glycerin solution

Treating old stains
Hold a clean cloth under the stain and apply a glycerin solution (see p. 33) with a second cloth. Leave for one hour, rinse, then treat as for fresh stains (see left).

Green Tip

Nature's stain remover
Rub the cut side of half a lemon on fresh fruit juice stains. Lemon juice is a natural bleaching agent.

TEA, COFFEE, AND COCOA STAINS

These stains tend to be a combination of the coloring of the drink and grease from any added milk. Blot the whole stain initially, then attack the grease, and finally use a method that will get rid of the color of the stain. Dried tea stains on fabric require special treatment.

ON FABRIC

● **Fresh tea stains** Rinse stains on clothes in lukewarm water, then soak in a laundry borax solution (see p. 33). Rinse stains on blankets at once in warm water, then launder. Rinse table linen immediately under cold water, then soak and launder, preferably in a detergent with enzymes.
● **Coffee and cocoa** Rinse in warm water. Soak in a warm enzymatic detergent solution (if suitable), or in a laundry borax solution (see p. 33).

DRIED TEA STAINS

If treating linen or cotton, water should be boiling

1 Drape the stained item over a bowl or basin. Sprinkle with laundry borax until the whole stain is thickly covered.

2 Pour a potful of hot water around the stain, working toward the center. Repeat treatment if necessary.

ISOLATING A STAIN

Tie off area with string

On a comforter or pillow, push the filling down and tie off the stained area, then wash it. This way you do not have to wash the entire item.

ON CARPETS

● **Coffee with milk and cocoa** Sponge with tepid water, or flush with a soda syphon. Apply a little carpet shampoo, and – when dry – use a liquid stain remover (but not on foam-backed carpets).
● **Black coffee** Sponge the stain repeatedly with tepid water, or flush it several times with a soda syphon, then blot.
● **Tea** Blot with paper towels, then sponge with tepid water, or apply a squirt from a soda syphon. Use a little carpet shampoo, and use an aerosol stain remover when dry.

ON FURNITURE

● **Coffee with milk and cocoa** Blot the stain with paper towels, then sprinkle with enzymatic detergent. Wipe off with a damp sponge.
● **Black coffee** Blot, sponge, and, if necessary, shampoo. Lubricate dried stains with a glycerin solution (see p. 33). Rinse, and blot well. Use a spray stain remover on any remaining marks.
● **Tea** Sponge off with a laundry borax solution (see p. 33), then wipe with a damp cloth. When dry, apply a spray stain remover.

MILK STAINS

If milk is not treated immediately after it is spilled on carpet, it will dry and leave a smell that is virtually impossible to remove. Move fast with the treatment, or you could find yourself having to replace an expensive item because of the permanent smell.

ON CLOTHES

● **Fresh stains** Rinse in tepid water, then launder as usual. Use a liquid stain remover if a grease mark persists.
● **Dried stains** Soak the item in enzymatic detergent if the fabric is suitable.

ON FURNITURE

● **General treatment** Sponge with tepid water (but do not overwet padded upholstery). Blot dry with paper towels, tissues, or a white cloth. Treat any remaining marks with a spray stain remover.

ON CARPETS

● **Fresh stains** Sponge with clear, warm water, then apply a spray cleaner.
● **Dried stains** If a stain is allowed to dry, the smell may return after cleaning. Use a professional carpet cleaner.

BIOLOGICAL STAINS

TREAT BIOLOGICAL STAINS IMMEDIATELY, since they can be difficult to remove if they are allowed to set. Also, they invariably carry unpleasant smells, which tend to linger if the stain is not cleaned up as quickly as possible.

BLOODSTAINS

Blood is a combination stain that soaks into surfaces and leaves a deposit on the top. The deposit is not as thick as some biological stains and therefore cannot be scraped off, but it should be wiped off with a clean cloth immediately. After that, treat the colored stain.

ON CLOTHES

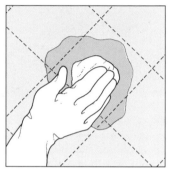

Add a generous handful of salt

Fill bucket with cold water

1 Add a handful of salt to a bucket of cold water. Soak the stained item of clothing for 15 minutes, making sure it is completely immersed.

2 Soak the item in enzymatic detergent next (if suitable), then launder as usual.

ON MATTRESSES

1 Follow the three steps in the box below. Next, apply a thick paste made up of baking soda and water to any stains that remain.

2 Let the paste dry, then brush it off with a dry cloth. Repeat if necessary.

ON CARPETS

● **General treatment** Sponge the area with cold water, and blot dry. Repeat until the stain disappears. If this does not work, use a carpet-spotting kit, followed by an application of carpet shampoo.

DRIED BLOODSTAINS

● **On clothes** Soak in a hydrogen peroxide solution (see p. 33) with ½ tsp (2.5 ml) added ammonia. (Do not use on nylon.)
● **On carpets** Use a glycerin solution (see p. 33), then treat as for fresh stains.
● **On untreated wood** Bleach stains with diluted household bleach, then stain the wood to its original shade.

REMOVING STAINS FROM MATTRESSES

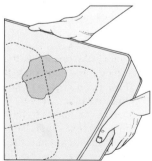 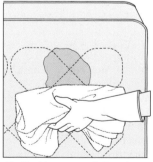 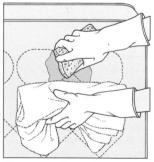

1 Turn the mattress on its side (this may take two people). Prop it up to prevent the stain and treatment from soaking in.

2 Position a towel directly beneath the stain. Always wear rubber gloves when treating biological stains.

3 Sponge the mark, repeating until it disappears. Hold the towel in place beneath the stain so that nothing trickles down.

URINE STAINS

Urine leaves an unpleasant stain that can result in a permanent mark and smell if it is not treated properly immediately. However, correct treatment is usually successful, so if this is a recurring problem in your house hold, keep the remedy on hand.

ON LEATHER SHOES
● **Fresh stains** Wipe polished shoes with a cloth wrung out in warm water. When dry, buff shoes well, then polish.

● **Dried stains** Wipe with a damp cloth to bring salts to the surface. Apply a product designed to remove salt stains.

ON SUEDE SHOES

Removing marks
Wipe gently with a damp cloth. Brush the damp area with a suede brush. On dry marks, use a shoe salt stain remover. Brush with a suede brush between applications.

Wipe with a cloth wrung out in warm water.

GREEN TIP

Neutralize urine smells
Using a plant-spray bottle, squirt a weak white vinegar solution onto pet stains on carpets to help remove the smell. Rinse with clean water.

ON CARPETS
● **Fresh stains** Use a carpet cleaner containing deodorant. Alternatively, sponge with cold water, pat dry, then rinse with a little antiseptic added to a bowl of cold water.
● **Dried stains** Treat as for fresh stains to remove the smell and the mark. Raise any faded color by sponging with a mild ammonia solution.

ON CLOTHES
● **Colored fabrics** Rinse in cold water, then launder according to fabric type.
● **Pale fabrics** Bleach dried urine stains with a hydrogen peroxide solution (see p. 33), to which a few drops of ammonia have been added. Alternatively, soak the item in enzymatic detergent, or use a commercial stain remover.

DRYING MATTRESSES

Clean urine off mattresses using the method opposite. Stand the mattress on its side, then prop it leaning slightly forward so liquid does not soak in more. Speed dry with a hair dryer on a cool setting.

VOMIT STAINS

With vomit, it is vital to get rid of all the deposit before tackling the underlying stain. Wearing rubber gloves, use the bowl of a spoon to lift off as much as possible, and use a metal ruler to scrape up the final traces. Be careful not to spread the stain.

ON CARPETS
● **Removing stains** Sponge with laundry borax solution (see p. 33), then with clear, warm water that includes a few drops of antiseptic. If any discoloration remains, work in the lather from some carpet shampoo with a sponge, or use an aerosol foam cleanser.
● **Removing smells** If the smell persists, continue rinsing with clear water and antiseptic until it disappears.

ON FURNITURE
● **Upholstery** Sponge the area with warm water containing a little ammonia, then pat dry. Or, use an upholstery cleaner that contains a deodorizer. Clean expensive or delicate items professionally.
● **Mattresses** Remove stains by following the method shown opposite. Sponge with a warm solution of dishwashing liquid. Sponge off with warm water that contains a little antiseptic.

ON CLOTHES
● **Removing stains** Rinse the area under cold running water until the mark begins to fade, rubbing the fabric gently between your hands to help the process. Soak, then launder in enzymatic detergent if the fabric is suitable. Alternatively, launder the garment as usual according to fabric type.
● **Removing smells** If the smell persists after laundering, launder the item again.

MUD STAINS

The key to removing any mud stain is to let it dry completely before tackling it. Do not be tempted to apply any treatment whatsoever until the deposit has become hard and you can brush it off easily. After that, you can work on the stain that has been left behind.

ON CARPETS
● **Persistent marks** Use either a carpet-spotting kit or a little denatured alcohol to remove traces of color that remain after removing the deposit.

ON FURNITURE
● **Basic treatment** Remove the deposit, then sponge the area with a weak, warm solution of dishwashing liquid or mild detergent. Wipe, then pat dry.

ON CLOTHES
● **Coats and jackets** Remove dry mud with a soft brush. Apply a commercial dry-cleaning product to any stains that do not brush off.

REMOVING DRIED MUD DEPOSITS

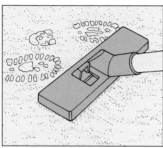

Brush mud off with a dry cloth

Vacuuming carpets
Let the mud dry (this usually takes one or two hours), then vacuum up the deposit. If necessary, use a stiff brush to loosen the dried mud first.

Brushing furniture
Use a soft brush to remove mud deposits on furniture without damaging the upholstery. Remove any remaining traces with a vacuum cleaner.

Wiping clothes
Brush dried mud off clothes with a dry cloth or a soft clothes brush. Launder to remove the remaining marks. Use denatured alcohol on persistent mud stains.

GRASS STAINS

Grass stains are inevitable if your household includes sports players or small children. They are very tricky to remove. As a rule, soak white cottons in bleach; a commercial stain remover help remove stains from other fabrics. Nonwashable fabrics should be dry cleaned.

ON WASHABLE FABRICS
● **Light stains** Provided the fabric is suitable, these stains should respond to a soak followed by laundering in enzymatic detergent. If marks remain, follow the treatment for nonwashable fabrics.
● **Heavy stains** Rub the stain with a heavy-duty hand cleaner – the kind used after serious do-it-yourself jobs. Apply a little denatured alcohol or a commercial stain remover to the area (test first), then rinse in cool, clean water before washing the garment according to fabric type.

ON CARPETS AND SHOES
● **Carpets** Pour a small amount of household detergent onto the stain, rub in, and let stand for a few hours. Scrub with a small brush. Wring out a clean cloth in clear water and wipe away the remains of the detergent.
● **Canvas shoes** Scrub grass stains with a nail brush dipped in a solution of dishwashing liquid and warm water. Wash the shoes in the washing machine, or on the top rack of the dishwasher (making sure all grit is removed first). Allow the shoes to dry naturally.

TRADITIONAL TIP

Treating old stains
Use egg white and glycerine in equal parts to loosen old grass stains on whites, then treat as for fresh stains.

OTHER BIOLOGICAL STAINS

Combat these stains on clothes by soaking in detergent with enzymes (if the fabric permits). Buy some disposable plastic gloves, or use a plastic bag over your hand when dealing with unpleasant deposits. Discard the bag or gloves after you have used them.

STAIN	SURFACE	TREATMENT
POLLEN STAINS	● These stains occur mainly on clothes and wall coverings, and can be very difficult to remove. Wear an apron when picking or arranging flowers, and keep floral arrangements well away from papered walls.	● Normal laundering will remove light stains on clothes. Failing this, dab lightly with denatured alcohol, then sponge off with warm water. ● Rub stains on wallpaper with a ball of white, crustless bread or an eraser. If this treatment fails, the wallpaper may need patching (see p. 18).
FLYSPECKS	● These tend to occur on lampshades, furnishings, and windows. Treat fabric lampshades with care.	● Wipe plastic lampshades with a dishwashing liquid solution. Use a spray stain remover on fabric lampshades, or apply a warm detergent solution with a soft toothbrush. ● Use denatured alcohol on windows, and a commercial stain remover on upholstery.
PERSPIRATION STAINS	● This appears as a yellowish or discolored patch in the armpit area of clothes.	● Sponge washable fabrics with an ammonia solution (see p. 33), then rinse. Where dye has run, sponge with 1 tbsp (15 ml) white vinegar diluted in 1 cup (250 ml) water.
PET STAINS	● These are urine, vomit, and fecal stains that occur mainly on carpets and furniture.	● See p. 43 for treating urine and vomit stains and for getting rid of unpleasant smells. See below for treating feces.
FECAL STAINS	● Always scrape up the deposit from carpets, furniture, and clothes with the bowl of a spoon immediately, taking care not to spread the stain.	● Sponge stains on carpets and furniture with a solution of warm water and a few drops of ammonia. Soak clothes in enzymatic detergent if suitable.
BIRD DROPPINGS	● Clothes drying on a wash line may sometimes become soiled by bird droppings.	● Remove the deposit, and relaunder washable fabrics. A bleach or hydrogen peroxide solution (see p. 33) may work on white and pale garments.
TOBACCO STAINS	● Nicotine can stain smokers' hands and fingernails with a yellowish tinge.	● Rub a pad soaked in a weak bleach solution over the stained areas. Use smoker's toothpaste on fingernails.

PIGMENT AND SYNTHETIC STAINS

Tʜᴇ ᴠᴀʀɪᴏᴜs ᴘᴀɪɴᴛs, ᴘᴇɴs, and crayons used around most homes produce marks that can be difficult to eradicate, especially since it is not always clear which dyes they contain, and therefore what will remove them.

PAINT STAINS

Every household will suffer at one time or another from spilled paint stains, especially when homes are undergoing redecoration. Unfortunately, paint stains are often left until the end of the day. Dried paint stains can be removed satisfactorily, but you must be careful.

ARTIST'S PAINTS
● **Fresh stains on clothes** Blot water-based paint stains with paper towels, then wash under a tap with soap and water. Launder as usual. Dab at oil-based paints with turpentine, holding a white pad beneath the stain. Sponge off, then launder as usual.

LATEX PAINTS
● **Fresh stains on fabric** Blot immediately, sponge with cold water, then launder.
● **Dried stains on fabric** Recently dried stains should respond to a commercial stain remover. Apply denatured alcohol to older stains (testing first), then launder as usual.

OIL-BASED PAINTS
● **On clothes** Dab with turpentine, then sponge with cold water. You may need to repeat this several times. Do not launder until all the paint is gone – if you do, you will set the stain. Bad stains and acetate and viscose fabrics need professional treatment.

Use a pad of absorbent white cloth

Sponge carpet with clear water

Dried stains on clothes
Hold a pad under the stain. Dab at the mark with a stain remover or denatured alcohol. For oil-based paints, use a paint solvent (available from art shops).

Spills on carpet
Using a sponge and cold water, dab at the stain, taking care not to spread it. Work from the outside inward. When clear, apply carpet shampoo.

Oil-based paint on carpet
Blot fresh spills with paper towels, then treat the area with carpet shampoo. For old stains, try using a commercial solvent, or snip off the top of the pile.

DYE STAINS

Dried dye never comes out, so mop up spills immediately. Use a dry cloth to wipe spills on hard surfaces – water will dilute and spread the mark. Wear protective clothing, and cover surrounding areas when using dye. Lemon juice will help remove dye from skin.

ON CARPETS
● **Basic treatment** Add a few drops of household ammonia to some denatured alcohol in a small container. Apply on a white pad, repeating several times if necessary, then apply carpet shampoo.

ON CLOTHES
● **Colorfast fabrics** Soak in an enzymatic detergent solution, then launder the item as usual.
● **Noncolorfast fabrics** Sponge with, or soak in, a hydrogen peroxide solution (see p. 33) for 15 minutes.

OTHER DYE STAINS
● **Laundry color run** If you accidentally include an item that runs in a load of wash, relaunder the whole load (but not the offending item!) using a commercial color-run remover instead of detergent.

BALLPOINT PEN INK MARKS

These are particularly difficult stains to remove. For bad stains, it may be worth contacting the manufacturer for a remedy for the type of ink used, since the company may sell its own solvent. Dried ballpoint pen ink is especially difficult to get out, so act quickly.

ON FABRIC

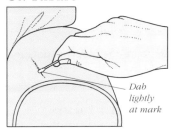

Dab lightly at mark

Blot the stain
Press paper towels against the stain to absorb as much of it as possible. Then apply denatured alcohol using a cotton swab.

ON WALL COVERINGS

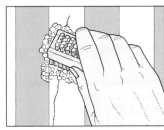

Treat immediately
Scrub vinyl wall coverings immediately with soap and water. Ordinary wall coverings may need patching (see p. 18).

ON OTHER SURFACES

● **Suede** Rub the stain with a fine emery cloth, emery board, or a commercial suede-cleaning block. Seek professional advice before cleaning valuable items.
● **Vinyl surfaces** Treat marks on vinyl immediately by gently rubbing the area with a nail brush and soapy water. If the ink is allowed to remain on the vinyl surface, it will merge into the plasticizer and leave a permanent mark.

FOUNTAIN PEN INK MARKS

Most fountain pen ink is washable, and it is worth making sure that the brand you use definitely is. Always screw on the cap of your pen firmly, especially when carrying it around with you. If you use ink from a bottle, rather than a cartridge, keep the top screwed on.

ON CARPETS

1 First dilute the stain by sponging repeatedly with clean water, or squirting with a soda syphon. Blot the area well with paper towels.

2 Make a hot, thick solution of soap flakes, and apply liberally on a white fabric pad. Let sit for 15 minutes.

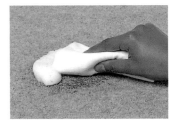

3 Wipe off the solution. If the mark persists, repeat Step 2 until it disappears.

ON SKIN

● **Removing marks** Scrub with a nail brush dipped in vinegar and salt. Or rub marks with the inside of a banana skin.

DRIED STAINS ON CLOTHES

1 If a fountain pen ink stain remains after you have washed a garment, rub the mark with half a lemon, or squeeze lemon juice onto it.

2 Press the stained area between two pieces of white cotton cloth. Repeat as necessary, then rinse. Launder according to the fabric.

TRADITIONAL TIP

Natural ink removers
Traditional wisdom recommends treating ink-stains with milk or tomato. Cover the stains with a little milk, or rub with the cut side of half a tomato. Rinse both treatments out well.

FELT-TIP PEN MARKS

Homes with small children are particularly susceptible to felt-tip pen marks on walls and furniture. Felt-tip pens also often leak into pockets of suit jackets – never attempt to tackle this yourself, but take the jacket to a dry cleaner and explain what the problem is.

ON FABRIC

● **Small marks** Press a paper towel on marks on clothes or furniture to remove as much ink as possible. Dab with denatured alcohol on a cotton swab, then launder using soap flakes, not detergent. (Soap is more effective than detergent on all types of ink.)
● **Large marks** Use a spray stain remover, repeating applications as necessary. Alternatively, buy a specific commercial stain remover.

ON WALL COVERINGS

● **Vinyl** Apply a nonabrasive household cleaner to marks, or use denatured alcohol.
● **Wallpaper** The best solution is to cover marks with a new patch of wallpaper (see p. 18).

ON OTHER SURFACES

● **Carpets and furniture** Blot stains with cotton swabs and paper towels, then dab with denatured alcohol.

Stains on vinyl
Wipe marks on vinyl surfaces such as toys with a white cloth wrapped around one finger and moistened with dishwashing liquid. Rinse with clear water.

OTHER PIGMENTS

● **Correction fluid** Let dry, brush off, then launder.
● **Crayon** Use a nonabrasive household cleaner for marks on vinyl. Painted walls may need to be repainted, and ordinary wall coverings may require patching (see p. 18).
● **Pencil** Use an eraser on walls and furniture. Sponge marks off clothes, then launder according to fabric.

STICKY SUBSTANCES

Chewing gum and colored plastic putty can be difficult to remove, especially from fluffy fabrics and carpets where rough removal can leave a bare patch. Freezing is the trick for removing chewing-gum stains; use a liquid stain remover on any marks that are left behind.

PLASTIC PUTTY

● **On clothes** Plastic putty does not freeze, so pick off as much as you can with your fingernails. Next, hold a folded white pad underneath the mark, and – using another white cloth – apply liquid stain remover until the deposit is dissolved. Rinse, then launder as usual.
● **On carpets** Pick off the deposit with your fingernails. Remove any residue with liquid lighter fluid (test on a hidden area, since lighter fuel may damage synthetic fibers). Do not overwet or allow the lighter fluid to reach the carpet backing.

CHEWING GUM ON CARPET

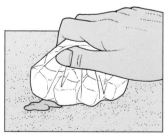

Use your fingers to lift gum

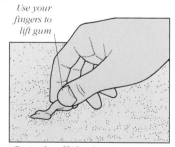

1 Hold a plastic bag filled with ice cubes over the chewing gum to harden it.

2 Pick off the hardened deposit, taking care not to remove the carpet pile.

CHEWING GUM ON CLOTHES

1 Place the stained garment in a plastic bag in the freezer for an hour, so that the chewing gum hardens.

2 Remove the item from the freezer. Bend the fabric across the stain to crack the gum. Pick off the pieces.

HOUSEHOLD PRODUCT STAINS

CLEANERS, MEDICINES, AND ADHESIVES are household substances that can cause difficult stains, particularly on carpets. Stains from cosmetics and candle wax are common in some homes. Tar and creosote stains require careful treatment.

POLISH STAINS

Try to avoid either spilling liquid household cleaners or getting polishes onto surfaces that are not intended for their use. Put caps on firmly when cleaners are not in use. Always store household cleaners in an upright position, away from children and direct sunlight.

SHOE POLISH
● **On carpets** Scrape off the deposit with a metal ruler. Apply turpentine or a liquid stain remover to dissolve any traces. Rinse with clear water, then use denatured alcohol to remove any remaining color. Apply carpet shampoo.
● **On fabrics** Washable fabrics will respond to either a stain remover or a little ammonia added to the rinse water when washing. Treat nonwashable fabrics as for carpet.

METAL POLISH
● **On clothes** Clean off any deposits with paper towels. Use a liquid stain remover, then launder as usual.

On carpets
Spoon and blot up as much polish as you can. Dampen the area with turpentine, and allow to dry. Brush off the dried deposit with a brush or cloth, then apply carpet shampoo.

● **On furniture** Sponge with warm water, let dry, and brush well. Apply a spray stain remover to lift marks.

Use a stiff-bristled brush

MEDICINE STAINS

These cause sticky, colored stains that should be treated quickly so that they do not set into a solid deposit. Ask your pharmacist what is in a particular medicine if you cannot get the stain out. Iodine is one of the worst offenders when it comes to medicine stains.

OINTMENTS

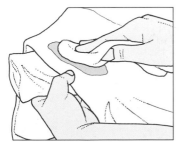

Spills on clothes
Ointments leave behind an oily residue. Scrape off the deposit, then treat the area with a grease solvent. If any color remains, apply denatured alcohol on a cotton pad (test first). Hold a pad beneath the stain to prevent any color transferring through.

LIQUID MEDICINE
● **On clothes** Laundering should remove most medicine stains from clothes. If any color remains, apply a little denatured alcohol. Hold a pad beneath the stain as you apply the denatured alcohol, testing this treatment on a hidden part of the item first.
● **On carpets and upholstery** Scrape up the deposit, then wipe the area with a damp cloth. Apply carpet shampoo.
● **Preventing stains** Keep a roll of paper towels nearby when giving liquid medicine. Use a bib made from a dish towel when giving medicine to small children.

IODINE STAINS

● **On carpets** To remove stains, use a solution of photographic hyposulfite (this is a chemical used in photography development, which you can purchase at camera stores). Dilute ½ tsp (2.5 ml) to 1 cup (250 ml) warm water. When clear, apply carpet shampoo.
● **On washable fabrics** Launder clothes by hand in soap flakes and water, with a few drops of ammonia. Wear rubber gloves.
● **On nonwashable fabrics** Have items professionally cleaned, or use a commercial tea-and-coffee stain remover.

COSMETICS STAINS

Cosmetics get spilled on and around the vanity, they come off on clothes and bedding, and they frequently leak inside handbags. Unfortunately, no all-purpose stain-removal technique exists for cosmetics stains. You must treat each item individually.

NAIL POLISH

Apply nail polish remover on cotton balls

On fabric

Hold a white absorbent pad beneath the stain, and dab with non-oily nail polish remover.

● **On carpets** Blot up as much as possible with paper tissues. Apply non-oily nail polish remover on a cotton ball, testing at the edge of the carpet first, since the backing can be damaged if the solvent soaks through. Treat any remaining traces of color with denatured alcohol applied on a white pad of paper tissue. Finally, apply carpet shampoo.
● **On furniture** Blot well, then apply non-oily nail polish remover, testing carefully first.

MASCARA

● **On clothes** Use a spray or liquid stain remover to remove mascara stains. If any marks remain after treatment, sponge, allow to dry, then apply a solution of one part ammonia to three parts cold water. Rinse, and launder.

LIPSTICK

● **On clothes** Sponge with denatured alcohol, then dishwashing liquid. Launder.
● **On walls** Rub marks gently with a damp cloth wrung out of a warm detergent solution. Use household cleaner on stubborn lipstick marks.

BRIGHT IDEA

Preventing spills
Make sure cosmetic bottles do not spill in luggage when traveling by taping the lids shut, or applying nail polish to the edges of the caps.

FOUNDATION CREAM

● **On clothes** Wipe off the excess cream, then soak in an ammonia solution (see p. 33). Launder according to fabric.

SCENT, SPRAY, AND LOTION STAINS

Sprays and scents tend to be cocktails of chemicals, usually containing some alcohol. They need to be treated with care in case they react with the chemicals used for removal. Creamy lotions usually contain oil or grease and should be treated accordingly.

PERFUME

● **On washable fabrics** Rinse out immediately, then launder the item. Apply a glycerin solution (see p. 33) to dried stains. Leave for an hour, then launder. Alternatively, rub with a laundry prewash stick.
● **On nonwashable fabrics** Apply a glycerin solution (see p. 33) as soon as possible. Let sit for one hour before wiping with a damp cloth. Take care not to wet any padding on furniture. Expensive items should be cleaned professionally.

DEODORANT

● **All surfaces** Blot, then sponge the area with warm water. Repeat if necessary. Use a commercial stain remover on remaining marks.

LOTION

● **Cleansing lotions** Blot with tissues, then treat the area with a grease solvent. Launder clothes; use carpet shampoo on carpets and upholstery.
● **Toning lotions** Squirt the area with soda water, or sponge with warm water. Allow to dry naturally.

HAIR SPRAY

On mirrors

Hair spray leaves a sticky deposit on mirrors, producing a blurred effect. Wipe off with a little denatured alcohol on a cloth.

CANDLE WAX STAINS

These are almost unavoidable if you enjoy candlelight. The wax is easy to remove, but colored candles may leave dye stains, which need to be treated after the wax has been removed. Wax does not set completely hard, so does not require immediate treatment.

ON CARPETS

Scoop up wax while it is soft

Place iron on a warm setting

1 Scrape up as much of the wax deposit as you can with a spoon. If the wax is hard, use your fingernails.

2 Place brown paper over the remaining wax. Iron with a warm iron until the wax melts into the paper.

ON OTHER SURFACES
● **Clothes** Use the treatment for carpets, left. Treat any residual color marks with denatured alcohol (testing first). Hold an absorbent white pad under the stain as you apply the denatured alcohol.
● **Furniture and wallpaper** Use the treatment for carpets, left, without lifting any wax first. Use denatured alcohol to remove color on furniture, and an aerosol stain remover for marks on wallpaper.
● **Wood** See page 16.

ADHESIVE MARKS

Adhesives stick to you as well as to whatever is being glued. Scrape up fresh spills immediately, then use the appropriate solvent. Dried stains are extremely difficult to remove. If you are doing a lot of gluing, buy the appropriate solvent when buying the adhesive.

FRESH ADHESIVE
● **Appropriate solvents** Use non-oily nail polish remover on clear adhesive. Remove contact adhesive with a manufacturer's solvent. Use a stain remover on airplane glue, liquid grease solvent on latex adhesive, and lighter fluid on epoxy.
● **On hard surfaces** Use denatured alcohol. Allow latex adhesives to set, then roll off with your finger.
● **On skin** Use lemon juice.

DRIED ADHESIVE

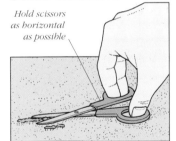

Hold scissors as horizontal as possible

On carpets
The best way to remove dried adhesive is to trim the top of the pile with a pair of scissors.

Apply solvent on cotton

On hard surfaces
To remove label residue marks, rub with lighter fluid, denatured alcohol, or cellulose thinners.

CREOSOTE AND TAR STAINS

These substances are best left outside, but they often creep in on shoes, swimwear, and beach towels – not to mention clothes. Because stains from creosote and tar are difficult to remove, take great care not to let them transfer onto any more surfaces.

● **On carpets** Blot gently, then apply a glycerin solution (see p. 33), and leave for one hour. Rinse with clear water, then use a carpet-spotting kit.

● **On clothes** Place an absorbent white cloth or tissue pad on top of the stain. Apply eucalyptus oil from below the stain with a cotton ball.

● **On shoes** Use lighter fluid, but test for affected color.
● **On furniture** Expensive furnishings should be dry cleaned professionally.

WEAR-AND-TEAR MARKS

WEAR AND TEAR IS INEVITABLE around the home. However, some problems, such as mildew, need to be controlled; otherwise, they may require professional treatment and can cause permanent damage to household items.

MILDEW PATCHES

Mildew tends to occur in damp parts of the home and should, if possible, be caught in the early stages. It appears as an unsightly growth of spores, which makes surfaces look as if they are covered in small dirty patches. Left unchecked, mildew develops a deposit.

ON CLOTHES
● **Whites** Bleach mildew with a hydrogen peroxide solution (see p. 33); do not use this treatment on nylon. Soak natural fabrics in a household bleach solution (see p. 58).
● **Colors** Dampen, then rub with a bar of hard soap. Let dry in the sun before laundering. Repeated washing will get rid of any remaining marks, and a specialized stain remover can be used on white and colorfast fabrics.

ON LACE

Cover mildew with soap

Using household soap
Rub the lace with soap so that a film develops. Leave in the sun for several hours, then rinse.

ON SHOWER CURTAINS

Removing marks
Sponge curtains with either a detergent solution, or a weak bleach solution (wear gloves).

ON WALLS
● **General treatment** Wash the whole wall (even areas where mildew does not show) with a mild detergent solution. Wipe the wall with a solution of commercial bactericide (a paint pad is good for this).

ON FURNITURE
● **Removing marks** Remove mildew spores as described below. If marks remain, have slip covers dry cleaned. Apply a hydrogen peroxide solution (see p. 33) to upholstery, then rinse thoroughly.

ON LEATHER
● **General treatment** Leather shoes, furniture, bags, and luggage all attract mildew in storage. Remove using the treatment below, then apply a coat of hide food or shoe polish. Rub in and buff well.

Tackling corners
Sponge carefully into corners of rooms. Be extra careful near windows in bathrooms and kitchens, where condensation could form pools that encourage mildew growth to develop.

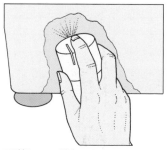

Killing mildew spores
Brush off as many of the spores as possible, then spray the item with a commercial solution designed to kill the spores. Do this outdoors so that the spores do not transfer to other items.

Treating leather bags
Sponge mildew with 1 tbsp (5 ml) disinfectant diluted in 2 cups (500 ml) of warm water. Alternatively, apply an antiseptic mouthwash on a cotton pad. Wipe dry, and buff well.

WATER MARKS

Water marking is caused by minerals in water, and often occurs after an area of a garment has been sponged. To prevent water marks from forming after removing a stain, sprinkle the damp area with talcum powder, cover with a dry cloth, then iron dry.

ON HIDES AND WOOD

● **On leather** Wipe off rain spots on shoes and handbags before they dry with a clean cloth. Allow to dry naturally. If salt marks appear or water marks persist, redampen the area with a sponge or cloth, then dry by rubbing with a soft, absorbent cloth.

● **On suede** Allow rain spots to dry, then brush with a soft-bristled brush, or use a suede-cleaning pad or stick.

● **On wood** See page 72.

ON FABRIC

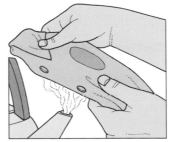

Rub toward center of mark

1 Hold the marked area over the steam from a boiling kettle. Take care not to burn your hands or the fabric.

2 Remove from the steam. Rub the area with a cloth over your finger. Start at the edge and work inward.

SCORCH MARKS

Scorch marks are usually the result of an accident with an iron left on clothing for too long, or cigarette and other tobacco burns. For severe burns on carpet, you may need to trim the top of the carpet pile, or to replace the burned area with a scrap (see below).

ON FABRIC

● **Washable fabrics** Rub the mark under cold running water, using another piece of the fabric rather than your fingers. Soak in a laundry borax solution (see p. 33), rubbing gently until clear.

● **Nonwashable fabrics** Apply a glycerin solution (see p. 33). Leave for two hours, then sponge with warm water.

ON CARPETS

Cigarette burns
Rub burns with fine sandpaper, using gentle circular motions until the mark disappears.

TRADITIONAL TIP

Natural alternatives
To treat light scorch marks on carpets, boil together 1 cup (250 ml) white vinegar, ½ cup (50 g) unscented talcum powder, and two coarsely chopped onions. Let the mixture cool, then spread over the stain. Let dry and then brush off. To remove small burns on polished wood, rub the area gently with very fine steel wool, then rub in a small amount of linseed oil. Leave for 24 hours, then polish well.

TREATING SEVERE SCORCH MARKS

1 Place a new piece of carpet over the burned area, and cut both layers together.

2 Insert the new patch into the space. Stick it down with double-sided tape.

RUST MARKS

Rust (iron mold) may seem like a difficult mark to remove, but in fact it does not require any drastic treatment. Lemon juice is useful as a gentle treatment for rust stains. If you do not have any fresh lemons on hand, lemon juice from a bottle works just as well.

ON CLOTHES

1 Hold a white, absorbent pad under the rust stain, and apply lemon juice from the cut half of a lemon.

Cover mark thickly with salt

2 Cover the lemon juice with salt, and let dry for an hour (if possible, in the sun). Rinse off, then launder.

OTHER SURFACES

● **On carpets** Remove rust marks with a commercial rust remover, following the instructions carefully.
● **On nonwashable fabrics** Use a commercial rust remover, then wipe with a damp cloth. A little lemon juice may help (be careful not to overwet the area).
● **On baths** Use a commercial cleaner that contains a rust remover. See page 24 for treating other bath stains.

SOOT MARKS

These are a common problem in homes that have open fires. Treat brick and stone fire surrounds as below; see page 21 for cleaning other fire-surround surfaces. Soot marks should wash out of clothes easily – but use a spray stain remover on any persistent stains.

LIGHT MARKS

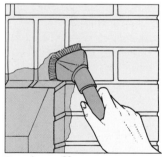

Dusting off soot
Keep soot marks at bay by cleaning your fireplace surround regularly, either with a vacuum-cleaner attachment or a brush.

ON CARPETS
● **Basic treatment** Vacuum well, or shake the carpet or rug. Do not brush the area because this will spread the mark. If this is not effective, apply unscented talcum powder, then vacuum. Have any large stains on carpets professionally dry cleaned.

SOOT STAINS

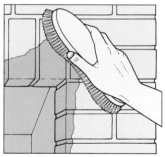

Scrubbing marks
If soot marks cannot be brushed or vacuumed away, scrub them vigorously with clean water, using a stiff scrub brush.

ON STONEWORK
● **Stubborn marks** Use a weak solution of dishwashing liquid on stubborn soot marks on stonework, then scrub the whole area with clear water. Treat heavy soot marking with a concentrated solution of household bleach, then rinse the area thoroughly.

PERSISTENT STAINS

Using acidic cleaners
Apply white vinegar on a sponge or brush to tough stains. Rinse well. If marks persist, treat with spirit of salts (see below).

WARNING
Spirit of salts is a solution of hydrochloric acid in water, and is poisonous and highly corrosive. Wear rubber gloves and protective goggles when handling this substance.

OTHER STAINS

OST STAINS CAN BE REMOVED using the methods described previously. If you are faced with a mysterious stain, follow the treatment for the most similar substance, testing carefully first. Refer to page 34 for removing mystery stains.

STAIN	TREATMENT	STAIN	TREATMENT
BABY FORMULA	Treat as for milk, p. 41. Do not allow the stain to set.	HAIR OIL	On wooden headboards, rub with turpentine.
CARBON PAPER	Dab stain with denatured alcohol.	HEAT MARKS	See scorch marks, p. 53, and marks on wood, p. 72.
CHUTNEY	Treat as for jams and preserves, p. 38.	MOLASSES	Treat as for jams and preserves, p. 38.
COAL	Brush off marks. Launder clothes in warm water.	NEWSPRINT	Apply denatured alcohol on a cloth, then rinse well.
COLA DRINKS	Blot spill, then treat as for fruit juice, p. 40.	SHELLAC	Act quickly. Dab with denatured alcohol.
COPIER TONER POWDER	Brush off deposit, then wash item in warm water.	SORBET	Remove deposit, then treat as for fruit juice, p. 40.
CREAM	Treat as for oil, fat, and grease, p. 36.	SOUP	Rinse or blot spill, then treat as for grease, p. 36.
DUPLICATING INK	Dab marks with undiluted dishwashing liquid.	SOY SAUCE	Treat as for tomato sauce, p. 38. Do not allow to set.
EMBROIDERY TRANSFER	Dab with denatured alcohol, then launder.	TOMATO	Blot, rinse, then treat as for tomato sauce, p. 38.
FRUIT	Rinse stain, then treat as for fruit juice, p. 40.	YOGURT	Scoop up deposit, then treat as for milk, p. 41.

STAINS ON DIFFICULT SURFACES

ON WOOD
● **Unvarnished wood** Stains on unvarnished wood are almost impossible to remove. Bleach what you can, then wash the area with detergent solution. Seal the surface with varnish to prevent future marks.
● **Varnished wood** See page 72 for treating marks on furniture; see pages 15–16 for special treatments for wood floors.

ON SKIN AND HAIR
● **Paint stains** Use turpentine to remove oil-based paint from skin and hair; or try vegetable oil on skin. Protect your hair with a cap when painting.
● **Inkstains** Scrub ink marks on the skin with a nail brush dipped in vinegar and salt.
● **Other stains** Use pure lemon juice to remove dye stains and adhesive marks on skin.

ON OTHER SURFACES
● **Paper** Remove grease spots by laying a piece of blotting paper over the mark and ironing with a warm iron.
● **Glass** Use white vinegar to remove grease marks on glass.
● **Leather and suede** See page 47 for removing ink stains; see page 53 for treating water marks; and page 83 for care and minor repairs to leather and suede.

CLOTHES & LAUNDRY

PROLONG THE LIFE of your clothes and your household linens by ensuring that they do not become heavily soiled before washing. Take advantage of the variable programming of washing machines to clean fabrics at the right temperature and spin speed. Do not forget about the launderette – it is the best bet for washing heavy items such as pillows, which could damage your machine at home.

DETERGENTS AND LAUNDRY AIDS

In addition to liquid or powder detergents for machine washing, use the the following aids to keep clothes looking their best.

- **Fabric softener** Use a commercial fabric softener, or add 2 tbsp (30 ml) white vinegar to the final rinse.
- **Starch** This keeps cotton shirts and table linen crisp and clean (see p. 63).
- **Bleach** For use on whites. Always dilute household bleach. Lemon juice is a natural alternative to bleach.
- **Detergent with enzymes** Use to treat built-up protein stains.
- **Soap flakes and hand-washing detergent** Use to hand-wash baby and delicate items.
- **Borax** This removes stains. Commercial prewash sprays or sticks are also useful.

Fabric softener

Liquid detergent

Spray starch

Bleach

Powder detergent

Detergent with enzymes

Soap flakes

Borax

INTERNATIONAL FABRIC CARE SYMBOLS

The symbols on care labels fall into five categories. An "X" through a symbol means that a specific treatment should be avoided. Some detergent packages feature a complete list of the symbols.

Washing symbol

Bleaching symbol

Ironing symbol

Dry-cleaning symbol

Drying symbol

FABRIC CARE

Certain fabrics need more careful treatment than simply machine washing. Check the care label – if it says hand wash or dry clean, follow these instructions. Use a dry cleaner for tailored clothing, items with special finishes, and anything made of more than one fabric.

FABRIC	WASHING	DRYING AND IRONING
ACETATES Temperamental fabrics. Never use enzymatic detergent.	Machine or hand wash at a low temperature. Do not wring or fast spin in a washing machine.	Do not tumble dry. Allow acetate items to dry naturally, and iron while still damp.
ACRYLIC Needs frequent washing since it can smell of perspiration.	Usually machine washable, but check the care label. Wash items at a low temperature.	Pull into shape after washing, and remove excess water (see p. 60). Dry flat or line dry.
BROCADE Take care not to flatten the raised pile when washing.	Hand wash at cool temperature or dry clean, according to the care label. Do not wring.	Iron on the wrong side with the pile over a towel (see ironing embroidery, p. 65).
CASHMERE Expensive, so it merits the specialized care that it needs.	Hand wash in cool water in well-dissolved soap flakes. Rinse well. Do not wring.	Dry, and shape or "block" while drying. Iron inside out while damp with a cool iron.
CORDUROY Tough in wear but needs care in washing to avoid crushing pile.	Always wash inside out. Hand or machine wash, according to the care label instructions.	Iron inside out while evenly damp, then smooth the pile with a soft cloth.
COTTON When mixed with other fibers, wash as for the most delicate.	Machine wash cotton at a high temperature, always keeping whites separate from colors.	Tumble or line dry. Do not allow items to dry completely, as they will be difficult to iron.
DENIM A strong fabric, but prone to shrinking, fading, and streaking.	Wash separately until you are sure there is no color run (see p. 59). Wash items inside out.	Tumble dry or line dry. Iron denim items while still very damp, using a hot iron.
LACE An extremely delicate fabric. Wash and dry carefully.	Treat stains before hand washing in a mild detergent. Never use bleach – it causes yellowing.	Dry flat on a white towel away from direct sunlight. Iron, if you must, over a white towel.
LEATHER AND SUEDE Sometimes washable, but check the care label.	Protect items with a leather spray after hand washing so that marks do not build up.	Rub suede with another piece of suede or a suede brush to keep the nap looking good.
LINEN A tough fabric that withstands the highest temperatures.	Machine wash according to the label. Test colored linen items for colorfastness (see p. 60).	Iron while still very damp. Starch will prevent some creasing (but not on bed linen).
SILK A delicate fabric that requires special care to prevent damage.	Hand wash in warm water. Some silk items can be machine washed on the delicate cycle.	Line dry naturally, and iron while damp. Use a pressing cloth to protect the fabric.
WOOL Wash and dry carefully, since items easily lose their shape.	Some woolens can be machine washed, others must be done by hand. Check the care label.	Wool can be dried flat, line dried, or dried on a sweater rack. Do not tumble dry.

WASHING CLOTHES

Always read the care label before washing clothes, to establish which method of cleaning is most suitable for the item. Soak heavily soiled clothes before washing. Treat stains as soon as they occur, then launder.

SOAKING CLOTHES

A good soak before washing loosens the dirt from clothes. Enzymatic detergent is best for protein-based stains. Soak clothes in the machine or in a bucket, immersing them completely. Be sure that enzymatic detergent is fully dissolved before you soak clothes.

DARK COLORS

● **Black garments** When these develop a "bloom" and do not look black any longer, it is because of a buildup of soap. Either soak the item in warm water with a little white vinegar, or add water softener (instead of detergent) to the machine's regular wash.

● **Color runs** Always wash dark colors separately until you are sure that the dye does not run (see washing colors, opposite). If dye from dark clothes runs onto pale fabrics in the wash, you can use a commercial dye-run remover to remove color from the lighter items.

DENIM ITEMS

Preserving color
To prevent a new pair of jeans from fading when washed, soak them in 4 tbsp (60 ml) of vinegar mixed with 5 quarts (5 liters) of water for about 30 minutes.

BRIGHT COLORS

Push items under water with a wooden spoon

Preventing fading
Preserve the brightness of colored clothes by soaking them in a bucket of cold water with a handful of salt added before washing them for the first time.

WHITENING DISCOLORED CLOTHES

Submerge socks with a wooden spoon

White cotton socks
Return white socks to pristine condition by boiling them in a saucepan with a few added slices of lemon. The lemon is a natural bleach. Dishwasher detergent also whitens socks – just add a little to the regular washload.

● **Cotton or linen** Soak items for 15 minutes in a solution of 1 tbsp (15 ml) household bleach to 10 quarts (10 liters) cold water. Rinse thoroughly before washing as usual.
● **Wool** Soak discolored wool overnight in one part hydrogen peroxide to eight parts cold water. Rinse, and wash according to care label.
● **Nylon** Soak nylon items in 6 tbsp (90 ml) of dishwasher detergent and 3 tbsp (45 ml) of household bleach to 5 quarts (5 liters) very hot water. Allow the mixture to cool to room temperature, then soak the nylon items in it for at least 30 minutes.

USING BLEACH

Always dilute bleach before you use it – straight bleach will "burn" holes in fabric. Follow the manufacturer's instructions for dilution. If in doubt, add a "glug" of bleach to a bucketful of cold water to make a standard bleach solution.

MACHINE WASHING

Sort clothes into matching loads, based on care label instructions. If you need to wash mixed fabrics together to make up a full load, set to the lowest recommended temperature. Do not be tempted to use more detergent than instructed – it will not get clothes any cleaner.

WASHING SYMBOLS

The washtub symbol contains details of the temperature and type of cycle to be used.

 The figure indicates the maximum water temperature (here in Celsius).

 Broken bars beneath the tub recommend using a gentle cycle.

 The hand in the tub means that the item should always be hand washed.

WASHING COLORS

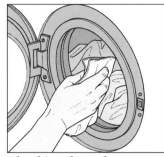

Checking for color run
Place an old, white handkerchief with colored garments to pick up any color run. When it stays white, all the excess dye has run out, and the colored items can be washed with white ones.

MACHINE BASICS

● **Cleaning machines** From time to time, clean your washing machine by running it empty on a hot cycle with 1 cup (250 ml) white vinegar in the detergent compartment, or added during the cycle. This cleans detergent deposits that may have built up.
● **Detergent quantities** Using too little detergent results in clothes remaining dirty; if you use too much, it will not rinse out of clothes completely.
● **Washing times** Whites may yellow if washed for too long at too high a temperature, and natural fibers may shrink.

SORTING CLOTHES

Close zippers and fasten buttons on garments before you machine wash them; otherwise they get battered, and they may not close when the wash cycle is finished. To avoid ending up with gray whites, do not mix whites and strong colors in the same load.

PREPARING CLOTHES FOR THE WASH

● **Checking pockets** Be sure to go through pockets before you put items in the wash – tissues disintegrate, pens leak, and money can be damaged.

Pin socks at tops

Keeping socks in pairs
Use safety pins to keep pairs of socks together in the wash, so that individual socks do not get lost. Leave the safety pins in while the socks dry (either in the dryer or on a clothesline).

Place items in pillowcase, then fasten at top

Protecting delicates
Place small or delicate items such as pantyhose and scarves in a pillowcase to machine wash. This will prevent them from snagging and from becoming tangled up with other garments.

MONEY-SAVING TIP

A stitch in time . . .
Mend holes and tears in clothes before you machine wash them. The machine's agitating action makes the damage worse, and you may have to replace items or have them professionally repaired. Fixing loose buttons before you launder an item ensures that the buttons will not get lost in the wash.

SPECIAL TREATMENTS

Set aside time each week to deal with delicate and unusual items that cannot be washed in the machine. Treat household linen with care to prolong the life of individual items. Air bedding regularly to keep it in good condition.

HAND WASHING

Hand wash wool, delicate fabrics, and colors that continue to run. Use warm water for hand washing, and if you use soap flakes, make sure that they are thoroughly dissolved. Do not skimp on rinsing: washing machines rinse several times, and so must you.

COLORFAST TEST

Using a steam iron
If you suspect that an item is not colorfast, steam iron an area between two layers of white fabric. If dye transfers onto the white, the item is not colorfast.

DELICATE FABRICS
● **Lace** Make a paper template of delicate lace items before you hand wash them. If they lose their shape, you can use the template to reshape the items correctly as they dry.
● **Silk** Add two lumps of sugar to the rinse water to give silk body; add a little lanolin to protect and restore silk.

RINSING TRICKS
● **Removing soap** Add 1 tbsp (15 ml) of white vinegar to the final rinse to remove soap.
● **Preventing freezing** Add a handful of salt to the final rinse to prevent clothes from freezing on the line in winter.

TIMESAVING TIP

Getting rid of suds
If you have too many suds after hand washing, sprinkle them with talcum powder to make them disperse. This saves having to let water out and add more fresh water.

DRY CLEANING

This is essential for fabrics that cannot take water. Use a professional dry cleaner for expensive items; cheaper garments can be cleaned in a coin-operated machine. The following tips will help minimize dry cleaning.

● **Outdoor clothes** Clean dirt from outdoor clothes as soon as you get home. Use an aerosol dry cleaner on coat and jacket collars and cuffs, which tend to get dirty faster than the main fabric.
● **Airing out clothes** Air non-washable items before putting away. Never wear items two days in a row.

WOOLEN CLOTHES

Drying woolens
Woolens can be distorted by machine spinning. After hand washing, roll them gently in a clean towel to remove excess water, then dry flat, shaping by hand on a dry towel (see p. 63).

Heat from hair dryer shrinks fibers on cuff

Reshaping stretched cuffs
Dip sweater cuffs in hot water, then dry them with a hair dryer on a hot setting. For a more permanent solution, stitch two or three rows of knitted elastic loosely around the cuffs.

BEDDING AND LINEN

Towels and bed linen get dirty quickly and require frequent laundering. Wash pillows and comforters only when it is necessary. When making beds, reverse pillows often to reduce wear on one side, and turn sheets from top to bottom – they will last twice as long.

PILLOWS

● **Hand washing** Wash pillows in the tub, using a soap flake solution. Knead vigorously, and rinse several times.

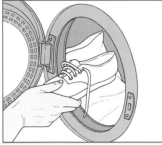

Drying pillows
Wet pillows are very heavy and may damage domestic machines. Remove all excess water before tumble drying, and add a clean tennis shoe to balance the load.

COMFORTERS

● **Dry cleaning** Comforters are too heavy to wash in home machines, and too large to be hand washed easily. Take them to a launderette or to a professional cleaner.

BATHROOM AND KITCHEN TOWELS

● **General care** Wash towels frequently, using hot water, to get rid of the skin debris that collects in the pile.

Vinegar removes soap residue

Soapy washcloths
Soak tired face cloths in 1 tbsp (15 ml) vinegar or lemon juice and 2 cups (500 ml) water before machine washing. This will remove all traces of soap.

● **Removing the "bloom"** Use a water-softening powder to remove any soap buildup and restore fading colors.

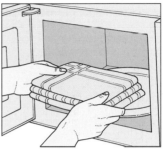

Sterilizing dish towels
Get rid of lingering bacteria in dish towels by placing them, newly washed, in a microwave. Turn on at a high setting for five minutes, then remove the cloths.

STORING AND CARING FOR SHEETS

● **Laundering** Wash sheets according to the care labels. Mixed-fiber sheets do not need ironing – simply fold them when dry. Natural-fiber sheets look better if ironed.

● **Storing** After laundering, place white linen or cotton sheets at the bottom of the pile in the linen closet. Regular rotation and use will prevent sheets from yellowing.

REMOVING DIRTY MARKS

Remove marks from clothes before washing, since laundering may cause stains to set. Use prewash sprays or sticks, soak items in enzymatic detergent if the fabric is suitable, or use the relevant stain-removal technique recommended on pages 32–55.

● **Collars and cuffs** Follow the method shown right to remove dirt from around collars and cuffs; alternatively, apply shampoo to these areas before washing. Using liquid or spray starch will keep collars and cuffs clean between washes.

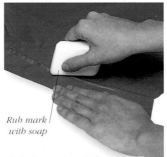

Rub mark with soap

1 Rub a piece of damp soap or a prewash stick along the mark or stain. Make sure that the mark is well covered.

Scrub the soap well

2 Use a wet toothbrush to work the soap into a lather. Rinse the area in warm water, then launder the item.

DRYING CLOTHES

IF YOU DRY CLOTHES PROPERLY, you can cut down considerably on ironing. After line or tumble drying, fold clothes or put them on hangers. When hanging items on the line, try to keep seams and creases in the right places.

LINE DRYING

Hang clothes to dry outdoors whenever the weather permits – this will save electricity, and is gentler on clothes than tumble drying. Sunlight makes white clothes whiter. If you are short of outdoor space, hang two lines parallel to each other, and drape items across them.

DRYING SYMBOLS
The four variants to the square symbol indicate which drying method should be used.

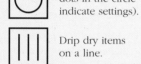 Tumble dry (any dots in the circle indicate settings).

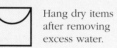 Drip dry items on a line.

 Hang dry items after removing excess water.

Dry items flat after removing excess water.

PREVENTING PROBLEMS
● **Fading** Turn colored T-shirts inside out, and hang them in the shade so that they do not fade in the sunlight.

Cleaning washing lines
Dirt collects on washing lines and may transfer to fabric. To clean lines, run a damp sponge or a split cork along the length of the line from time to time.

DRYING SWEATER

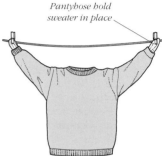
Pantyhose hold sweater in place

Preventing stretching
Sweaters will not stretch on a clothesline if you string an old pair of hose through the arms, and pin the pantyhose – rather than the sweater – to the line.

TIGHTS AND SOCKS
● **Reducing snags** Clip clothespins to the feet of socks and or tights. This prevents them from blowing around and tangling or snagging.

Drying socks
To save space on lines, hang pairs of socks on a hanger. This will also enable you to remove the socks quickly if it rains.

DRYING TRICKS
● **Belts** To dry belts without creating a clothespin mark, loop around the washing line and fasten the belt buckle.
● **Pleated skirts** After washing, hang on the line from the waistband. Clip clothespins at the bottom of each pleat so that the pleats dry in place.

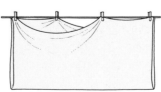

Quick-drying sheets
Pin the sheet at both ends first, then pin each side one-third of the way along. This "bag" shape allows air to circulate easily.

MONEY-SAVING TIP

Handy helpers
Use ordinary clothespins around the house to clip things together. They reseal food packages and hold notes and telephone messages together as effectively as gadgets sold for the purpose.

TUMBLE DRYING

Dryers work best when the drum is only half full – clothes will dry most quickly if they can move around freely. Do not let tumble-dried items become bone dry – if you do, you will find that they are difficult to iron. Clean the dryer filter after each use.

USING DRYERS

● **Avoiding creases** Certain items require little ironing if tumble dried – in particular, clothes made from polyester and cotton mixtures. Remove items as soon as the dryer stops, and fold or hang them.

● **Fabric softener sheets** Use these in the dryer to keep items from creasing – particularly items that you do not wish to iron, such as sheets. Use half a sheet – it is as effective as a whole one.

● **Spin drying** You can use a no-heat setting to spin dry hand-washed items. Put woolens in pillowcases to prevent stretching.

FABRIC SOFTENER

A cheap softener
For an alternative to commercial fabric-softener sheets, soak a washcloth in a solution of fabric-softener liquid and water for a few minutes. Squeeze out excess liquid, then put the wash-cloth in with the clothes being dried in the dryer.

FLAT DRYING

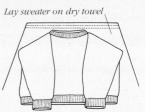
Lay sweater on dry towel

Clothes made from delicate fabrics should always be dried flat. Roll them in a towel to remove excess moisture, then pat them into shape and let dry on a towel (as shown above). Do not expose colored items to direct sunlight while drying them, since this may cause fading.

AIRING AND STARCHING

Large items are best aired along parallel washing lines, which will not only take the weight but allow air to reach the entire area of fabric. Air items such as pillows and blankets on the clothesline. To improvise an airing rack indoors, use the method shown below.

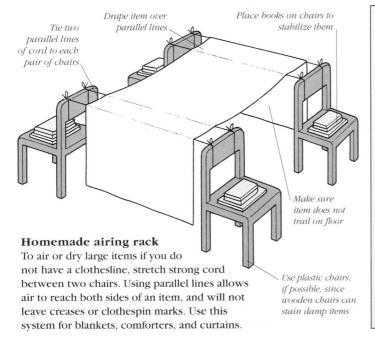

Tie two parallel lines of cord to each pair of chairs

Drape item over parallel lines

Place books on chairs to stabilize them

Make sure item does not trail on floor

Use plastic chairs, if possible, since wooden chairs can stain damp items

Homemade airing rack
To air or dry large items if you do not have a clothesline, stretch strong cord between two chairs. Using parallel lines allows air to reach both sides of an item, and will not leave creases or clothespin marks. Use this system for blankets, comforters, and curtains.

USING STARCH

Apply starch to right side of fabric

Starching clothes and bed linen makes fabric crisp and helps reduce soiling. Rinsing kitchen towels used for drying dishes in a weak starch solution will prevent lint from coming off on glasses. Always apply starch to the right side of fabric, once the item is dry and just before it is ironed. Spray starch is easier to use than starch dip, but it does not last as long.

IRONING CLOTHES

ALWAYS IRON FABRICS that need the coolest setting first, and work up to the hottest setting. Iron as many items as possible at once, since irons use a lot of electricity heating up. Ironing is easiest if clothes are slightly damp.

IRONING BASICS

Use long, smooth strokes when ironing, and iron clothes until they are dry. Freshly ironed clothes crease easily, so hang them carefully afterward – do not simply drape them over chairs (especially not over wooden ones, which can transfer color onto clothes).

IRONING SYMBOLS

There are four ironing symbols: hot, warm, cool, and do not iron.

 Hot iron: 410°F (210°C).

 Warm iron: 320°F (160°C).

 Cool iron: 248°F (120°C).

 Do not iron.

EQUIPMENT
- **Iron safety** Check the cord frequently to make sure you have not accidentally burned it with the iron and destroyed the protective coating.
- **Steam irons** Empty steam irons after each use to prevent them from becoming clogged. Descale using a commercial descaler or white vinegar.
- **Ironing boards** Choose an ironing board that can be adjusted to your height, since ironing at the wrong height can cause backache. Starch your ironing-board cover so that it stays clean and crisp.

GREEN TIP

Energy-efficient ironing
Place aluminum foil under ironing-board covers to reflect heat onto garments.

SIMPLE IRONING TECHNIQUES
- **Fastenings** Iron around zippers and buttons, since metal zippers could damage the iron, and nylon zippers and buttons could melt.
- **Seams and hems** To avoid creating a line over seams and hems, iron the garment inside out, and stop just short of the seam or hemline.

CLEANING IRONS

Unplug your iron before you clean it. Unless your iron is nonstick, clean the base (the sole plate) with toothpaste, applied on a soft cloth. Rub persistent marks gently with fine-grade steel wool. Clean nonstick sole plates with a sponge dipped in a detergent and warm water solution, or use denatured alcohol.

Protecting delicates
Iron delicate fabrics over a clean cloth or tissue paper to avoid damaging the fabric. Make sure the garment is evenly damp.

Ironing collars
Always iron collars on both sides, wrong side first. Iron inward from the point to avoid pushing any creases to the tip.

SPECIAL ITEMS

Some fabrics need special attention when ironing. Acetates, triacetates, and some polyesters should be ironed on the wrong side when evenly damp. Iron acrylics from the back when dry. Always iron corduroy and crêpe on the wrong side, covered with a damp cloth.

HOUSEHOLD LINEN

● **Timesaving technique** Fold large items such as sheets and tablecloths double, and iron one side. Fold in half again and iron the other two sides. This also works for smaller items such as tea towels, napkins, and handkerchiefs.

● **Large items** Stop sheets and other large items from trailing on the floor by putting the ironed half over a chair back. Cover wooden chairs with a towel to prevent stain from transferring from the wood.

PLEATED SKIRTS

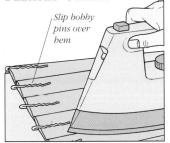

Slip bobby pins over hem

Hold pleats in place
Use bobby pins to keep pleats firmly in place. Press all but the hem, then remove the bobby pins and press the rest.

HEAVY FABRICS

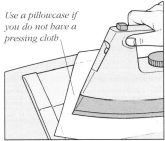

Use a pillowcase if you do not have a pressing cloth

Preventing shininess
Iron heavy fabrics such as wool and viscose rayon over a damp pressing cloth to prevent the fabric from becoming shiny.

IRONING SMALL AND UNUSUAL ITEMS

● **Trimmings** If items have trimmings that need a cooler setting than the main fabric, iron these first, before ironing the rest of the garment.

● **Hair ribbons** To "iron" in a hurry, grasp both ends and pull the ribbon back and forth against a tea kettle that has just been used to boil water.

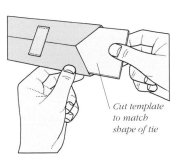

Cut template to match shape of tie

Creaseless ties
Slip a cardboard template into ties before ironing, so that the impression of the seam does not show through on the front.

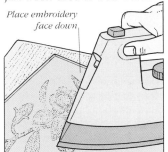

Place embroidery face down

Ironing embroidery
Lay the piece of embroidery face down on a towel, and iron the reverse side. This way you will not flatten the embroidery.

DAMPENING ITEMS

Items that are too dry are difficult to iron. Use a plant-spray bottle to dampen dry clothes. Alternatively, put all the clothes into the tumble dryer together with a wet towel, and run the dryer on a no-heat setting. If you cannot finish a load of ironing, keep it damp by putting it in the freezer in a plastic bag.

ALTERNATIVES TO IRONING

● **Tumble-dry clothes** Take synthetic fabrics (cotton and polyester mixtures) out of the dryer as soon as the drying cycle is finished. Hang the items on coat hangers while they are still hot; creases will drop out as the items cool.

● **Drip-dry clothes** Straighten collars, seams, and pleats while still damp to ensure that they dry straight.

● **Velvet and silk** Hang silk and velvet items in a steamy bathroom to dry – the steam will make creases drop out.

● **Caught without an iron?** If you must press something but have no iron, put the item under your mattress overnight. The weight of your body will give it a thorough pressing. Dampen creases on pants with a wet towel first.

CARING FOR CLOTHES

CLOTHES NEED ATTENTION if they are to remain in good condition. Hang them properly after you take them off. Brush, remove stains, and make any repairs before wearing again. Never wear clothes or shoes two days in a row.

SOLVING PROBLEMS

Loose buttons, stuck zippers, and runs in pantyhose are common clothes problems. If a zipper is stuck remember to pull the zipper down, ease out the material, and start again. For back zippers that are difficult to reach, thread string through the tab, and pull.

BUTTONS

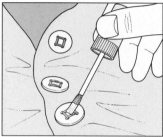

Long-lasting buttons
Buttons will not come off easily if you dab the threads of the buttons on new garments with clear nail polish. Sew children's buttons on with dental floss.

ZIPPERS

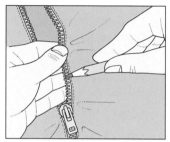

Fixing sticking zippers
Rub an ordinary pencil over a sticking zipper – the graphite will help it slide smoothly. See page 149 for repairing zippers damaged close to the base.

CARING FOR HOSE

To prolong the life of pantyhose, wet them when new, and place them in a plastic bag in the freezer for a few hours. To stop holes from running, apply clear nail polish as a barrier.

MINOR REPAIRS

Prevention is always better than cure, so do not rush into wearing new garments when a simple treatment might keep them looking better longer. Mend holes and remove stains as they occur – and always before washing a garment. See pages 148–149 for sewing tips.

RING MARKS

Hold water mark over steam

Steaming off marks
Sponging a small area of a garment often leaves behind a ring mark. Hold the stained area in the steam of a boiling kettle until the mark disappears.

SHINY PATCHES

Sponging with ammonia
Areas that get a lot of wear, such as knees and elbows, often become shiny. Sponge with 1 tbsp (15 ml) ammonia diluted in 1 cup (250 ml) of water.

RECYCLING ITEMS

Use old socks for dusting and for cleaning behind radiators (see page 21). Old pantyhose can be used to tie plants to stakes. Sew old shoulder pads inside the knees of old jeans for comfortable gardening.

MAINTAINING CLOTHES

Storing and hanging clothes properly is essential to keep them looking good. After wearing clothes, hang them to air before putting them in a closet. Remove lint from clothes with a piece of adhesive tape wrapped around your hand, or with a damp sponge.

CREASELESS CLOTHES

● **Drawer storage** Fold clothes across their width when storing in drawers. Creases will drop out more quickly than if folded lengthwise.

SPACE SAVERS FOR CLOSETS

● **Hanging items** Slip shower curtain hooks on the rod in your closet and hang belts and bags from them. Hang a string bag to hold socks.

● **Odds and ends** Plastic shoe containers with pockets can be hung in a closet and then used for storing socks and other small items.

SCARVES

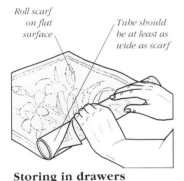

Roll scarf on flat surface

Tube should be at least as wide as scarf

Storing in drawers
Roll silk scarves around the paper tubes from aluminum foil or plastic wrap. This will prevent the scarves from creasing when they are stored.

LONG DRESSES

Hanging out
Prevent a long evening dress from trailing by sewing loops at waist level inside the dress. Turn the bodice inside out, and hang the loops from a hanger.

BRIGHT IDEA

Storing skirts
If you do not have any room in your closet to hang skirts, roll them around plastic bags or tissue paper to prevent creasing, then store them in a drawer.

ADAPTING HANGERS

Wind rubber bands around hanger

Cut away from yourself when using craft knife

Nonslip hangers
Prevent clothes from slipping off wire hangers by winding two or three rubber bands around the ends of the hangers.

Making a skirt hanger
Cut V-shaped notches near the ends of a wooden hanger to hold skirt loops securely. Use a sturdy craft knife to cut the notches.

ACCESSORIES

If you must get rid of good-quality accessories (they may come back in fashion!) donate them to charity.

● **Hats and bags** Paint straw hats and bags with a coat of clear varnish to prevent the straw from splitting.
● **Gloves** Marks on light gloves can often be removed by rubbing with a pencil eraser. Wash gloves in special glove shampoo and put them on your hands while they dry – this restores the shape.
● **Buttons** When throwing out garments, snip off the buttons. Keep sets of buttons in small plastic bags so you know how many you have.

CARING FOR FURS AND SKINS

● **Suede** Pick up threads and lint on suede bags and shoes by rubbing the suede with a piece of velvet fabric. This also works for dark clothes.

● **Fur care** When wearing furs, always wear a scarf to prevent makeup from rubbing off onto the collar. Do not spray on perfume when wearing fur.

STORAGE

Do not allow clothes in your closets to become crowded – if they do, they will not air properly and will become creased. Make space in closets by storing out-of-season clothes elsewhere. Alternatively, use a free-standing clothing rack kept in a spare room.

DAMP CLOSETS
● **Cure for dampness** Fill a coffee can with charcoal briquets. Punch holes in the lid, and put in the closet.

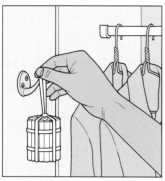

Using chalk
Tie 12 pieces of ordinary chalk together, and hang them inside a damp closet. The chalk will absorb moisture from the air.

STORING BED LINEN
● **Avoiding yellowing** Establish a separate closet for linen items – linen may yellow if stored on open shelving.

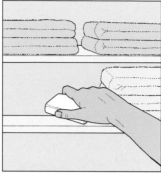

Scented linen closets
Store unwrapped soap in linen closets – the soap scents the linen and, at the same time, hardens to become long lasting.

VACATION PACKING

When packing for vacations, put makeup and toiletry bottles, however tightly closed, into plastic bags with twist ties. Mix the family's clothes in different suitcases – if one is lost, no one has to do entirely without extra clothes.

● **Saving space** Use small items such as underwear and socks to fill shoes, which should, in their turn, be packed in plastic bags.
● **Planning ahead** Pack two large plastic bags for the trip home – one for dirty laundry, the other for damp items.
● **Suitcase storage** When you return home, put a couple of sugar cubes in your empty suitcase to absorb odors.

MOTHPROOFING

Moths breed in dust and dirt, so clean and air items before you store them. Clean closets and cabinets out annually. Do not line drawers with prepasted wallpaper, since this may attracts moths. See page 52 for tackling mildew, which also affects items in storage.

NATURAL MOTH DETERRENTS

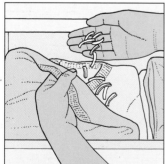

Citrus peel and cloves
Scatter dried citrus peel among clothes and shoes in closets and drawers. Put whole cloves in the pockets of coats before storing them for the summer, and into plastic bags for woolen sweaters.

Tie top of muslin bag with ribbon

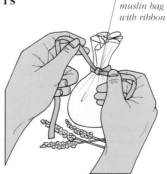

Lavender sachets
Make your own lavender bags by tying a handful of lavender into a square of muslin. Place the bags in drawers and chests. They help keep moths away and also scent clothes and linen.

BED LINEN
● **Heat cure** If you suspect moth eggs are in your bed linen, hang the items in bright sunlight for a few hours or put them in your dryer on the appropriate cycle.
● **Moth-proofing mixture** For washing a blanket for storage, mix 3 tbsp (45 ml) eucalyptus oil, 1 cup (225 ml) denatured alcohol, and 1 cup (225 g) soap flakes in a jar, and shake well. Add 1 tbsp (15 ml) of this mixture to 1 gallon (4.5 liters) of warm water, and soak the blanket, agitating until it is clean. Do not rinse. Spin dry without heat, then hang out in fresh air.

SHOE CARE

SHOES ARE A VITAL AND EXPENSIVE PART of any wardrobe. Keep shoes clean, inspect them regularly, and repair them at the first sign of damage. Air shoes after wearing and use shoe trees to help shoes maintain their shape.

CLEANING SHOES

Well-cleaned leather shoes resist scuffs. Apply polish, leave overnight, then buff in the morning. White canvas shoes benefit from being starched. Nail a metal bottle cap to the back of your shoe brush, and use this for removing dirt and mud from heels and soles.

PATENT LEATHER

Buff with a soft cloth

Raising a shine
Rub patent leather shoes with petroleum jelly – this shines the shoes and prevents them from sticking together. Buff well.

SUEDE

Ensure that shoe is dry

Use a clean eraser

Erasing marks
Use an eraser to remove mud and surface soil, and to raise crushed pile on suede shoes. Use a stain remover on grease.

CANVAS

Rub in shampoo until it creates a foam

Using carpet shampoo
Clean dirty canvas shoes with a toothbrush dipped in carpet shampoo. Treat new canvas shoes with fabric protector.

MAINTAINING SHOES

Coat new leather soles with castor oil or linseed oil to preserve them. Store your shoes and boots away from direct sunlight (rubber boots, in particular, may deteriorate if care is not taken). Touch up scuff marks on shoes with a felt-tip pen or a wax crayon.

USING NEWSPAPER

Stuff wet shoes and boots with newspaper to speed the drying process. Stretch tight shoes by stuffing them with wet, crumpled newspaper and letting them stand overnight. Stuffing rolls of newspaper into boots will help them to keep their shape.

COMMON PROBLEMS

● **Muddy shoes** Let the shoes dry thoroughly, then scrape off the mud with a blunt knife or a piece of wood. Sponge any marks with a damp cloth, and stuff with newspaper or shoe trees to keep the shoes in shape. Polish when dry.

● **Polish substitute** If you run out of shoe polish, try using a similarly colored furniture polish instead. Buff well.

● **Heel preserver** Paint the heels of new and newly repaired shoes with clear nail varnish – this prevents scuffing the finish and will keep cork heels from being damaged.

GREEN TIP

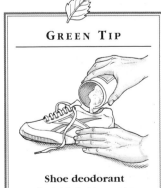

Shoe deodorant
Sprinkle baking soda liberally into smelly shoes. Let stand overnight, then shake out the baking soda before wearing.

CARE & REPAIR

*S*OME OF THE OBJECTS *and surfaces in your home require more attention than a regular cleaning routine provides. Make it a rule always to mend items as soon as you can – letting things go just makes it harder to do repairs. During regular cleaning, watch out for problems that call for prompt remedial action. Keep a kit of the repair equipment and professional cleaners you are likely to use so you can swing into action at any time.*

CARE AND REPAIR EQUIPMENT

In addition to your cleaning kit (see p. 10-11), it is a good idea to assemble a kit of items that you might need for professional cleaning and repairs. A selection of adhesives, sandpaper, and brushes is useful, as are different types of solvent and polish.

● **Brushes and steel wool** Use clean, soft paintbrushes, old toothbrushes that have been sterilized, and steel wool to apply and remove substances.
● **Sandpaper** Keep a supply of different grades that can be used for a variety of tasks.
● **Adhesives** Use the correct adhesive for the material that you are mending. Adhesives are difficult to remove, so keep the appropriate solvent on hand during use. See page 51 for removing adhesive marks.
● **Solvents** Keep ammonia and denatured alcohol for cleaning. Store out of the reach of children. Always wear gloves when handling ammonia and open the bottle away from you.
● **Oil and polish** Linseed oil is a useful treatment for wood that also conditions leather. Metal polish will clean various metals and remove scratches from glass and acrylic surfaces.

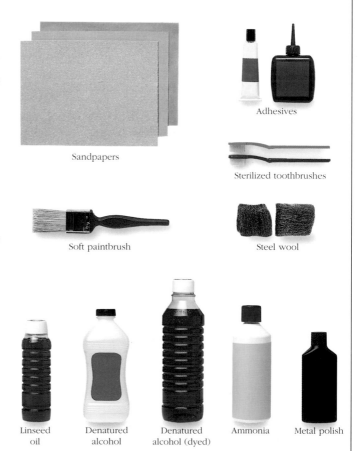

Sandpapers

Adhesives

Sterilized toothbrushes

Soft paintbrush

Steel wool

Linseed oil

Denatured alcohol

Denatured alcohol (dyed)

Ammonia

Metal polish

WOOD

MOST HOMES CONTAIN WOOD surfaces, furniture, and objects, finished in a variety of ways. Although tough, wood is easily damaged. Polish protects wood, but will build up after time. Antique wood needs special care.

CARING FOR WOOD

Different types of wood vary in terms of hardness and color, but all can be damaged by dry air and exposure to sunlight. Position wooden furniture away from direct sunlight. Humidify rooms with houseplants and by concealing bowls of water nearby.

TEAK

Wear gloves when handling steel wool

Applying teak oil
Once or twice a year, rub teak furniture with a small amount of teak oil or cream, applied with fine steel wool. Buff well with a soft cloth. Dust regularly.

OAK

Apply polish with a soft brush

Homemade polish
Polish oak with a mixture of 2 cups (600 ml) beer, a small lump of melted beeswax, and 2 tsp (10 g) of sugar. Buff well with chamois leather when dry.

CONDITIONING WOOD
● **Mahogany** To remove the bloom from mahogany, mix 1 tbsp (15 ml) each of linseed oil and turpentine in 4 cups (1.2 liters) of water, and wipe. Rub well, and polish.
● **Ebony** To revive dull ebony, apply petroleum jelly, let sit for half an hour, and rub off.
● **Other woods** Pine, beech, elm, and walnut need dusting regularly. Polish occasionally with wax polish that matches the color of the wood. To keep oak in good condition, wipe occasionally with warm vinegar. Dry before polishing.

MAKING BEESWAX POLISH

Polish antique furniture with natural beeswax polish; silicone polish gives antiques an unnatural sheen and is difficult to remove. Use the recipe below to make your own beeswax polish. Store it in a wide-necked jar so that you can dip a cloth into it. If the polish becomes hard, stand the jar in warm water.

Use coarse part of grater

1 Coarsely grate 2 oz (50 g) of natural beeswax. If the beeswax is too hard to grate, warm it in a microwave on low for several seconds.

Pour turpentine onto beeswax

2 Place the grated beeswax in a screw-top jar. Add 5 fl oz (150 ml) of turpentine (do not use turpentine substitute), then place the lid loosely on the jar.

Water should be hot, not boiling

Cover jar loosely

3 Stand the jar in a bowl, and pour hot water in the bowl to melt the beeswax. Shake the jar gently so that the mixture forms a paste. Let cool.

REMOVING MARKS FROM WOOD

Wood is easily damaged by heat and scratching. Avoid placing hot objects directly onto wood – always use a trivet. Wipe up spills quickly. Check that ornaments do not have bases that could scratch a surface. If necessary, stick felt pads to their bases.

MARK	NOTES	TREATMENT
ALCOHOL STAINS	Alcohol damages polished wood surfaces and leaves white marks. Spills should be blotted or wiped immediately; apply treatment as soon as you can.	Rub the area vigorously with your usual polish. If this does not work, rub along the grain of the wood with cream metal polish on a soft cloth.
MINOR BURNS	Minor burns on solid wood can usually be repaired. On veneered surfaces, you may need to cut out the damage and insert a new piece of veneer.	Rub with metal polish. If the wood is rough, scrape and sand the surface. Place wet blotting paper over the mark, and cover with plastic wrap. Leave overnight.
SERIOUS BURNS	These need more drastic treatment than light burns. Do not attempt to repair expensive pieces yourself; they require professional attention.	Scrape out the burned wood with a sharp knife. Fill with matching wood filler. When dry, sand, then paint the area to match the color of the grain with artist's paints.
HEAT MARKS	If hot dishes are placed on wood surfaces they can cause white marks to appear. Use trivets to protect wood from hot dishes and saucepans.	Rub cream metal cleaner along the grain. Alternatively, apply a paste of vegetable oil and salt. Leave for a couple of hours, then apply polish.
DENTS	Treat as soon as possible. Dented veneer may split, in which case you will have to cut out the damaged piece and replace it with a new one.	Fill the hollow with warm water, and let it stand to swell the wood. Alternatively, cover with damp blotting paper, and apply a warm iron to the dent.
SCRATCHES	These must be filled. You can buy scratch-disguising sticks in a variety of shades to match different woods. Alternatively, use the treatment at right.	Rub with beeswax polish and a little linseed oil. Rub over the scratch, and buff well. Alternatively, use a colored wax crayon or suitable color of paste shoe polish.
WATER MARKS	Water marks wood and causes unvarnished wood to swell. Mop up as soon as possible, and allow the surface to dry before applying any treatment.	Rub with cream metal polish along the grain of the wood, or mix a little cigarette ash with petroleum jelly and rub it over the marked area.
GREASE MARKS	Spilled grease will leave a permanent dark patch on wood unless treated quickly. Remove excess grease at once, using paper towels or a dish towel.	Use straight vinegar to dissolve the grease, then wipe over the surface with a cloth wrung out with a solution of equal parts vinegar and warm water.

WOODEN FURNITURE

Modern furniture is not always solid wood, but may consist of particleboard or plywood covered with veneer. Minor repairs, such as fixing sticking drawers and wobbly legs, are relatively easy and do not take much time. Major repairs require expert attention.

SPECIAL TREATMENTS

● **Reviving dull polish** Use a mixture of 2 tbsp (30 ml) each of turpentine, white vinegar, and denatured alcohol, and 1 tbsp (15 ml) of linseed oil. Shake, and apply on a cloth.

● **Surplus polish** Use vinegar and water to remove a polish buildup. Rub off at once. This also removes finger marks.

● **Stuck paper** Moisten paper that is stuck to wood with baby oil. Let stand for a few minutes, then roll paper off.

● **Cane chairs** If the seat of a cane chair is sagging, saturate the seat with very hot water, then let it dry in the sun.

WOBBLY TABLES

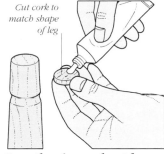

Cut cork to match shape of leg

Lengthening a short leg
If a table is wobbly because one leg is shorter than the others, cut a piece of cork to the right depth and width. Attach the piece to the bottom of the leg with woodwork adhesive.

STICKING DRAWERS

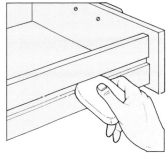

Greasing the runners
If a drawer does not slide in and out smoothly, rub the runners with soap or candle wax. If the drawer still sticks badly, rub the runners with fine sandpaper, and reapply the soap or candle wax.

WOODEN OBJECTS

Most homes contain a variety of wooden objects, such as ornaments, kitchen utensils, and musical instruments. These items need regular attention to prevent the wood from drying out and cracking. Keep wood out of direct sunlight, which may cause fading.

CARING FOR KITCHEN UTENSILS

● **New utensils** Soak new wooden utensils in cider vinegar overnight to prevent them from picking up food smells. Dry on paper towels.

● **Old tableware** Restore stained tableware by rubbing along the grain with fine steel wool (wear gloves to protect your hands). Apply a little vegetable oil, and rub in well.

OTHER OBJECTS

● **Boxes** Give ornamental wooden boxes a sheen and scent by rubbing them with lemon-balm leaves. Sanding wooden boxes lightly will bring back their natural scent.

Salad bowls
Rub new wooden salad bowls with a little olive oil on a soft cloth. Do not clean with soap. Instead, rinse in warm water, and reapply olive oil when dry.

Cover whole board

Cutting boards
Seal splits in a cutting board (caused by the wood drying out) by covering it with a damp cloth for several hours. This will make the wood fibers swell.

Pour in a handful of dry rice

Musical instruments
Remove dust inside stringed instruments, such as guitars and violins, by pouring raw rice through the center. Shake gently, then pour the rice out.

METAL

METAL ITEMS MUST BE CLEANED regularly, or they will tarnish and, on some metals, verdigris may appear. This is much harder to remove than a layer of dirt. If you do not have time to clean thoroughly, there are ways to restore shine.

CLEANING SILVER

Silver tarnishes easily so must be cleaned frequently. There are a number of different methods to choose from, some more suitable for particular types of silver than others. You may need more than one product, depending on the sizes of your silver objects.

SILVER-CLEANING EQUIPMENT

Keep silver polish or cloths impregnated with cleaning fluid for polishing large silver items. A silver dip is useful for cleaning jewelry. Use soft toothbrushes to clean embossed items, and dusters for buffing polish. If you use your silver only rarely, store it in a tarnish-proof bag, or wrap items in acid-free tissue paper – both of these will keep tarnish from developing in storage. Silver keeps best if it is used.

Tarnish-proof bag

Dust cloths   Impregnated cloths

Silver polish   Silver dip

Acid-free tissue paper

Soft toothbrushes

BASIC CLEANING TECHNIQUES

● **General care** Wash your silver regularly in hot water and dishwashing liquid, and you will not have to polish it very often. Dust and wash ornaments once a week.

Scrub blackened areas gently but firmly for several minutes

Cleaning embossed silver
Use a soft toothbrush to apply silver polish to embossed silver. Alternatively, apply polish on a cotton swab, or on an orange stick wrapped with cotton.

● **Dos and don'ts** Clean silver near an open window to stop fumes from collecting. Do not rub hallmarks too hard – you will wear them away and reduce the value of the piece.

Gloves prevent fingerprints

Handling clean silver
After you have cleaned silver, wrap it in acid-free tissue paper or place in a tarnish-proof bag if you plan to store it. Wear gloves to avoid leaving finger marks.

KEEPING SILVER CLEAN

● **Preventing tarnish** Do not store silver items in plastic bags or plastic wrap. These trap condensation, which will encourage tarnishing.

● **Alternative cleaners** To remove bad tarnish from silver objects, first dissolve a handful of washing soda in hot water in an aluminum pan. Place the objects in the solution, and remove them as soon as the tarnish disappears. Rinse, and polish. Alternatively, use a paste made from salt and lemon juice. Brighten silver quickly with a drop of turpentine on a soft cloth.

● **Homemade cleaning cloths** Make your own impregnated cloths by saturating cotton squares in a solution of two parts ammonia, one part silver polish, and ten parts cold water. Let cloths drip dry.

PROTECTING SILVER OBJECTS

Polish silver at the first hint of tarnish. Buy a tarnish-proof bag with compartments for each piece of sliver – or make your own from baize. Avoid overcleaning antique silver – its charm lies in its slightly aged look; there is no need to make it look brand new.

SILVER TABLEWARE

● **Salt shakers** Do not put salt directly into a silver shaker – use a glass liner. Remove the salt after each use.

● **Coffeepots** Remove stains from silver coffeepot interiors by rubbing them with a piece of fine steel wool dipped in white vinegar and salt.

● **Teapots** To clean tea-stained interiors, fill teapots with boiling water, and add a handful of washing soda. Soak overnight, then rinse.

● **Candlesticks** Remove wax by pouring hot water over the candlestick. Melt wax on the base with a hair dryer.

STORAGE

Sugar lumps absorb dampness

Preventing mustiness

Place a couple of white sugar lumps inside a silver coffee pot between uses to prevent a stale smell. Store with the lid off.

TRADITIONAL TIP

Silver tarnishers

Salt, egg yolk, broccoli, and fish are all notorious enemies of silver – they cause it to tarnish. Wash silverware immediately after it has been in contact with any of these foods. Then rinse and dry the silver thoroughly.

CLEANING SMALL ITEMS

Nail polish will prevent allergic reaction

Silver earrings

Paint clear nail polish on the posts of earrings to stop tarnish from causing ear infections.

Use toothpaste as a mild abrasive

Napkin rings

To clean intricate engravings on silver napkin rings, rub in a little toothpaste with a soft cloth.

SILVERPLATED ITEMS

● **Cleaning** Treat silverplated items as if they were solid silver – but with more care, since the coating can come off. Do not polish silver gilt; you may rub it off. Just dust every now and again.

● **Restoring silverplate** Dip worn silverplate in a special solution that applies a silver coating to it. This will wear off with polishing and must be reapplied. Do not use the solution on valuable pieces.

CARING FOR SILVER CUTLERY

Cover all the silver with water

Always wash silver cutlery as soon as possible after it has been used – this prevents food from causing tarnish stains. To clean a lot of silver cutlery quickly, put strips of aluminum foil in a large bowl, and place the silver cutlery on top. Cover the cutlery with boiling water, then add 3 tbsp (45 ml) of baking soda, and soak for 10 minutes.

● **Dishwashing silver** Never wash silver and stainless-steel pieces of cutlery together in a dishwasher, since the silver may cause the stainless steel to pit.

● **Decorative handles** Whiten bone handles with a paste of lemon juice and soapstone, applied and left for an hour. Do not immerse bone or mother-of-pearl handles in water, since they may be damaged.

CHROME AND STAINLESS STEEL

It is important not to use abrasive cleaners on chrome, since the plating can be damaged easily. To treat corrosion, use a special chrome cleaner. Although stainless steel is easy to care for, it can become stained by deposits from hard water, grease splashes, and silver cleaner.

CHROME
● **Minor marks** Remove these by wiping over with a little dishwashing liquid and water.
● **Shining faucets** For a quick shine, rub a handful of plain flour on faucets, then polish with a soft cloth. See page 25 for cleaning bathroom taps.

Cleaning chrome
Gently clean chrome with white vinegar. Remove stubborn marks with a solution of baking soda and warm water. Rinse.

STAINLESS STEEL
● **General care** Dry stainless steel thoroughly after washing, to prevent a buildup of white film. Do not soak stainless steel – it may become pitted. To shine stainless steel, use a commercial cleaner, or one of the methods below.

Buff flour well with a clean, soft cloth

Shining stainless steel
Give stainless-steel pans a good shine by rubbing with flour. Remove heat marks with a scouring pad and lemon juice.

CARING FOR KNIVES

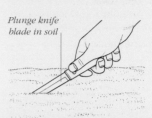

Plunge knife blade in soil

● **Removing smells** If strong fish or garlic smells cling to a knife blade, plunge it into soil. Wash well before use.
● **Keeping knives sharp** Store knives in a wooden knife block, or on a magnetic rack. If you store them with other utensils, the blades will become blunt – and you may cut yourself when reaching into drawers. Alternatively, keep knives in plastic sleeves or in fabric rolls (available at restaurant-supply stores).

IRON AND PEWTER

Cast iron must always be dried thoroughly after being washed; otherwise, it will rust. Season it well with cooking oil before use. Pewter should have a soft glow rather than a shine. Wash it in soapy water, and buff well. Remove grease marks with denatured alcohol.

CAST IRON

Rub in oil with paper towels

Caring for cast iron
After washing and drying cast-iron pans, rub with vegetable oil. If the pans are rusty, rub them with 1 tbsp (15 ml) citric acid and 2 cups (600 ml) water.

PEWTER

Freezing does not damage metal

Chip wax off with your fingers

Removing wax
To remove wax from pewter candlesticks, place them in the freezer, and the wax will chip off. Use a hair dryer on low to melt away any remaining traces.

TRADITIONAL TIP

Pewter cleaners
Rub pewter objects with cabbage leaves, or immerse them in leftover water that has been used to boil eggs.

BRASS AND COPPER

Use the same methods to clean brass and copper. Apply a thin layer of lacquer to the surface of these metals to reduce the need for polishing. Use a cardboard template when cleaning brass and copper details on furniture, so that no metal polish spills onto the wood.

CLEANING BRASS AND COPPER

● **Removing tarnish** Use a paste of salt and lemon juice, or rub items with half a cut lemon dipped in salt. Rinse.

● **Copper pans** Have copper pans relined when the interior starts to show signs of wear. Copper reacts with food acids.

Salt is dissolved in ammonia

Removing verdigris
If brass or copper turns green, rub with a solution of ammonia and salt. Always wear gloves when using ammonia.

Cleaning ashtrays
After washing a brass or copper ashtray, spray a little wax polish on the inside. In future, you will be able to wipe it out easily.

CARING FOR BRONZE

Shoe polish shines bronze

● **Shining bronze** Wipe bronze objects with a little shoe polish or vegetable oil to maintain a sheen.
● **Cleaning** Dust bronze with a soft cloth. Clean intricate areas with a cotton swab. Apply turpentine to remove any marks, then polish.

OTHER METALS

Precious metals, such as gold and platinum, are most commonly found in the home in the form of jewelry. Protect gold jewelry by storing it separately. Gold leaf is sometimes used on picture frames; it needs to be handled with care to prevent it from coming off.

CARING FOR GOLD

● **Gold chains** Wash in a bowl of soapy water. Use a soft toothbrush to get inside links. Drip dry on a towel; then rub with chamois leather.

Storing gold jewelry
Wrap clean gold jewelry in chamois leather to maintain brightness. Wash gold jewelry occasionally in soapy water.

LARGE GOLD ITEMS

● **Cleaning** Clean large gold objects such as goblets and plates with an impregnated cloth for silver cleaning. Buff with a chamois leather.

Apply paint with a soft paintbrush

Replacing gold leaf
If a modern gilt frame becomes damaged, use gilt paint, available from art suppliers, to touch up marks. (Gilt paint is poisonous.)

CLEANING METAL

● **Platinum** Clean platinum by immersing it for a few minutes in a jewelry dip. Use a soft toothbrush for intricate areas. Rinse and dry it thoroughly.
● **Lead** Scrub with turpentine. Place very dirty objects for approximately five minutes in a solution of one part white vinegar to nine parts water, with a little baking soda added. Rinse in distilled water.
● **Ormolu** Clean by making a solution of 2 tsp (10 ml) ammonia in a cup of warm water. Apply the solution to the object with a cotton swab. Rinse with clear water on a cotton ball, and dry with a soft cloth. Do not use metal polish on ormolu.

GLASS AND CHINA

Glass and china look best when sparkling clean. Items that you do not use often should be washed from time to time, or dust will build up and produce a grimy finish. Wipe regularly with a soapy cloth, then a damp one.

CRYSTAL AND GLASSWARE

Wash delicate glasses by hand – using a plastic bowl to prevent breakage – and dry carefully. Never put cut glass or fine crystal in a dishwasher; the strong detergents used will eventually cause a white bloom known as etching, which is impossible to remove.

CLEANING CRYSTAL AND GLASSWARE

Stemmed glasses
When drying stemmed glasses, hold the dish towel steady, and twist the glass around inside it. If you do it the other way around, you may snap the stem.

Making glass shine
Put some lemon peels in the rinse water used for glassware. Lemon cuts grease, and the acid released gives a clear shine and brilliance to the washed glasses.

TRADITIONAL TIP

Polishing glasses
Make a thin paste from baking powder and water, and rub it onto glass. Rinse well, and dry with a soft cloth to create a bright shine. This polish also works well on car windshields.

CARING FOR GLASS

● **Preventing heat damage** Do not expose glassware to high temperatures, or to extreme changes in temperature – the glassware may break. Gilt and silver decorations on glassware will come off if items are washed or soaked in hot water for too long.
● **Storing glasses** Store wine glasses upright. If you store them upside down, they will develop a musty smell and the rims may be damaged.
● **Removing smells** If bottles or jars smell strongly, wash them, then steep in a solution of 1 tsp (5 g) dry mustard to 4 cups (1 liter) warm water overnight. Rinse well.

MAKING REPAIRS TO GLASSWARE

Inner tumbler is filled with ice cubes

Pour hot water into bowl

Unsticking glasses
If one glass becomes stuck in another, stand both in a bowl. Put ice cubes in the top tumbler to make it contract. Pour hot water into the bowl – this will make the outer tumbler expand and release its grip on the inner one.

Hold glass steady

Use a small piece of sandpaper

Treating chips
There is no need to throw away glasses that get chipped. Rub the chip with a piece of extra-fine sandpaper until it is smooth. Then rub the surrounding area of the rim to smoothen it and make the repair less obvious.

SPECIAL GLASS ITEMS

Glass items around the home will attract dust and look dull unless they are cleaned regularly. Do not let dirt build up, or cleaning will become a chore. If you have to carry glassware to another room for cleaning, put it in a wastepaper basket filled with newspaper.

CLEANING AND CARING FOR MIRRORS

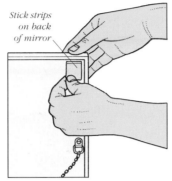

Stick strips on back of mirror

Polishing mirrors

Create a sparkling finish on a mirror by applying a few drops of denatured alcohol. Do not allow any liquid to seep under the sides of the frame and behind the glass. Buff with a soft, dry, lint-free cloth.

Large, heavy mirrors

These can often damage the wallpaper or paint on the wall they hang from. Prevent this by attaching strips of foam rubber or pieces of cork to the back corners of mirrors, using adhesive or double-sided tape.

DECANTERS AND VASES

● **Cleaning** Put a handful of salt and 2 tsp (10 ml) of white vinegar in dull decanters and vases. Shake vigorously, then rinse. Alternatively, use a solution of white vinegar and water, and a little coarse sand. Shake well, then rinse.

● **Stains in crystal vases** To remove stains and grime deposits, fill a vase with water and 2 tbsp (30 ml) ammonia. Leave for several hours, then wash and rinse. Always wear gloves when using ammonia.

● **Stains in decanters** Use a solution of household bleach to remove port stains from decanters. Be sure to rinse thoroughly – until all trace and smell of bleach has gone.

● **Storing decanters** Place a small silica packet (available from florists) in decanters to absorb any moisture and prevent mustiness.

WATCHES

● **Caring for watches** Get a professional to clean the insides of a watch. Always remove a watch off before putting your hands in water to prevent damage to the works.

Use metal polish to buff away scratches

Rub in circular motions

Treating scratches

Remove scratches from watch crystals by rubbing firmly for 10 minutes with a piece of cloth wrapped around your finger and dipped in thick metal polish. Polish the face afterward.

CHANDELIERS

● **Regular dusting** Use a long-handled, fluffy brush to regularly dust a chandelier. This will reduce the need for frequent thorough cleaning.

● **Cleaning** Turn off the electricity at the fuse box, and cover each bulb with a plastic bag. Cover the ground below to catch drips. Standing on a ladder, wipe all glass parts with a solution of dishwashing liquid. Spray cleaners are available for glass beads. Unscrew and clean each bulb. Use a metal polish on the metal parts. If you have to dismantle the chandelier, make a diagram, so that you can put it together again.

SPECTACLES

● **Loose screws** If the screws of your eyeglasses tend to come out easily, dab the ends of the screws (while they are properly screwed in) with clear nail varnish.

Dip spectacles in soapy water

Cleaning eyeglasses

Wash eyeglasses regularly in a dishwashing liquid solution. Rub with undiluted dishwashing liquid to prevent eyeglasses from clouding over; or polish with eau de cologne.

CHINA AND DISHES

Take good care of your china and dishes; otherwise, you could end up with a set of mismatched, chipped items for which you cannot obtain matching replacements. If you break a piece from a set, replace it as soon as possible – some designs go out of production.

CHINA PLATES
● **Storing fine china** When stacking clean china plates, place a paper plate on top of each one – this prevents the base of a plate from damaging the decorated surface of the one sitting below it.

CASSEROLE DISHES
● **Preventing damage** Before using an unglazed casserole dish, season the outside by rubbing it with a cut onion or garlic cloves. This will give it added strength to withstand high temperatures.

CLEANING INTERIORS OF TEAPOTS

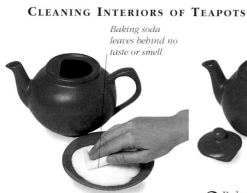

Baking soda leaves behind no taste or smell

Rub all stained areas firmly until clean

1 Clean a china teapot by dipping a damp cloth into baking soda. (Roll up the cloth to clean the spout.)

2 Rub the inside of the teapot with the cloth, then rinse it well. Store it with the lid off. An old glove thumb will protect the spout.

CHINA VASES

Sand will scour interior of vase

● **Cleaning** Pour a handful of sand or salt into dingy vases. Fill with a dishwashing-liquid solution, or pour in a little straight vinegar, and shake well. Let the mixture soak overnight, then rinse.
● **Deep vases** If a china vase is too deep for cut flowers, simply place some crumpled paper towels or newsprint in the bottom of the vase.

REPAIRING BROKEN CHINA

You can repair minor damage to china yourself, but valuable pieces are best repaired by an expert. Keep all broken pieces in a plastic bag until they can be reassembled. Do not eat or drink from chipped dishes, since the chipped parts may harbor germs.

REPAIRING CHINA
● **Using adhesive** Before you spread glue on broken china, wipe the edges with a piece of lint-free material (do not use cotton, which will leave lint). Try not to get fingerprints on the broken edges. Use epoxy for making repairs – this will allow you to expose the piece to low heat after the repair.
● **Improvised clamps** When gluing small pieces of china, use modeling clay or clothespins to hold the pieces.

MENDING A BROKEN HANDLE

Sand holds mug in position while you work

Check seam for extra adhesive

1 Place the mug in a box of sand, handle side up, to hold it in place. Apply adhesive to the broken edges of the handle and to the mug.

2 Glue the handle in position. Wipe away any extra adhesive around the seam. Leave the mug in the sand until the glue is dry.

ORNAMENTAL SURFACES

ORNAMENTAL SURFACES NEED MORE CARE than common substances such as wood, metal, and plastic. You cannot always use a basic household cleaner. Surfaces such as marble, alabaster, onyx, and jade each require a special treatment.

STONE SURFACES

Stone can be used for many surfaces, not just walls and floors. Special stone surfaces are often porous, so should not be wetted. They may also stain easily, so it is important to treat spills and marks quickly. Be careful when carrying stone items – they may be very heavy.

CARING FOR STONE

● **Marble** This is a porous stone, so treat stains at once. For wine, tea, or coffee stains, rub with a solution of one part hydrogen peroxide to four parts water. Wipe off at once, and repeat if necessary. For other stains, see right.

● **Alabaster** This is highly porous. Clean it with a little white spirit or turpentine. Remember not to put water in alabaster vases – they leak.

● **Jade** You can wash jade, but you must dry it at once with paper towels. Never use abrasive cleaners.

REMOVING STAINS FROM MARBLE

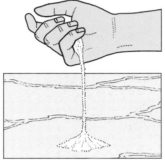

Sour milk will keep salt damp

1 Cover stains on marble surfaces with salt. If the stain is not serious, brush off and reapply the salt as the stain is soaked up.

2 If the stain persists, pour sour milk over the salt, and leave it for several days. Then wipe it off with a damp, wrung-out cloth.

BONE AND HORN

In general, bone, horn, and antique ivory should be wiped gently, not washed. Do not immerse bone knife handles when doing dishes. Keep bone and horn out of strong sunlight and away from high heat. Rinse horn goblets immediately after use, and dry them thoroughly.

CARING FOR BONE

● **Hairbrushes** Clean tortoiseshell hairbrushes with furniture cream, and ivory hairbrushes with turpentine. When washing brushes, rinse the bristles without wetting the backs, and dry with the bristles face down.

● **Bone handles** Wipe bone handles clean with denatured alcohol. Lay discolored handles in sunlight, or rub them with a paste of equal parts hydrogen peroxide and whiting (available from hardware stores).

IVORY

Cleaning piano keys
Use toothpaste on a damp cloth to clean piano keys. Rub gently so as not to damage them. Rinse with milk, and buff well.

CARING FOR PIANOS

● **Plastic keys** Dust regularly and wipe occasionally with a solution of warm water and vinegar on chamois leather.

● **Ivory keys** Leave the piano open on sunny days so that the keys will be bleached and not turn yellow. See left for cleaning. Keys that are badly discolored must be scraped and polished by a professional cleaner.

● **Casework** Use a vacuum cleaner to blow dust away from the inside casework.

UPHOLSTERY FABRICS

THE BEST WAY TO CARE FOR CURTAINS and upholstery is to vacuum them frequently. Do not let fabrics get grimy before they are cleaned. Wash or dry clean them as necessary. Regular cleaning makes these items last longer.

UPHOLSTERED FURNITURE

Upholstery is subject to much wear and tear and needs care, but simple techniques can make furniture look new. A few mothballs dropped down the backs of sofas prevents musty smells and keeps moths away. See pages 32–55 for removing stains on upholstery.

RENOVATIONS
● **Covering seats** Disguise worn-out chairs and sofas by covering them with large sheets of fabric. Alternatively, make replacement slipcovers, or dye existing ones.
● **Patching** Patch holes and worn areas as soon as they occur. First expose the new fabric to sunlight, so that it fades to match the old fabric.
● **Tapestry furniture** To revive dull colors and remove dust, rub damp salt into tapestry. Leave for half an hour, then dust off with a soft brush.

REPAIRS TO UPHOLSTERED FURNITURE

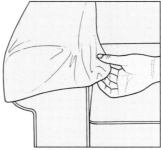

Adding slipcovers
Arms are the first part of a chair to show signs of wear. Make a slipcover to place over a worn area to protect it from further damage.

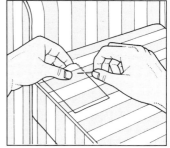

Applying a patch
To patch upholstery, cut a piece of matching fabric, and fold or tack the edges under. Sew the patch in place with tiny stitches.

LEATHER FURNITURE

Keep leather furniture out of direct sunlight; otherwise, it may dry out and crack. Use hide food once or twice a year to ensure that the leather remains supple. Rub it in well so that it does not come off on clothes. Dust or vacuum regularly, and clean with saddle soap.

REMOVING STAINS

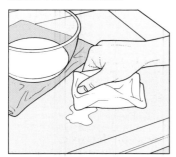

Ballpoint ink
Treat ballpoint ink with milk applied on a soft cloth. Wipe up other ink spills immediately, then sponge the area with tepid water or a little turpentine.

CARING FOR LEATHER
● **Treating leather** Keep leather upholstery looking new by wiping clean, then rubbing well with a soft cloth dipped in beaten egg white. Polish with a clean cloth.
● **Checking for washability** To see if leather is washable, drip a tiny amount of water onto an inconspicuous area. If the water remains as droplets on the surface, then the leather is washable. If the water is absorbed, the leather must not be washed – dust regularly, and wipe over with a barely damp cloth instead.

GREEN TIP

Natural leather polish
Boil 1¼ cups (300 ml) of linseed oil. Let cool and add 1¼ cups (300 ml) vinegar. Apply on a cloth, then buff.

CURTAINS AND HOUSEHOLD LINEN

Take care of your bed linen and curtains to prolong their useful life. If you move, curtains can be altered for your new home.

Bed linen can be repaired or recycled when it shows signs of wear. See page 68 for moth-proofing household linen in storage.

SOLVING CURTAIN PROBLEMS

● **Rings and rods** Boil rusty curtain rings in vinegar to make them bright again. Rub soap on old curtain rods to make them run smoothly.

● **Sheer curtains** To stop sheer curtains from being snagged when you are replacing them on rods, slip a finger cut from an old glove over the rod end.

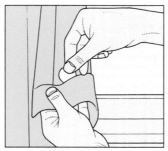

Lengthening curtains
Attach a ruffled edge to the bottom in a matching or similar fabric to lengthen a curtain. Use a fabric of the same weight.

Straight hanging
To keep light curtains hanging properly, place coins inside the hem. Distribute the coins evenly, and stitch them in place.

BEDDING AND LINEN

Use all your linen in rotation, rather than saving some for guests. If linen is stored too long, it deteriorates along the folds and attracts moths. See page 61 for laundering linen.

● **Comforters** Shake daily spread the filling evenly. Comforters will last longer if aired regularly outdoors.
● **Electric blankets** Remove the wires before washing. Return blankets to the manufacturer for servicing about every three years.
● **Dish towels** These wear out all over. When worn, double them and sew the edges together to make them last for another few months.

LAMPSHADES

Clean lampshades regularly, or they will be difficult, if not impossible, to clean. In most people's homes lampshades are in full view, so they need frequent dusting with a vacuum cleaner or feather duster. Always unplug lamps before cleaning them.

CLEANING TIPS
● **Parchment shades** Dust gently, and remove marks with an eraser.
● **Plastic and glass shades** Wash in a dishwashing liquid solution, then rinse and dry.
● **Silk shades** Have silk shades cleaned professionally before dirt starts to show.
● **Straw shades** Vacuum raffia and straw shades frequently, since they tend to trap dust.
● **Vellum shades** Mix together one part soap flakes, one part warm water, and two parts denatured alcohol. Wipe the lampshade with this solution. Rinse with a cloth dipped in denatured alcohol, and apply a little wax furniture polish.

PAPER SHADES

Wipe dirt from creases

Regular dusting
Use a dustcloth to clean paper shades, and pay special attention to any creases. Do not use water, since it will cause distortion. Paper shades can be relatively cheap – consider replacing shades that become very dirty.

FABRIC SHADES

Vacuum cleaning
Use the upholstery tool on your vacuum cleaner to clean a fabric lampshade. Do not wash the shade – the fabric could shrink, and the metal frame may rust. If the shade is very dirty, have it professionally cleaned.

AROUND THE HOME

T HE MODERN HOME is full of items that need frequent cleaning and maintenance to keep them functioning properly and looking good. Electronic equipment, books, candlesticks, and pictures all need regular care.

ELECTRONIC EQUIPMENT

D ust is the enemy of electronic equipment, so items should be kept covered or protected when not in use. Situate equipment where it is least likely to sustain damage, and do not attempt any repairs unless you are certain that you know what you are doing.

CLEANING TIPS
● **Telephones** Use denatured alcohol to clean off marks. Clean the ear- and mouth-pieces with antiseptic fluid, applied on a cotton ball.
● **Portable radios** Dust these often. Clean occasionally with denatured alcohol applied on a cotton ball.
● **Cameras** Leave cleaning to a professional. Store cameras in their cases between uses.
● **Compact discs** Clean discs and players with special kits available from record stores.
● **Other equipment** See page 26 for caring for kitchen appliances. See page 64 for cleaning and caring for irons.

TELEVISIONS

Cleaning a television
Keep dust from settling on a television screen by spraying it with an antistatic product. Clean weekly with denatured alcohol or a window-cleaning product and buff with a paper towel.

CARING FOR VIDEO CASSETTE RECORDERS

Prevent dust from getting into your VCR by keeping the cover on. If the room is damp, keep silica packets (available from florists) on top of the VCR. Keep away from children and pets.

● **Cleaning VCRs** Clean VCRs occasionally, using a cleaning tape to ensure good-quality pictures on playback.
● **Storing videos** Store video-tapes in cardboard or plastic cases. Number each case and keep a log of what you have recorded. Keep a supply of labels for relabeling tapes when you record over them.

COMPUTERS

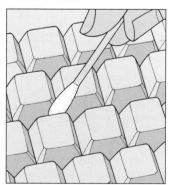

Cleaning computers
Dust between the keys of your computer with a cotton swab. Clean the key tops with denatured alcohol on a cotton swab. Dust the screen and spray with an antistatic product.

OFFICE EQUIPMENT
● **Safety** Before cleaning any electrical equipment, make sure it is unplugged.
● **Computer care** Make sure computers are situated out of direct sunlight, which can cause overheating. Sunlight also makes it difficult for the user to see the computer screen clearly.
● **Answering machines** Dust regularly with a feather duster, particularly inside the machine. You can use an aerosol cleaner, but make sure that the machine is dry before you replace the cassette.
● **Fax machines** Keep these dusted, and occasionally wipe them with denatured alcohol.

DECORATIVE OBJECTS AND BOOKS

The objects in your home are what gives it a distinctive character. Keep pictures and books clean and in good repair. Hang pictures with plexiglass away from open fires; do not smoke near them. Keep watercolor paintings away from direct sunlight to prevent fading.

PICTURE CARE

● **Cleaning picture glass** Apply denatured alcohol or vinegar on a tissue, then wipe off with a dry tissue. Do not use water, since it may seep around the edges and cause damage.

● **Drying damp prints** Place damp prints or drawings between several pieces of blotting paper under an even weight (a piece of board and a few books are ideal). Change the blotting paper as you find it necessary.

MISCELLANEOUS ITEMS

● **Clocks** Clean clock faces with denatured alcohol. Cover a valuable small clock with a plastic bag when doing your regular house cleaning.

● **Umbrella stands** Cut a piece of thick foam to put in the base of your umbrella stand to catch excess drips.

PICTURE FRAMES

● **Cleaning** Rub furniture polish into wooden frames. Wipe plastic frames with a dishwashing liquid solution.

Cleaning frames

Warm a turpentine bottle in hot water, and rub the warm liquid over the frame. Then clean it with 3 tbsp (45 ml) vinegar in 2¼ cups (600 ml) cold water. Dry and polish with a soft cloth.

CANDLES

● **Securing a candle** Dip the candle end in hot water before placing it in a tight holder. For a loose holder, wrap the candle end in tape.

Wipe candles with denatured alcohol

Caring for candles

Wipe decorative candles that become dirty with denatured alcohol. Place new candles in the freezer for a few hours to help them burn longer.

HANGING PICTURES

● **Marking the spot** When you have chosen the spot for your picture, cover it with a cross of masking tape. This will prevent the plaster from cracking when you hammer in the nail and picture hook.

● **Preventing slips** If a picture keeps slipping to one side, twist tape around the center of the picture wire to give it a better grip on the hook.

CLEANING BOOKS

● **Dusting** Once a year, remove books from shelves and dust the tops of the leaves with a fluffy acrylic duster. Keep the books firmly shut.

Leather-bound books

Clean leather-bound books once a year with a mixture of lanolin and neat's-foot-oil (available in leather stores). Neutral shoe cream is a passable substitute.

CARING FOR BOOKS

● **Storing books** If you have doors on your bookshelves, leave them open from time to time to let the books air and to prevent mildewing. Do not pack books tightly on shelves; keep similar-sized books together. Beware of storing books above a radiator, which may cause the bindings to crack.

● **Preventing mildew** Oil of lavender, eucalyptus, or cloves, sprinkled onto bookshelves, will prevent mildew from developing.

● **Removing mildew** Cover mildew patches on books with cornstarch for a few days before brushing off.

● **Grease stains** See page 55 for treating grease on paper.

ACCESSORIES

Mᴏꜱᴛ ᴘᴇᴏᴘʟᴇ ʜᴀᴠᴇ ᴠᴀʀɪᴏᴜꜱ ɪᴛᴇᴍꜱ that they treasure, even if they are not particularly valuable. Keep them clean, and repair them if necessary. Insure valuable objects and take photographs of them in case they are stolen.

CARING FOR JEWELRY

Cᴏꜱᴛᴜᴍᴇ jewelry needs minimal care, but valuable pieces should be cleaned often. Do not wear rings with stones during cleaning, since you could cause damage to the settings. See pages 74–75 for cleaning silver, and page 77 for cleaning gold and platinum.

PREVENTING DAMAGE

● **Checking jewelry** Check jewelry each time you wear it for any damaged links and faulty clasps. Have rings checked by a jeweler a few times a year for loose stones.
● **Chains** Fasten chains when you are not wearing them to prevent knotting. Do not wear gold chains when you go swimming – the chlorine in pools makes gold brittle.

COSTUME JEWELRY

● **Cleaning** Cover costume jewelry with baking powder, then brush off gently with a soft toothbrush.

CLEANING VALUABLE JEWELRY

Place items to soak before brushing them

Put down each piece to dry separately

1 Soak jewelry in a solution of dishwashing liquid in a bowl for a few minutes – do not use a sink. Brush items gently with a toothbrush.

2 Rinse the jewelry and lay it on a dish towel. Dry it with a hair dryer on a low setting. Check the water for stones before you discard it.

PRECIOUS STONES

Amber

● **Fragile stones** Amber, coral, and jet are fragile stones. Wash using the method above. Do not use chemicals on them.

Ruby

● **Hard stones** Clean rubies, diamonds, and other hard stones as above, or use a special jewelry solution.

Emerald

● **Emeralds** These are soft and chip easily, allowing water into cracks. It is best to have them cleaned by a professional jeweler.

Jade

● **Jade** This should be washed, then dried immediately. Use a soft cloth – any abrasive surface or grit will scratch it.

Opal

● **Opals and turquoise** These are porous stones, so they should not be washed. Shine them with a chamois leather. Brush settings with a toothbrush.

Pearl

● **Pearls** The best way to keep these stones clean is to wear them. If you wear yours only infrequently, rub them gently with a chamois leather occasionally.

JEWELRY REPAIR AND STORAGE

Have a safety chain added to valuable brooches to back up the clasp. Wrap gold items in tissue and store in separate boxes to avoid scratching them. If a gold or silver ring is causing skin discoloration, coat it with clear nail polish – it will not damage the metal.

MAKING MINOR REPAIRS TO JEWELRY

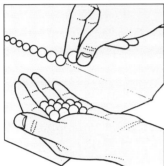

Restringing a necklace
Place the beads in the correct order along a crease in a piece of paper. Restring using fishing line – it is extremely strong.

Untangling chains
Lay a knotted chain on a piece of wax paper, and put a drop of baby oil on the knot. Untangle with a pair of needles.

STORING PIECES OF JEWELRY

● **Necklaces** Prevent necklaces from tangling by hanging them from cup hooks screwed into a wooden clothes hanger.

● **Costume jewelry** Use egg cartons to store jewelry – the bottom for small items, the lid for necklaces and bracelets.

STUCK RINGS

● **Using soap** Loosen a stuck ring by wetting your hands and rubbing soap lather above and below the ring until the ring slides off.
● **Using ice** If a ring is stuck because your finger has swollen in hot weather, put your hand in a bowl of ice water. Soak your hand until the ring can be slipped off.

MISCELLANEOUS ITEMS

Objects such as combs, fountain pens, and handbags need regular attention to keep them in good condition. Clean canvas bags with household detergent, then rinse well. Rub leather bags with neutral shoe polish. See page 79 for cleaning watches and eyeglasses.

PERSONAL ITEMS

● **Handbags** To prevent metal handbag frames and clasps from tarnishing, paint them with two coats of clear nail polish before use. If a handbag handle breaks, replace it with chandelier chain from a hardware store.
● **Combs** Wash combs in cold water with a few drops of ammonia or 2 tsp (10 g) baking soda. See page 81 for cleaning brushes.
● **Stuffed toys** To clean non-washable stuffed toys, shake in a plastic bag that contains baking soda. Brush well, preferably outdoors.

PLAYING CARDS

Rub mark gently with piece of white bread

Cleaning off marks
Rub playing cards with crustless white bread to remove dirt and grease. Dust with talcum powder occasionally to keep them free from grease and grime.

FOUNTAIN PENS

Cleaning a fountain pen
Occasionally, take fountain pens apart and soak the pieces in vinegar. Let stand for an hour, then rinse them in warm water, and let dry on a paper towel.

HOME IMPROVEMENTS

K EEPING YOUR HOME IN *good condition maintains, and may even increase, its value. You will also save a great deal of money by doing your own decorating and simple home repairs. However, unless you are an expert, do not expect to save time. Make sure you have all the equipment you need before you begin, and plan everything ahead. Begin jobs only when you are sure that you have the time and energy to complete them.*

BASIC HOUSEHOLD TOOL KIT

A good-quality set of household tools will last a lifetime – invest in the best you can afford. Keep tools together in a sturdy box with a handle so that you can locate them easily. The items listed below can be used for most DIY jobs in the home.

● **Pliers** These can be used for bending, straightening, or cutting wire; and for gripping nails and tacks for removal.
● **Wrenches** Buy wrenches in several different sizes. They are useful for tightening and loosening nuts and bolts.
● **Screwdrivers** You will need regular and Phillips-head screwdrivers in different sizes.
● **Claw hammer** This can be used both for driving in nails and for taking them out.
● **Cutting tools** You will need a pair of sharp scissors and a craft knife with extra blades.
● **Other equipment** Buy sturdy gloves to protect your hands. You will need sandpaper in a variety of grades; various sizes of nails, screws, and wall anchors; a tape measure; string; masking tape; and oil for keeping tools free of rust.

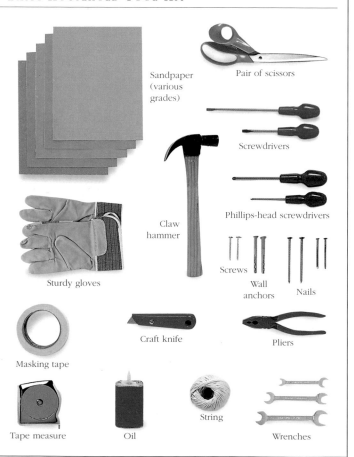

Sandpaper (various grades)

Pair of scissors

Screwdrivers

Phillips-head screwdrivers

Claw hammer

Screws

Wall anchors

Nails

Sturdy gloves

Masking tape

Craft knife

Pliers

Tape measure

Oil

String

Wrenches

ADDITIONAL EQUIPMENT

The following equipment is useful if you are going to do a lot of home improvements.

● **Gripping pliers** Good for pulling out nails and tacks.

● **Extra screwdrivers** A ratchet screwdriver is a good buy, as is a short-bladed screwdriver.

● **Extra wrenches** An adjustable wrench and mole wrench are useful, especially for plumbing.

● **Saws** You will need a crosscut saw and different sizes of hacksaw, depending on the type of job you are doing.

● **Extra hammers** A cross-peen hammer is useful for panel pins. Use a mallet with a chisel for any masonry work.

● **Chisels** You can use these for woodwork, as well as for various masonry jobs.

● **Other equipment** Use a bradawl to start screw holes, a pair of safety goggles to protect your eyes, and a sponge for dirty jobs. A power drill and bits, a stepladder, and a workbench are also useful.

Cross-peen hammer

Mallet

Chisel

Small chisel

Ratchet screwdriver

Sponge

Safety goggles

Adjustable wrench

Short-bladed screwdriver

Bradawl

Gripping pliers

Large hacksaw

Small hacksaw

Crosscut saw

Power drill

Mole wrench

Masonry drill bits

General-purpose drill bits

Stepladder

Portable workbench

HOUSEHOLD TOOLS

KEEP TOOLS IN GOOD CONDITION for maximum efficiency. Keep cutting tools sharp to avoid cutting yourself by pressing too hard. Wear safety goggles to avoid getting debris in your eyes, and sturdy gloves to protect your hands.

CARE AND STORAGE

Improve the efficiency of your tools by taking good care of them. You can sharpen cutting tools yourself, or take them to a hardware store to be ground professionally. Clean tools after each use, no matter how tired you are, before putting them away in a safe place.

CARING FOR CHISELS

Wear gloves to protect hands from steel wool

Oiling chisel blades
To keep a chisel blade sharp and free from rust, rub on oil with steel wool. Protect your hands with gloves. Wipe off the oil with a paper towel before storing.

SANDING SAWS

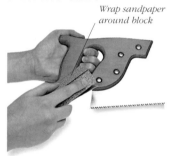

Wrap sandpaper around block

Smoothing handles
Wrap sandpaper around a sanding block, and use it to rub off any roughness from a saw handle – otherwise your hand may blister or get splinters.

CLEANING HAMMERS

Protect a solid surface with newspaper

Cleaning the head
If you keep mishitting with a hammer, the head may be dirty. Rub it in sand or soil, or use fine sandpaper. Try the hammer on a test piece of wood first.

STORING TOOLS IN CONTAINERS

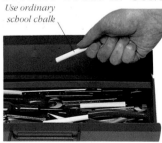

Use ordinary school chalk

Nail shows exact contents

Using a toolbox
Put a few pieces of chalk in each section of your toolbox. Chalk attracts dampness and will prevent rust from developing.

Labeling storage cans
Make a foolproof label for cans of nails or screws simply by taping an example of what is in each can onto the outside.

PREVENTING TOOLS FROM RUSTING

● **Small items** Store tools such as hammers, screwdrivers, and chisels indoors in a bucket filled with dry sand to keep them clean and prevent rust.

● **Screws and nails** Use polish cans or cold-cream jars for storing screws and nails. Any remaining grease will help prevent the nails from rusting.

MAINTAINING TOOLS

● **Removing rust** To remove rust, rub with a rust solvent on steel wool until the metal becomes bright again. Finish by rubbing with a little oil.
● **Waxing blades** Rubbing a little automobile paste wax into tool blades will help stop them from corroding.
● **Rope and cord** Prevent rope from fraying by applying shellac to the ends. To stop nylon cord and twine from fraying, heat the ends over a flame until the strands have bonded together securely.
● **Using a pegboard** Hang tools on a pegboard using special pegboard hooks. Do not store your tools loosely in a drawer; they are liable to be damaged or blunted.

USING TOOLS

It is important that you use tools correctly, otherwise you could end up with crooked saw lines, bent nails, or missed screw holes – or you may injure yourself. Always concentrate when working with tools; only use tools for the purpose for which they were designed.

USEFUL SAWING TECHNIQUES

● **Scoring** For a straight saw line, score the wood with a knife along a steel rule. Cut a small triangular wedge along the score line and on the waste side of the wood. Then start sawing in the groove.

● **Improvising a sawhorse** If you do not have a workbench, improvise one by turning a wooden stepladder on its side and laying the wood across it. Clamp the wood on both sides of the ladder for safety.

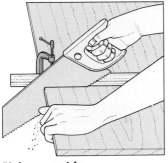

Using a guide
To make a straight sawcut, place a length of wood over the piece that you want to cut. Clamp the length of wood in position, then use its edge as a cutting guide.

Tape marks starting point

Splinter-free plywood
Keep plywood from splintering as you cut it by putting a piece of masking tape at the start of the sawline. Mark the spot with a pencil before starting to saw.

PRACTICAL SANDING

Wrap damp sandpaper around block

● **Using a cork block** Wrap sandpaper around a cork or wood sanding block to give yourself a good grip. When sanding awkward surfaces, use a pack of playing cards instead of a block – the cards will move slightly to fit the surface being sanded.

● **Good sanding sense** Always wear gloves when sanding – otherwise you may roughen and hurt your fingers. Rent an electric sander if you are going to sand large areas.

WORKING WITH NAILS AND SCREWS

● **Tight screws** To undo tight screws, turn the screwdriver slightly in the tightening direction, then immediately in the opposite direction.

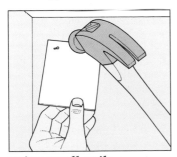

Using small nails
If a nail is too small to grasp firmly, push it through an index card to hold it in position during hammering. Tear away the card when you have finished.

● **Loose screws** If screws on appliances keep coming loose, apply a little shellac or clear nail polish under the heads before tightening them.

● **Filling screw holes** If you have made a screw hole in the wrong place and need to drill just beside it, put a matchstick in the first hole to fill it.

● **Awkward spaces** To start a screw in a hard-to-reach spot, rub some beeswax on the screw head so that the slot is filled with wax. This will give the screwdriver a firmer grip, and help it stay in place until the screw gets started.

● **Nails in plaster** Prevent plaster from chipping as you bang in a nail by putting clear tape over the spot first.

TIMESAVING TIP

Quick screw finder
Pour screws onto newspaper to find the right size quickly, then funnel the remaining screws back into the can.

HOUSE PAINTING

PAINTING IS ONE OF THE CHEAPEST and quickest ways to give a fresh look to a room. It is best that you decide on fabrics and floor covering – which are considerably more expensive than paint – before choosing the paint itself.

PAINTING EQUIPMENT

Painting is such a large job that you must assemble all your equipment before you start work. Make sure you have enough brushes or rollers of the right size and type for the job you are intending to do.

● **Brushes** Natural-bristle brushes are expensive but have a longer life than synthetic ones, and the bristles do not fall out as easily. Buy brushes in several different sizes. A brush with angled bristles makes painting around windows easier.
● **Roller and paint pad** These are suitable for covering a large area quickly. Both are best used to apply water-based paints.
● **Containers** If you are using a roller or pad you will need a paint tray. Pour paint into paint buckets if you are working with brushes – you can also paint straight from the can. Store any leftover paint in a glass jar.
● **Other equipment** Additional useful items include a scraper for removing old paint, a dampened sponge for wiping off fresh paint marks, and masking tape for keeping glass free from paint while painting windows.

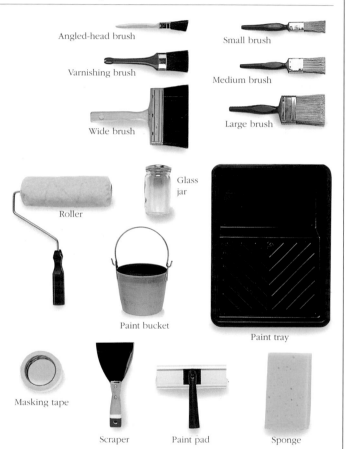

Angled-head brush

Small brush

Varnishing brush

Medium brush

Wide brush

Large brush

Glass jar

Roller

Paint bucket

Paint tray

Masking tape

Scraper

Paint pad

Sponge

PROTECTION FROM PAINT

Before you start to paint, cover any furniture that you cannot take out of the room with drop cloths. Cover the floor with newspaper, and wear clothes kept especially for messy jobs. Protect your eyes with safety goggles when painting ceilings.

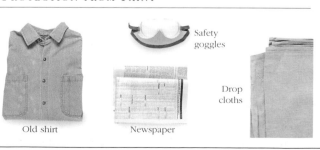

Safety goggles

Drop cloths

Old shirt

Newspaper

PREPARING SURFACES

The quality of a final paint finish depends to some extent on the preparation of the surface before you begin painting. Cleaning surfaces, smoothing them, providing a key for the paint to adhere to, and filling in holes will all help ensure a professional end result.

TYPES OF SURFACE

Plaster
Make sure plaster is perfectly dry before sealing it with primer prior to painting.

Brick
Remove mold, replace damaged mortar, brush well, and apply a coat of sealer before painting.

Bare wood
First treat knots with knotting solution. Apply a wood primer according to wood type.

Painted wood
Sand down the finish if the surface remains uneven. Then wash with TSP, rinse, and let dry.

Tempera
Scrub off tempera with water and a nylon pot scourer. Paint with stabilizing solution.

Latex
Wash latex walls with TSP. Hang lining paper (see p. 102) first if you are wallpapering.

Wallpaper
Paint over paper, or wet it well in sections, and scrape off (see p. 101). Then treat as for plaster.

Ceramic tiles
Clean with an ammonia solution, then sand down to prepare for paint. Use enamel paint.

REPAIRING SURFACES

Fill any holes or cracks in the surface to be painted with cellulose wall filler, and allow to dry thoroughly. Sand the surface until it is level, then paint. Stuff deep holes and cracks with newspaper before applying wall filler. Make sure that it will not flake off when dry.

REMOVING OLD PAINT

Sanding flaky paint
Vacuum away any dust, then sand flaky paint using sandpaper wrapped around a block. Wash the area, and allow to dry.

FILLING A HOLE BEFORE PAINTING

1 Remove as much dust as possible from the hole with a paintbrush. Wet the hole with a damp cloth so that the filler will be held in place.

2 Apply filler with a putty knife, smoothing it as level as possible. Scrape off as much extra as you can, let dry completely, and sand.

HOW TO PAINT

BEFORE STARTING TO PAINT, remove pictures, ornaments, and as much furniture as you can. Big pieces need to be moved around while you paint the ceiling. After that, they can be grouped in the middle of the room and covered.

WORKING WITH PAINT

Cover the floor with newspaper or drop cloths (do not use plastic sheeting, which is slippery). Put on protective clothing. Try to avoid interruptions – they can cause accidents such as paint spills or lines on walls where you have suddenly stopped painting.

PAINT CANS

● **Opening paint** Dust the rim of the can so debris does not fall into the paint. Pry open with a blunt knife.

Keeping rims clean
Stick masking tape around the rim of the paint can to prevent paint from getting into it. The lid will still fit securely when closed.

PAINT BUCKETS

● **Dust-free paint** Pour small amounts of paint at a time into the bucket to keep the rest of the paint dirt-free.

Foil keeps paint bucket clean

Lining a paint bucket
To keep a paint bucket clean, line it with foil before you pour in the paint. Discard the foil when painting is finished.

TYPES OF PAINT

● **Primer** This is used before painting porous surfaces such as bare plaster, wood, and various metals.
● **Undercoat** This is painted over the primer coat before the topcoat is applied.
● **Latex** This comes in a variety of colors and is easy to apply. It also dries quickly.
● **Oil** These oil-based paints are long lasting. They are particularly good for woodwork, but can be more difficult to apply than paints that are water based.
● **Textured paints** These hide cracks and irregularities. They are generally thick and have a rough finish.

PROBLEM SOLVING

Excess paint drips into can

Protect work surface with paper plate

Drip-free painting
To avoid drips down the side of a can, tie a piece of string across the can, and use this to wipe excess paint off a brush. Stand the paint can on a paper plate to protect the floor from drips.

Stocking sieves debris out of paint

Straining lumpy paint
If paint is lumpy or has bits of debris in it, strain it through a "sieve" before using. Use an old stocking, a pair of hose, or a piece of muslin, stretched over a paint bucket, to strain the paint.

BRIGHT IDEA

Removing fumes
Cut down on paint smells during decorating by leaving half an onion, cut side up, on a plate in the room. Replace the onion daily until the smell of paint disappears.

BASIC TECHNIQUES

Rollers and paint pads are ideal for covering large areas, but they can be messy to use. Painting with brushes will give the best finish, although the task may take a little longer. Remove dust particles from clean paint brushes by brushing them against your hand.

BRUSHES

Avoiding brush marks
Work your brush both vertically and horizontally over the area to avoid brush marks showing in a particular direction. Overlap sections until the wall is evenly covered with paint.

ROLLERS

Covering a large area
Rollers cover an area quickly. Pour the paint into a tray, and dip the roller in it, rolling along the ridged part to spread the paint evenly. Roll paint on the wall in the shape of a W.

PAINT PADS

Working in all directions
Paint pads are cheap, disposable, and come in different sizes. Starting near a corner, carefully smooth the pad over the wall in all directions without lifting it. Work in wide bands of color.

PAINTING ROOMS

Painting a room in the correct order helps minimize the risk of splashing paint onto newly painted surfaces. Work on small sections at a time. If you stop for a break, paint up to a corner of a wall first; a stop in the middle for any length of time will leave a line.

ORDER OF PAINTING AROUND A ROOM

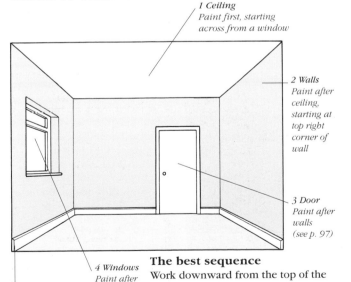

1 Ceiling
Paint first, starting across from a window

2 Walls
Paint after ceiling, starting at top right corner of wall

3 Door
Paint after walls
(see p. 97)

4 Windows
Paint after doors
(see p. 97)

5 Baseboards
Paint last, first masking any surrounding paint (see p. 96)

The best sequence
Work downward from the top of the room to the bottom. Start with the ceiling, followed by the walls, and finally paint all of the woodwork, including doors, window frames, and baseboards.

ESTIMATING PAINT QUANTITIES

To estimate the quantity of paint you will need, visualize the walls as a series of rectangles. Multiply the heights of the rectangles by the widths, and add the total. Treat any windows with moldings as a whole rectangle. Calculate the area of a flat door as above. If the door is paneled, work out the area and add 25 percent.

PAINT GUIDELINES
These are only estimates; see a dealer for precise information.

Primer:1 gal (3.8 liters) covers 590 sq ft (55 sq m).

Undercoat:1 gal (3.8 liters) covers 772 sq ft (72 sq m).

Latex:1 gal (3.8 liters) covers 590 sq ft (55 sq m).

SPECIAL AREAS

SOME AREAS OF THE HOME require more effort than others when painting. These include ceilings, baseboards, doors, and floors, as well as behind pipes. It is worth taking time and care to paint these areas properly.

CEILINGS

The general rule when painting ceilings is to paint away from the window. However, if you are covering white paint with more white paint, work toward the window so that you get the benefit of the light showing what has already been done. Paint ceilings in strips.

REACHING THE CEILING

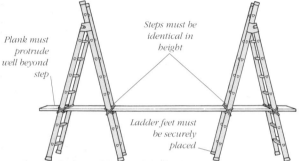

Plank must protrude well beyond step

Steps must be identical in height

Ladder feet must be securely placed

CEILING BRUSH

Avoiding drips
When painting a ceiling, stop paint from running back down the brush handle by pushing the handle through a paper plate.

Making a platform
If you cannot afford scaffolding to reach a ceiling, put a plank securely between two ladders.

Do not be tempted to stand on a table or chair, since they will be unsafe and may fall over.

AWKWARD SPACES

There are several tricks you can employ to make it easier to paint awkward areas. For example, paint alternate stairs, and wait until they are dry before painting the others. Cover taps and handles with plastic bags held with rubber bands to keep them paint-free.

PAINTING WOODWORK

Baseboards
Hold thick cardboard above a baseboard as you paint to protect the surface of the wall. Paint the baseboards on one side of a room at a time.

PAINTING METALWORK

Painting pipes
When painting pipes, hold cardboard behind to protect the wall. Use oil-based paint. Use anticlimb paint on outside pipes. It never dries, so deters burglars.

DIFFICULT AREAS
● **Radiator** Make a pad for painting behind a radiator by winding fabric around a straightened coat hanger.
● **Bricks** Be careful when painting near bare brickwork, since it will be impossible to remove splashes of paint.
● **Gutters** Instead of painting metal outdoor pipes and gutters, consider replacing them with plastic ones. Plastic pipes last much longer and do not need painting. If you need to paint the wall underneath them, unclip and remove them first.

DOORS AND WINDOWS

These need to be cleaned off really well before you paint or varnish them. When painting casement window frames, paint the frame that opens first, since it will dry most quickly. Paint the side edges last so that you can close the window while painting.

PAINTING DOORS AND FRAMES

● **Door edges** Do not forget to paint the edge of a door. Shut it while painting the face, then wedge it open until dry.

● **Hinges** Rub petroleum jelly on doorknobs and hinges before painting the door. Paint smears will wipe off easily.

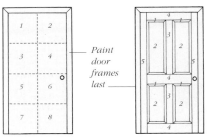

Flat door   Paneled door

Paint door frames last

Painting doors
Follow the numbered sequences, left, when painting flat doors and those with panels. Start at the top, and paint downward in narrow horizontal bands. Paint moldings on paneled doors with a small brush.

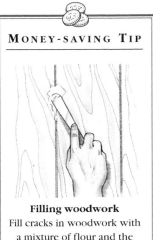
PAINTING WINDOWS

● **Start early** Open windows and paint them early in the day so that they will be dry by night and you can close them without fear of them sticking.

● **Wet paint** If you need to close a window and the paint is not completely dry, rub talc along the contact area.

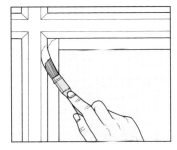

Taping windows
When painting window frames, stick masking tape around the edges of the glass so that you do not get paint on it. Remove the tape when the paint is dry.

VARNISHING WOODWORK

Bare wood is easily stained and will show marks unless sealed with varnish. A varnished finish is also easier to clean than bare wood. Polyurethane varnish is the best type to use, since it resists stains, water, and heat. For bare wooden areas that get a lot of wear, use a durable marine varnish.

1 Apply knotting to seal any knots. Then wrap a cloth around your forefinger, and rub varnish into the wood in the direction of the grain.

2 When the varnish is dry, rub the surface with extra-fine sandpaper to give a smooth finish. If a knot still leaks resin, apply more knotting to it.

3 Dust the surface well, then apply a second coat of varnish. Work in line with the grain. Sand down the finish before applying the final coat.

FINISHING UP

IT IS VITAL TO CLEAN YOUR TOOLS at the end of every painting session. If you do not, a skin will form on top of the paint, and brushes and rollers will harden and become difficult to clean. You may then have to throw them away.

CLEANING EQUIPMENT

Turpentine or warm water and detergent will clean off most paint. Some paints need special solvents – read the instructions on the paint can carefully. When brushes and rollers are clean, shake them to remove excess water, and wipe dry with a lint-free cloth.

CLEANING BASICS
● **Avoid fumes** Ventilate the room well when cleaning painting equipment with turpentine or solvents, since these chemicals may release dangerous fumes. Do not smoke in the cleaning area.
● **Latex** Water-based paints can be washed off in warm water and detergent.
● **Oil-based paint** Clean brushes by wiping thoroughly on newspaper. Swirl the brushes in turpentine, and rinse in warm, soapy water followed by clean water.

ROLLERS AND BRUSHES

Cleaning a roller
Run the roller over several sheets of old newspaper to remove as much paint as possible. Then wash the roller in warm water and detergent.

Nail keeps brush suspended

Bristles are not bent

Soaking a brush
To soak a brush in solvent, drill a hole in the handle, and push a long nail through it. Balance the nail across a jar. This will keep the bristles from bending.

STORING EQUIPMENT

When storing brushes for a long time, make sure that the bristles are straight, then wrap the brushes in foil or heavy paper, or hang them up. To replace the lid on a paint can, lay a piece of wood across the rim and gently tap it all around with a hammer.

TEMPORARY MEASURES

Protecting brushes
When taking a break, wrap brushes in foil or plastic to keep them moist. Alternatively, place the bristles in a plastic bag and immerse the bag in water.

PAINT STORAGE

Color-code paint can

Upside-down cans
Store paint cans upside down to prevent a skin from forming on the paint. Dab paint on the base of the can so that you can find the right color next time.

BRUSH STORAGE

Hanging brushes
Drill a hole in the handles of new brushes to hang them up. Never store brushes standing on their bristles, since resulting bends are difficult to remove.

AFTER PAINTING

Once you have finished cleaning your equipment, make sure that it is ready for your next painting session. Soften old brushes that have hardened, update your decorating log book (see below), and put equipment away where you can easily find it again.

KEEPING BRUSHES IN GOOD REPAIR

● **Softening brushes** If a paintbrush has become stiff through not being cleaned properly, simmer it in vinegar until it is soft. Scrape off the old paint with a wire brush.

● **Oiling brushes** Work a few drops of oil into clean, dry brush bristles to keep them soft and ready for the next use. Wipe off excess oil before hanging up for storage.

CLEANING UP SPILLS

● **Paint stains** See page 46 for removing paint stains from clothes and furnishings. To remove dried paint from hair, rub with a little turpentine, applied on a paper towel.

CLEANING HANDS

Rub oil well into hands

Use ordinary cooking oil

Natural paint remover
Rub vegetable oil into your hands to remove dried paint from the skin. Wipe them dry with a paper towel. The vegetable oil will not dry out your hands as turpentine does.

TOUCHING UP

Pour leftover paint from bucket into jar

Storing sample paint
Pour a little paint into a clean, dry, screw-top jar for touching up paint work. This is especially important if the color is not premixed – producing an exact match will be difficult.

BRIGHT IDEA

Color swatch
Apply some paint to a piece of heavy white paper. Carry the swatch with you when shopping for furnishings that will match the paint.

KEEPING A DECORATING LOG BOOK

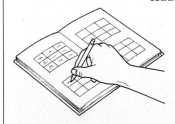

It will be of enormous help when you come to redecorate or sell your home if you have kept a log book of the materials you have used for decorating, as well as the quantities. Make notes while you are decorating. Later you can refer to your log book, and all the details will be there at your fingertips.

● **Format** Use a notebook, or create a decorating section in your home log book (see p. 9).
● **Recording details** Note the quantity, color, code number, type, and cost of wallpaper or paint, and where you bought it. If you make a paint color swatch, store it in this section.
● **Flooring** Use a color picture cut from the manufacturer's literature to record new floor coverings. Samples may be too bulky to put in the log book.
● **Shopping** When you redecorate, take the log book with you to stores. You can then be certain that whatever you buy will match what you have.

● **Fabric samples** Stick fabric samples in your log book. Note details such as the manufacturer, the fabric's name, and the code number. For curtains, note the heading used and the curtain maker's name. For blinds, note color, brand and where bought.

HANGING WALLPAPER

Using a wall covering, whether paper or vinyl, allows you to decorate walls in a variety of patterns and a mixture of shades and colors. Hanging wallpaper is trickier than painting, so it is best to begin with a small room.

WALLPAPER EQUIPMENT

These are the basic items you will need for hanging wallpaper. You may prefer to rent some of the bulkier items if you do not have adequate storage space for them in your home.

● **Equipment quality** Use tools of good quality: blunt scissors will tear paper, and a cheap pasting brush will shed bristles.
● **Plumb line** There is no need to buy a plumb line – you can make your own (see p. 103).
● **Extras** Use a clean broom for holding up pasted paper when working near the ceiling.

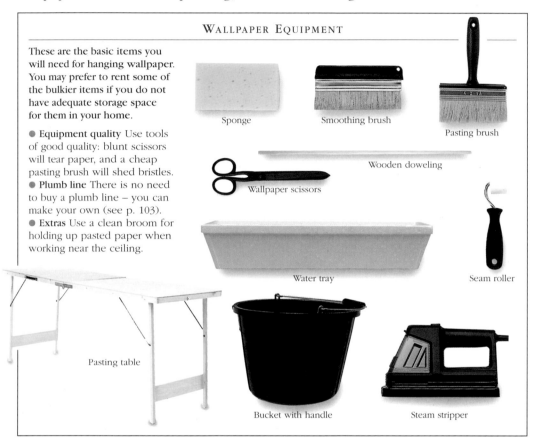

Sponge

Smoothing brush

Pasting brush

Wooden doweling

Wallpaper scissors

Water tray

Seam roller

Pasting table

Bucket with handle

Steam stripper

TYPES OF WALLPAPER

Different types of wallpaper serve different functions. Make sure the wallpaper you choose is suited to the condition of the walls and the use of the room.

● **Quantity** Always buy one more roll than you think you need. Mistakes happen and there can be color changes from one dye lot to another.
● **Thick paper** Buy thick or textured paper if you want to cover rough or cracked walls. These will not stretch or tear as easily as thin paper would.

LINING
This is good for covering slightly uneven walls before hanging decorative paper.

VINYL
A wipe-clean surface makes this good for kitchens, bathrooms, and children's rooms.

TEXTURED
This is ideal for uneven walls. It must be painted and may be hard to remove.

DECORATED
A wide range of decorative colors and patterns is available. Try a sample at home.

BEFORE YOU START

Remove all old wallpaper before applying new. If working on a previously painted surface, first wash it well, and allow it to dry. Make sure bare plaster is dry before painting with size so that wallpaper paste will stick. Wear overalls or old clothes for protection.

REMOVING OLD WALLPAPER

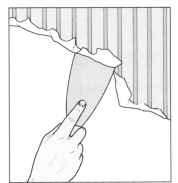

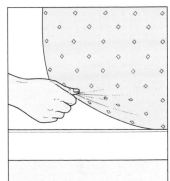

By hand
Using a sponge, thoroughly soak a small area of wallpaper with water. Make a few random slits in the area with the corner of a scraper, and begin scraping off the paper, working upward.

Using a steamer
A steamer will dissolve the paste behind the old wallpaper with blasts of steam. You can work on a larger area than by hand, but you still need to scrape the paper off afterward.

Peeling off vinyl
Starting at the bottom, peel off vinyl with care – you should find walls lined with backing paper underneath. This backing can either be removed or covered with fresh wallpaper.

PREPARATION

Make sure any painting has been done in the room first, since wallpaper paste can easily be wiped off painted surfaces. Get all your equipment ready, and cut several lengths of paper to the correct size, allowing at least 4 in (10 cm) more than the height of the wall.

STARTING WORK
● **Ceilings** Always paper the ceiling before starting on the walls so that paste will not drip onto the new paper.

WALLPAPER PASTE
● **Using a roller** Consider using a roller rather than a sponge to apply paste to paper more quickly.

Applying size
If you first apply a coat of size to the walls, it allows you to slide the paper around for a perfect pattern match. Size also reduces the absorbency of the surface.

Mixing paste
Follow the manufacturer's instructions for mixing together the powder and water. Mix well with a dowel, and let stand until the bubbles subside.

BRIGHT IDEA

Covering grease spots
Paint any grease spots on the walls with latex before wallpapering. This will prevent the grease from soaking through the paper.

USING LINING PAPER

Lining paper provides a smooth surface for the top layer of wallpaper. It is sold in several thicknesses. Let dry for 48 hours before wallpapering. Hanging lining paper will also give you practice in fitting paper around obstacles such as light switches.

ON CEILINGS

ON WALLS

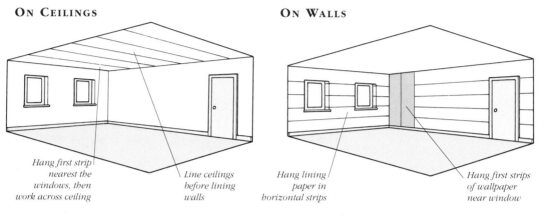

Hang first strip nearest the windows, then work across ceiling

Line ceilings before lining walls

Hang lining paper in horizontal strips

Hang first strips of wallpaper near window

ORDER OF WORK

Begin on the most important wall. With a dominant pattern, start by hanging the central piece above the focal point – probably a fireplace. Otherwise, start to the left of a window. Finish at a corner nearest to the door so that any minor mismatches will not be seen.

The right order
Begin papering near a window or at the focal point of a room. Work away from the starting point in both directions, and finish off in a corner near a door.

FINISHING WORK
● **Trimming edges** Press the paper into the corner of the wall and ceiling at the top, and the wall and floor or baseboard at the bottom. Pull the paper away and trim along the crease with scissors.

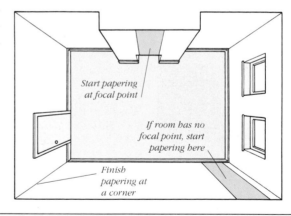

Start papering at focal point

If room has no focal point, start papering here

Finish papering at a corner

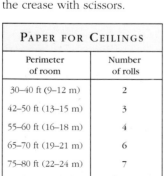

PAPER FOR CEILINGS	
Perimeter of room	Number of rolls
30–40 ft (9–12 m)	2
42–50 ft (13–15 m)	3
55–60 ft (16–18 m)	4
65–70 ft (19–21 m)	6
75–80 ft (22–24 m)	7
85–90 ft (25–27 m)	9
95–100 ft (28–30 m)	10

PAPER FOR WALLS									
Number of rolls according to perimeter of room									
Wall height	30 ft (9 m)	38 ft (12 m)	46 ft (14 m)	52 ft (16 m)	59 ft (18 m)	69 ft (21 m)	75 ft (23 m)	85 ft (26 m)	92 ft (28 m)
7 ft (2.14 m)	4	5	6	7	8	9	10	12	13
8 ft (2.45 m)	5	6	7	9	10	11	12	14	15
9 ft (2.75 m)	6	7	8	9	10	12	13	14	15
10 ft (3 m)	6	8	9	10	12	13	15	16	18

USEFUL TECHNIQUES

When you have finished wallpapering the room, record the amount of paper that you used in your decorating log (see p. 99), or write it somewhere inconspicuous – behind a light switch, for example. This saves having to recalculate quantities next time you decorate.

WALLPAPERING AIDS

● **Screw holes** To locate screw holes for fixtures when repapering, place a matchstick in the wall anchor, protruding about ⅛ in (3 mm). Brush the wallpaper over it, so you will see where to put the screws.

● **Protecting paper** If you need to protect wallpaper, paint a commercial protective sealant over it once the wallpaper paste is dry.

● **Excess paste** Tie a piece of string across the paste bucket so that you can remove excess paste from the brush.

LIGHT SWITCHES

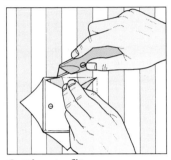

Cutting to fit
When papering around a light switch, cut a diagonal cross in the paper. Peel back the paper triangles, and trim flush.

MONEY-SAVING TIP

Homemade plumb line
Tie a pair of scissors to a string to make your own plumb line in an instant.

WALLPAPERING PROBLEMS

Careful preparation of walls and wallpaper will help minimize most common wallpapering problems. Minor faults, such as bubbles, shiny patches, and uneven edges, can be corrected relatively easily. However, if you have damaged a length of wallpaper, it is best to start again with a fresh sheet.

1 To remove bubbles of air, use a craft knife and carefully slit a small cross in the paper at the center of the air bubble.

2 Gently fold back the flaps and, using a small, narrow brush, carefully insert fresh wallpaper paste into the slits.

3 Replace the flaps and rub the edges together with a smoothing brush. Wipe over the seam with a damp sponge.

Lifting seams
If seams have come loose, lift edges with a craft knife. Apply paste, and sponge in place.

Shiny patches
These are due to paste drying on the surface. Use a ball of soft white bread to remove them.

OTHER PROBLEMS

● **Uneven edges** It is easy to cut an uneven edge, particularly at the junction of the wall and ceiling. An uneven edge can be disguised by a thin border.

● **Creases** These can be caused by applying paper to an uneven wall. Cut along the crease, and repaste the paper. Sponge it flat.

● **Damp patches** Damp patches and stains cannot be remedied. Strip the paper and start again.

OTHER TECHNIQUES

Most homes contain woodwork, tiling, and shelving, as well as different types of flooring. These will need repairing or replacing at some stage if you want to redecorate your home properly. Call an expert if you are unsure.

WOODWORK

Good-quality bare wood can just be sealed or stained, rather than painted. Always sand down well and use knotting to seal any knots before you apply the paint or varnish. Cover wood to be painted in primer, then with undercoat before applying a top coat of paint.

WOODWORK BASICS
● **Woodworm** Be alert for tiny holes in wood with particles of sawdust coming out of them – these usually indicate woodworm infestation. If a large area of woodwork has been infected, professional treatment is essential. This should carry a guarantee covering it for several years.
● **Painting wood** Before painting wood, wipe over it with a cloth soaked in turpentine to provide a key for the paint. Apply several coats of oil-based paint.

STRIPPING WOOD

Use fine sawdust

Applying wood stripper
When stripping vertical surfaces, sprinkle sawdust onto the wood stripper – this makes it drip off slowly and gives it time to work.

TRADITIONAL TIP

Reviving scent
Restore natural scent to cedar chests or closets by lightly sanding the interiors.

TILING

Tiles enhance decor by providing a different type of surface from either paint or paper. Mirror tiles will help make a room look bigger. Tiles are ideal in the kitchen and bathroom, since they can withstand heat, grease, and moisture better than paint or wallpaper.

BEFORE TILING
● **Choosing tiles** Buy self-adhesive ceramic tiles if you can afford them. They are not as messy to lay as ordinary tiles that need adhesive. For large areas, buy mosaics of tiles already joined together.
● **Sound surfaces** Make sure that the surface to be tiled is firm, dry, and undamaged. Do not lay tiles over wallpaper – it may tear, causing the tiles to fall off and break. Make sure that paint on a painted wall is not flaking. You can lay new tiles over old ones if the old tiles are not cracked or loose.

LAYING TILES
● **Preparing walls** Rub down the surface of the wall with coarse-grade sandpaper to provide a rough key to help the tiling adhesive to stick.
● **Installing accessories** To hang accessories on tiled walls, you will have to drill holes in the tiles. First scrape a small hole in the required spot with a sharp tool. Then put masking tape in a cross over the hole to prevent the drill bit from slipping. Do not use a hammer and nail to make a hole in a tile – the tile will probably shatter.

REPAIRS TO TILES

Replacing tiles
If a tile is cracked, you do not need to retile the whole wall. Chip out the damaged tile, using a cold chisel and mallet, and replace it with a new one.

FLOORING

Most types of flooring can be laid by an amateur. However, poor laying can ruin the look of flooring, and of the whole room, so if you are not confident about doing a good job, leave it to an expert. See pages 14–17 for caring for different types of floor surface.

VINYL FLOORING
● **Laying vinyl** Begin in front of a window and lay the vinyl running away from it. Lay it at right angles to floorboards, or on a sheet of hardboard.

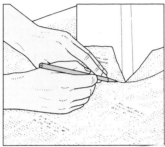

Laying around fixtures
Trim vinyl flooring to fit around awkward shapes by first tracing the shape onto newspaper with a thick pen. Cut out and use as a template for a perfect fit.

LAYING CARPET
● **Carpet tiles** Hammer several small nails through a piece of wood and use to grip the carpet with the nails when pushing the tiles together.

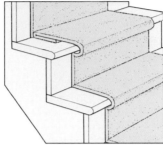

Stair carpeting
Leave a little extra carpet at the top and bottom of the stairs. This way, you can move the carpet each year to even out wear along the step edges.

OTHER FLOORING
● **Cork** This type of floor is easy to lay, but take care to get the grain running in the right direction unless you want it to look random. Cork is a good insulator, muffles noise, and is warm to walk on. Use PVC-coated cork in areas subject to heavy wear.
● **Linoleum** When laying linoleum, allow for the fact that it tends to stretch. Lay it out flat first and leave it for a while before cutting it to size.
● **Quarry tiles** These must be laid professionally, on a solid subfloor. See page 16 for treating white patches on newly laid floors.
● **Wood tiles** Allow wood tiles to acclimatize to the room for several days before laying.

SHELVES

When putting up shelves, it is important to consider what you will store on them. Books in particular are heavy and need to be supported at regular intervals, so that the shelves do not sag in the center. Choose a style that will match the decor of the room.

CHOOSING SHELVES
● **Using bricks** Construct a cheap shelf unit using piles of bricks with planks of planed wood laid between them at appropriate intervals.
● **Using glass** Glass shelves should be made from plate glass with a beveled front edge so that you cannot cut yourself on them. Use double-sided adhesive pads between glass and supports to prevent the glass from slipping.
● **Brackets** Use strong shelf brackets to support heavy equipment such as a stereo system or a television. Make sure that the walls are strong enough to support the weight.

PUTTING UP SHELVES

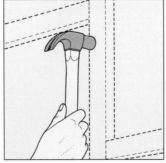

On partition walls
Attach shelf brackets to the load-bearing points – studs – of partition walls. To locate the studs, tap along the wall gently with a light hammer until the quality of the sound changes.

ADAPTING SHELVES

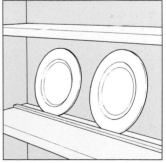

Displaying plates
Nail molding along a shelf that will be used to display items such as plates upright. The molding prevents the plates from slipping off. Varnish or paint the added molding to match.

HOME MAINTENANCE

K EEPING YOUR HOME *in good repair means that all fixtures and equipment work properly and that long-term problems are avoided. Good repair maintains the value of your home if you own it, and helps safeguard your deposit if you rent it. Treat any problems as soon as you spot them, with sweat equity or by calling in professional help.*

A WELL-MAINTAINED HOME

Take time to look at your home with an outsider's eye. It is only too easy to accept that a faucet drips or a lightbulb needs replacing and to live with the problem. Failure to put things right immediately can cause inconvenience – and sometimes even danger.

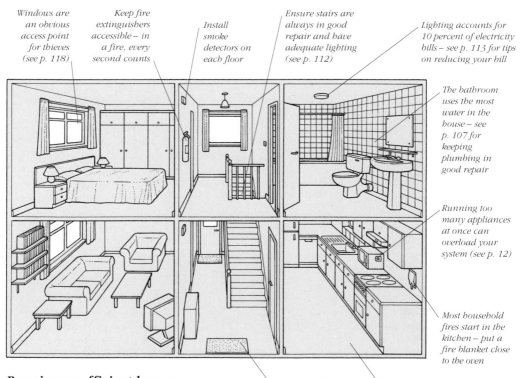

Windows are an obvious access point for thieves (see p. 118)

Keep fire extinguishers accessible – in a fire, every second counts

Install smoke detectors on each floor

Ensure stairs are always in good repair and have adequate lighting (see p. 112)

Lighting accounts for 10 percent of electricity bills – see p. 113 for tips on reducing your bill

The bathroom uses the most water in the house – see p. 107 for keeping plumbing in good repair

Running too many appliances at once can overload your system (see p. 12)

Most household fires start in the kitchen – put a fire blanket close to the oven

Place floor mats inside exterior doors to keep floors clean

Keep floors well insulated, and use a smooth, easy-to-clean surface in kitchens – see p. 116 for floor repairs

Running an efficient home

This costs extra time and money, but forestalls disasters such as burglaries, fires, and floods. Install smoke alarms, fire extinguishers, and burglar alarms, and place secure locks on doors and windows. Always make repairs immediately.

PLUMBING

DRIPS AND LEAKS MAY SEEM like minor irritations but can, if left unrepaired, cause flooding and damage. Leaks are also dangerous near electrical wiring. Call in a plumber if you cannot handle these problems yourself.

BASIC PLUMBING KIT

Be prepared for plumbing problems by keeping a tool kit for routine maintenance and emergencies. Buy the best tools you can afford, since they will be easier to use than cheap ones and will last longer. Make sure you know how to use them safely and effectively. Store your tools where you can easily find them in an emergency.

Mole wrench

Sink plunger

Resin

Insulating tape

Adjustable wrench

DRIPPING FAUCETS

Drips are extremely wasteful – particularly if they come from a hot-water tap. Drips also create a buildup of lime on sinks or tubs.

A dripping faucet may just need a new washer, it may need to be replaced, or may indicate a major problem, such as a cracked pipe.

REPLACING WASHERS

1 Turn off the water supply feeding the faucet. Use an adjustable wrench to unscrew the faucet cover, inserting a soft cloth between the faucet and the wrench to avoid scratching the finish.

2 Unscrew the large nut inside with an open-ended wrench. Remove the valve mechanism, lift out the old washer, and replace it. Reassemble the faucet.

PLUMBING BASICS
● **Water supply** Make sure you know where to turn off the water in your home. Turn it off and on from time to time so that you can easily shut it off in an emergency.
● **Timing jobs** It is always best to start plumbing jobs early in the morning. That way, if you have to make a trip to the hardware store for any missing parts, it will be open.
● **Buying washers** When buying a replacement washer, get several spares at once. Store where you can find them easily, for example, near the main shutoff valve.

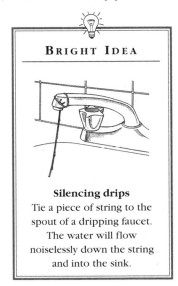

BRIGHT IDEA

Silencing drips
Tie a piece of string to the spout of a dripping faucet. The water will flow noiselessly down the string and into the sink.

STEMMING LEAKING FAUCET HANDLES
● **Old faucets** Leaking handles indicate that the gland, which prevents water coming past the spindle when the faucet is on, needs replacing.

● **Modern faucets** These have O-ring seals instead of glands. To buy a new O-ring, you need to know the name of the manufacturer of the faucet.

DRIPPING PIPES

Burst and dripping pipes can cause floods that will ruin furnishings and even bring down ceilings. Therefore, you must act quickly when you find that there is damage to a pipe. Before attempting any repairs, turn off the water. You may have to call in a plumber.

TEMPORARY REPAIRS

● **Copper pipes** Enclose the cracked pipe in a piece of garden hose split along its length. Secure with hose clips.

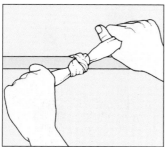

Lead and plastic pipes
Squeeze petroleum jelly into the crack. Wrap a rag or waterproof tape around the pipe until you can get it fixed properly.

WARNING
If a pipe is leaking near electrical fixtures or outlets, turn off the power immediately.

PERMANENT REPAIRS

1 Rub the pipe with abrasive paper so that epoxy adhesive will stick to it. Smear the adhesive over the crack.

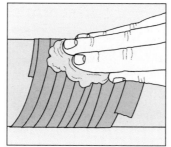

2 Bind fiberglass tape or plumber's waterproof tape around the damaged area at least twice. Smear more resin over the newly taped surface.

3 Let the adhesive to set hard before you turn on the water. Leave all the taps on until water comes through to prevent airlocks forming in the pipes (see below).

WHAT TO DO WHEN A PIPE BURSTS

1 Turn off the main water supply and open all the taps to drain the system.

2 Turn off the water heater to prevent the metal of the pipes from overheating and cracking.

3 If water is running through light fixtures, switch off the lights, and take the appropriate fuse out of the main fuse box.

4 Try to find the source of the leak. Bind the crack with a rag or waterproof tape. Keep a bucket under it, and call a plumber.

5 Meanwhile, if ceiling plaster is bulging, move furniture and carpets away, and place a bucket under the area. Pierce the bulge to let the accumulated water out. This will limit the damage to one area.

NOISY PIPES

Most pipe noises are caused by pipes vibrating against one another because they are not supported properly. If the pipes are not secure, put foam rubber between them and the walls, or secure them to a strip of wood. If this fails, you may have an airlock.

CAUSES OF NOISE

● **Airlocks** Air may get into pipes if a lot of water is suddenly drawn off the system. Try tapping along the pipes with a mallet wrapped in cloth to move the air.
● **Other causes** The main storage tank may need a larger ball float. You could also try installing a special equilibrium ball valve in place of a standard one. This will move less under water pressure, so will be quieter.

CURING AN AIRLOCK IN A PIPE

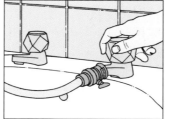

1 Turn all taps on full to run water through the pipes.
If this fails, connect a piece of garden hose between a main tap and the problem faucet.

2 Turn on the problem tap, then the clear one. The pressure of the water should push the air out of the pipe and back into the tank.

3 Turn off the taps when the noise in the pipe stops. Remove the hose from the main tap, and drain it before disconnecting the other end. Reduce the pressure of the main water supply to prevent the airlock from recurring.

FROZEN PIPES

Frozen pipes should be thawed out as soon as possible to prevent them from cracking. Thaw U-bends under a sink by wrapping them in rags wrung out in hot water. You can thaw frozen outdoor pipes by pouring boiling water around the area of the pipe that is frozen.

THAWING A FROZEN INDOOR PIPE

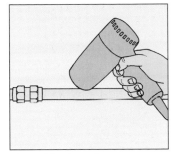

1 Turn off the water. Turn on taps fed from the frozen pipe to let the water out. Feel all the way along the pipe to locate the frozen area.

2 Hold a hair dryer on a warm setting close to the frozen part of the pipe. Do not put it too near plastic pipes, or they may melt.

PREVENTING FREEZES
● **Keeping cold air out** Keep bath and basin plugs in place to prevent waste pipes and drains from freezing.
● **Keeping water moving** For pipes that tend to freeze regularly, leave water faucets dripping overnight during cold spells in the winter.
● **Traditional cure** Put a handful of table salt down drains last thing at night to prevent pipes from freezing.
● **Insulating pipes** Insulate pipes using foam secured in place with duct tape.

BLOCKED DRAINS AND SINKS

Sinks and drains often become blocked because grease, food scraps, or other solid waste has been poured down them. Keep drains open with a mixture of salt, baking soda, and cream of tartar. Do not use lye decloggers – it will combine with fat to form a hard plug.

REMOVING BLOCKAGES FROM PIPES
● **Sinks and baths** Bale out water in a blocked sink into a bucket. Pour a cupful of washing soda followed by boiling water down the drain. Repeat if necessary.

● **Outside drains** Use the treatment for indoor drains to remove blockages outdoors. For serious blockages outdoors, you may have to use a snake or call a plumber.

SMELLY DRAINS
● **Keeping drains fresh** Flush baking soda down a drain with hot water to stop odors.

Using a plunger
If the treatment above fails, use a plunger. Smear the rim with petroleum jelly, place it over the plughole, and run water until the cup is covered. Pump the handle in an up-and-down movement.

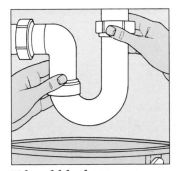

U-bend blockages
If the blockage is in the U-bend, it will not respond to a plunger. Place a bucket underneath the bend, and unscrew the U-bend. Carefully poke a piece of wire up the pipe until you free it.

TIMESAVING TIP

Unscrewing U-bends
Before replacing a U-bend, smear petroleum jelly around the threads of the screw. Next time you need to undo it, it will come off easily.

TOILETS AND APPLIANCES

Blocked toilets usually occur if something unsuitable has been flushed. You will know a toilet is blocked if water rises to the rim and drains slowly. Overflowing from toilet tanks and appliances such as dishwashers can cause major flooding if not fixed immediately.

UNBLOCKING TOILETS

1 If your toilet is blocked, stop flushing and let the water drain away as close to its usual level as possible.

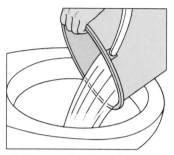

2 Throw a bucket of water into the bowl, all at once. If the blockage remains, push a toilet plunger to the bottom of the bowl, and pump up and down vigorously.

OVERFLOWING TANKS

● **Causes** Overflows may be caused by a damaged ball float, the float arm being at the wrong angle, or a worn washer in the inlet valve.

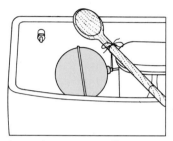

Stopping an overflow
If a toilet tank is overflowing, **raise the ball float arm. Tie it to a wooden spoon to hold it in a raised position until you can get a new float arm installed.**

OVERFLOWING APPLIANCES

● **Soap problems** Some washing machines and dishwashers may overflow if you use the wrong detergent, or too much. Turn the dial until the machine begins to empty. Run a rinse cycle with the machine empty before rinsing clothes or dishes to get rid of the excess soap.
● **Machine problems** If the detergent is not a problem, check that the filter and soap compartment have been put in properly. If you cannot locate the cause, unplug the machine, empty it, and call a repair person. Turn off electricity if the water is near switches or outlets.

SAVING WATER

Simple measures around the home will help you conserve water and save money on your household bills. Bathing uses more than 25 percent of all household water, so shower instead if possible. Never leave the bathroom faucet running while you brush your teeth.

KITCHEN
● **Washing dishes** Dishwashers are only economical if you have a full load of dishes. Wash small loads by hand.

Leftover water
Use water left in cups and kettles to water your indoor plants. Dishwater can be used to water outdoor plants if you do not use harsh detergents.

LAUNDRY
● **Washing machines** When buying a new washing machine, remember front-loading machines use less water than top-loading ones. Save water by washing full loads only (unless your machine has a half-load or short-cycle option).

OUTDOORS
● **Car washing** Use a bucket to wash your car, and use a hose only for rinsing. Leaving the hose running idly wastes hundreds of gallons of water.
● **Cleaning driveways** Sweep driveways and sidewalks clean with a stiff broom instead of hosing them down.

BATHROOM
● **Wasted water** Dripping taps waste hundreds of gallons of water each year. Drips from hot-water taps waste energy as well as water.

Food coloring stains water

Test for leaks
Your toilet tank may be leaking water. To test for leaks, drip food coloring in the tank. If the dye appears in the toilet bowl, call a plumber to fix the seal.

ELECTRICITY AND FUEL

ELECTRICITY CAN KILL, so it is vital to treat it with respect. Before working on anything electrical, turn off the power and remove the fuse that protects the circuit on which you are working. Check that the circuit is dead.

BASIC ELECTRICAL EQUIPMENT

Keep your electrical repair tools together in a box, so that in the event of a power outage you will know where to find everything. A flashlight is vital in such cases, so keep one especially for emergencies and check regularly that its batteries are still working. Make sure that you know how to use the repair tools safely and correctly.

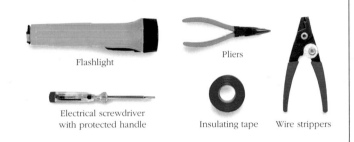

Flashlight

Pliers

Electrical screwdriver with protected handle

Insulating tape   Wire strippers

SAFETY WITH ELECTRICITY

Check all plugs and cords regularly for damage. Fix loose connections right away; otherwise, they may become dangerous. Never run cords under carpets, since they may become worn and the wires may be exposed. Do not hammer nails into walls near sockets.

BASIC SAFETY
● **Dry hands** Do not touch electrical equipment with wet hands, feet, or cloths. Water conducts electricity, and you may get a shock.
● **Avoid overloading** Do not use an adapter to plug in more appliances than a circuit can safely accommodate. You could overload the system.

Wrap tape tightly around damaged area

Repairing cords
If a cord has become worn, wrap it tightly in insulating tape to make it safe. Replace it with a new cord as soon as possible.

APPLIANCES
● **Grounding** Ensure all metal appliances are grounded to prevent electric shocks,.
● **Plugs** Always unplug small appliances like irons and hair dryers immediately after each use. If you make this a habit, you will never have to worry "Did I turn off the coffee maker?" when you go out.

Electrical fires
Use a special fire extinguisher on electrical fires. Never use water – it will cause a short circuit and electrical shocks.

DANGER SIGNALS

Call an expert in to deal with electrical wiring problems, for example, if the wiring looks dangerous, or if an appliance is not working and you cannot discern the cause. Be aware of the warning signs of electrical problems given below, and familiarize yourself with the emergency treatment for electrical shock given on pages 167 and 171.

● A "fishy" or burning smell This can indicate that an appliance plug is overheating and starting to melt. Switch off the appliance and remove the plug from the outlet.
● **Warm plugs** If a plug feels warm, switch it off, and take it out of the wall. Turn off the power at the circuit breaker. Check the wiring in the plug and outlet. A problem with either, if left may cause a house fire.

LIGHTS AND APPLIANCES

Good lighting is essential in the home. Turn off lights in empty rooms, and put timer switches on lights in halls and outside so that they come on when the house is empty. Keep appliances in good repair – faulty items can cause fires, power failure, or electrical shock.

LIGHT CARE

● **Correct bulbs** Always use the recommended wattage bulb for each lamp. Clean lamps regularly.

Keep bulbs clean
Dust can reduce the light given out by a bulb by as much as 50 percent. Use a feather duster to clean ceiling bulbs and light fixtures. See also page 20.

LIGHTING YOUR HOME

● **Lighting plans** Take time to make a lighting plan before you decorate a home. Use the right wattage bulb for each area – dim lighting may suit eating areas, while kitchen, bathroom, and reading areas require bright lighting.
● **Light switches** Put luminous paint or stickers on all light switches so that you can find them easily in the dark.
● **Lighting and safety** In a home with small children, use childproof safety outlets and outlet covers. Use a night-light for children afraid of the dark. Illuminate hazards such as outdoor steps at night with low-level lights.

APPLIANCE PROBLEMS

● **Outlets** If an appliance stops working, check the manufacturer's handbook for information. If it continues to fail, plug in an appliance that you know is in working order to see if there is a problem in the outlet.
● **Overloading** Do not plug too many lights and appliances into the same outlet – you may overload it and cause a fire.
● **Dangerous appliances** If an appliance gives you a shock, the plug or cord may be poorly insulated. Do not use the appliance until an electrician has repaired it.

POWER FAILURE

If you suddenly lose electricity, it may mean that a fuse needs replacing, or that there is a widespread blackout. If you have advance warning of a power outage, turn refrigerator controls to maximum, and put candles and matches where you can find them easily.

CIRCUIT FAILURE

1 If several appliances or lights in one area fail at once, a circuit fuse in the fuse box has probably blown. Switch off everything on that particular circuit.

2 Replace the blown fuse. If the fuses are not labeled, look for scorch marks. Check for and repair broken wires.

3 Check for and repair any visible damage to plugs and cords used on the circuit.

4 Switch on appliances and lights one at a time. If the fuse blows again, the circuit may be overloaded or an appliance may be faulty.

BLACKOUTS

● **When power returns** Reset electric clocks and timer switches. Do not open the freezer for at least six hours.

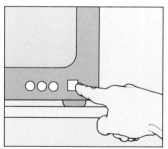

During a blackout
Turn off all your appliances and lights - apart from one bulb, and the refrigerator and freezer. A power surge when electricity is restored could blow a fuse.

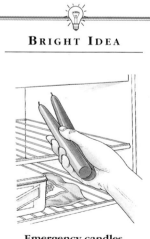

BRIGHT IDEA

Emergency candles
Keep a pair of candles in the refrigerator or freezer at all times, so that you are sure to find them in a power failure.

OTHER FUEL SOURCES

Fuels such as gas and coal can be hazardous and should be treated with caution. If you smell gas or burning, investigate immediately. A gas leak could lead to an explosion, while an uncontrolled fire in a fireplace can burn down a building. Both can be fatal.

EMERGENCY ACTION FOR GAS LEAKS

1 If there is a strong smell of gas, extinguish cigarettes, candles, and gas stoves. Switch off any machines that might produce sparks, such as a vacuum cleaner. Leave lights either on or off.

2 Cut off the supply of gas to the house by turning off the valve beside the gas meter. In most cases, turn the handle of the valve until it is at a right angle to the pipe.

3 Open as many windows as possible to let in fresh air to dissipate the gas fumes. Evacuate the whole building, and warn neighbors. Take anyone unconscious outside for treatment (see p. 168).

4 Call the gas company's emergency number and report the problem. Never enter a room to investigate the smell of gas – the fumes may quickly overpower you.

OPEN FIRES

● **Safety** If an open fire gets out of control, pour water on it to put it out. If the chimney is on fire, call the fire department. Have chimneys swept regularly to prevent soot from building up.
● **Slow fires** Quicken a smoky fire by holding an open newspaper across the fireplace. Leave a 1–2 in (3–4 cm) gap at the bottom for air to reach the fire.

SAVING FUEL

Using fuel economically can save quite a bit of money. Even simple ideas, such as turning down the thermostat on the hot-water tank, can save fuel. Major tasks, such as insulating the attic or lagging your pipes, will make a considerable difference in the long run.

KETTLES

Use a mug as a measure

Boiling water
Do not overfill a tea kettle - boil only as much water as you require for the immediate need, using a mug or cup to measure the right amount. Turn off the heat on the stove as soon as the water comes to the boil.

ELECTRONICS
● **Televisions** Unplug the television if it has an "instant on" feature to cut down on the amount of energy it uses.
● **Choosing appliances** Buy energy-efficient appliances, and choose the best you can afford – they will last longest.

IN THE KITCHEN
● **Appliances** Buy energy-saving small appliances such as electric frying pans, slow cookers, and deep fryers. They use considerably less energy than ovens and stoves.
● **Ovens** When using a standard oven, make sure you benefit from its capacity. Rather than baking a single pizza, for example, cook several items at once.
● **Stoves** Keeping stoves clean will maximize reflective heat.
● **Microwave ovens** Use a microwave whenever possible. It uses far less energy than standard ovens.
● **Freezers** Open the freezer as infrequently as possible. Every time you let cold air out, the freezer works harder to regain its temperature.
● **Pots and pans** Make sure saucepan lids fit tightly. Use pots the same size or slightly larger than cooking elements.

MONEY-SAVING TIP

Paying for energy
Keep a money jar by main light switches, and fine family members each time a light is left on in an empty room.

LIGHTING
● **Reflecting light** Place lamps in corners of rooms to reflect light. Pale walls in a room will require less lighting than those with dark walls.

HEATING AND COOLING

INSULATING YOUR HOME WILL HELP to keep it warm in winter and cool in summer, and will also save you money on your heating and cooling bills. The initial expenditure on insulation could easily be recouped in just a couple of years.

A COOL HOME

A WARM HOME

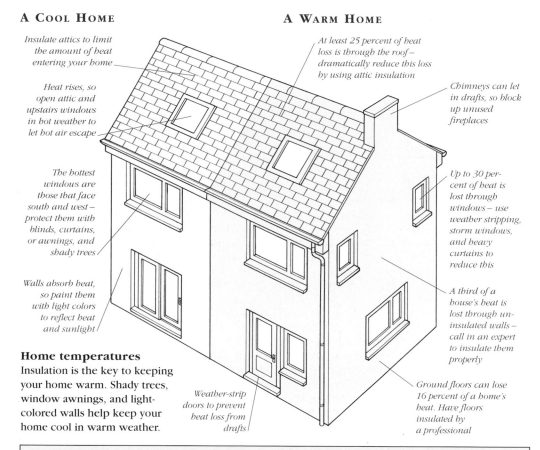

Insulate attics to limit the amount of heat entering your home

Heat rises, so open attic and upstairs windows in hot weather to let hot air escape

The hottest windows are those that face south and west – protect them with blinds, curtains, or awnings, and shady trees

Walls absorb heat, so paint them with light colors to reflect heat and sunlight

At least 25 percent of heat loss is through the roof – dramatically reduce this loss by using attic insulation

Chimneys can let in drafts, so block up unused fireplaces

Up to 30 percent of heat is lost through windows – use weather stripping, storm windows, and heavy curtains to reduce this

A third of a house's heat is lost through uninsulated walls – call in an expert to insulate them properly

Weather-strip doors to prevent heat loss from drafts

Ground floors can lose 16 percent of a home's heat. Have floors insulated by a professional

Home temperatures

Insulation is the key to keeping your home warm. Shady trees, window awnings, and light-colored walls help keep your home cool in warm weather.

REDUCING COOLING AND HEATING BILLS

COOLING BILLS

● **Windows** Install awnings over sunny windows to shade them, or plant shady trees and use trellises to protect them.
● **Fans** Install an attic fan to pull heat out of the house. A low-speed ceiling fan in the kitchen will be more efficient than a high-speed one.
● **Air conditioners** Put air conditioners on the shadier side of the house, or put up awnings over them. Make sure you clean air filters regularly.

HEATING BILLS

● **Thermostats** Turn down your central heating and hot water thermostats by a couple of degrees to save 10 percent off your electricity bills.
● **Insulating** The heat-saving benefits of insulating hot-water pipes and cylinders will be obvious almost immediately.
● **Storm windows** Storm windows are expensive to install, but will eventually pay for themselves in savings on your heating bill.

● **Floor insulation** Fill in cracks in floorboards, and insulate floors with carpets. Call an expert to insulate under the floor – it will be worth the cost in the long run.
● **Attic insulation** A quarter of a home's heat is lost through the roof. Prevent this by insulating the attic with fiberglass or other insulation.
● **Weather stripping** Buy adhesive insulation strips for drafty doors and windows.

KEEPING WARM

The cost of keeping warm in winter does not need to be high. Wear more or warmer clothes. Keep doors to heated rooms closed, and close off unused rooms so that you do not have to heat them through the winter. Block off unused chimneys at the top.

RADIATORS
● **Heat channel** Install a shelf directly above a radiator so that heat flows into the room rather than rising away.

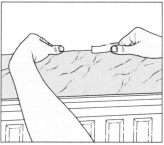

Heat reflector
Make radiators more efficient by taping aluminum foil to cardboard behind them, shiny side in. Foil will reflect heat into the room, not through the walls.

DRAFTS
● **Draft finder** Close doors and windows, and walk around with a candle. Where it flickers, you have a draft.

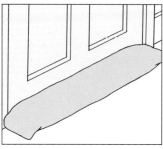

Draft protector
Stuff an old jacket sleeve with padding, and sew it up to make a draft protector for a door. Use a bright color so that no one will one trip over it.

DOUBLE GLAZING
● **Temporary measures** Use sheets of plexiglass or heavy plastic as "double glazing", secured with strong tape.

Using plastic sheeting
Clear plastic sheeting, stuck to windows with tape, provides instant "double glazing." Shrink it to fit with a hair dryer, and peel it off in the summer.

KEEPING COOL

Insulating your home properly will help keep it cool in summer and warm in winter. Wear loose clothing around the house in hot weather, and avoid using the oven in the heat of the day. Open attic or top-floor windows, and try to circulate air with cross ventilation.

NATURAL SOLUTIONS
● **Avoid artifical light** Light-bulbs give off more heat than you might imagine. Use natural daylight as long as possible, and do not switch lights on until it is essential.
● **Landscaping for shade** Plant trees outside to shade your home. Deciduous trees will provide shade in summer and allow light in when their branches are bare in winter.

REDUCING HUMIDITY
● **Showering** Steam can dramatically increase the level of humidity in your home. When showering, open the windows to let as much moisture escape as possible.

KEEPING HEAT OUT
● **Draw curtains** Draw blinds and curtains during the hottest part of the day to shade rooms from the rays of the sun.

Reflect solar heat
Staple or tape aluminum foil inside the roof space to reflect the sun's heat outward. Heat passing into the house will be reduced by at least 20 percent.

GREEN TIP

Reduce humidity
Keep lids on saucepans to reduce the humidity caused by steam. You will also use less energy to cook foods and so save money. Close internal kitchen doors while cooking to keep other rooms cool.

GENERAL REPAIRS

YOU CAN SAVE A LOT OF MONEY by doing simple repairs around the home yourself. Minor problems with floors, doors, windows, and stairs can be fixed without much expense. More complex jobs may require a professional.

FLOORS

Creaks and gaps in wooden floorboards cause irritation and drafts, but can be easily fixed. Concrete floors may sometimes be uneven, so bumps should be chipped away with a chisel and club hammer. Lift damaged vinyl tiles with a hot iron over aluminum foil.

WOODEN FLOORS
● **Square-edged boards** If a board is cracked or split, find the joists by locating the nails at each end. Drill close to the joists and cut out the board with a saw. Replace with a new piece of wood.
● **Tongue-and-groove boards** Saw out a damaged tongue-and-groove board along the edge. It cannot be replaced, so substitute it with an ordinary floorboard, supported at each end by a block of wood screwed to each joist.

QUICK INSULATION

Using homemade filler
Fill spaces between floorboards with papier-mâché made from newspaper and wallpaper paste. Sand smooth when dry.

SQUEAKY FLOORS

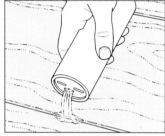

Using talcum powder
To silence squeaks, shake talcum powder between floorboards. Attach loose boards to the joists with long nails at an angle.

DOORS

To prevent a door from slamming, install a spring-door closer or use a doorstop. Stop a door from rattling by moving the lock catch, or put a draft protector inside the frame. Lift a sagging door by tightening or moving the hinges. Repair rotten parts of wood quickly.

STICKING DOORS

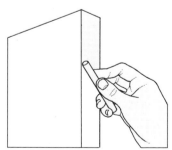

Finding the problem
Rub chalk down the edge of the door, then close it. The chalk will leave a mark on the frame at the contact point. Plane the area. If sliding doors stick, apply floor polish to the tracks.

STICKING HINGES

Lubricating a hinge
Treat a sticking hinge by rubbing pencil lead along the spine. Alternatively, smear a little light oil along the hinge with a cloth, working the hinge back and forth until it moves freely.

BRIGHT IDEA

Oiling sticking locks
To loosen a sticking lock, put a little oil on the key. Put the key in the lock, and give it a few turns to loosen the lock.

STAIRS

The best way to deal with creaking stairs is from below. If you cannot get underneath, take up any carpet and firmly screw the front of the tread to the top of the riser. Make sure that stairs are well lit and that any carpeting is securely laid so that no one can trip over it.

THREE WAYS TO REPAIR CREAKING STAIRS

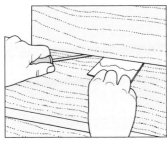

Gluing a riser
Push a screwdriver between the tread and the riser and insert a piece of cardboard covered with wood glue. Leave it there. Repeat until the squeak is gone.

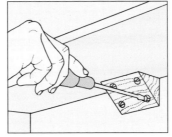

Adding a wood block
A persistent squeak may need tackling from under the stairs. Glue a triangular block of wood into the corner of the tread and riser. Secure it with screws.

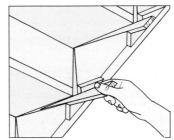

Replacing wedges
With old stairs, you may have to replace the stair wedges to fix a squeak. Clean off the old glue, reapply, then hammer the new wedges back into place.

WINDOWS

If a window has broken and you cannot repair it at once, board it up with chipboard. Always wear heavy gloves when dealing with glass. Cover small cracks temporarily with heavy plastic and masking tape. Be sure window panes are sealed properly.

BROKEN WINDOWS
● Handling broken glass Wear thick gardening gloves when handling broken glass, and use goggles if you have to break any glass. Dispose of broken glass in newspaper.

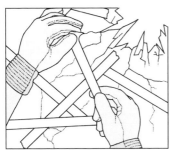

Removing glass
Carefully crisscross pieces of masking tape over a broken windowpane. Cover the glass with a heavy cloth, then tap gently with a hammer to break away the pieces from the window without splintering.

REPLACING PANES
1 Buy a pane of glass that is ¹⁄₁₆ in (1.5 mm) smaller than the window opening on all sides. Chip out any old putty. Clean out the recess, and paint it with primer.

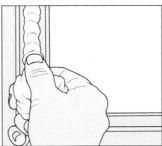

2 Lay a bed of fresh putty in the rabbet in the window frame. Press the new piece of glass into position around the edges – not in the center, where it could break. Insert glazing brads or clips to keep the pane of glass in place.

WINDOW PROBLEMS

● **Damaged putty** As putty hardens, it may crack and fall out. Chip it out with a chisel, and replace all the putty – not just the damaged section.
● **Sticking windows** A build-up of paint may cause a wooden window to stick. Strip paint off the edge, and plane it to fit the frame. Repaint the wood.
● **Condensation** Install secondary double glazing to prevent condensation on metal window frames.

HOME SECURITY

Making your home more secure will help deter burglars. Install security locks on doors and windows, a good-quality burglar alarm, and outdoor lights. Join the local neighborhood crime watch if one exists in your area.

VULNERABLE AREAS OF THE HOME

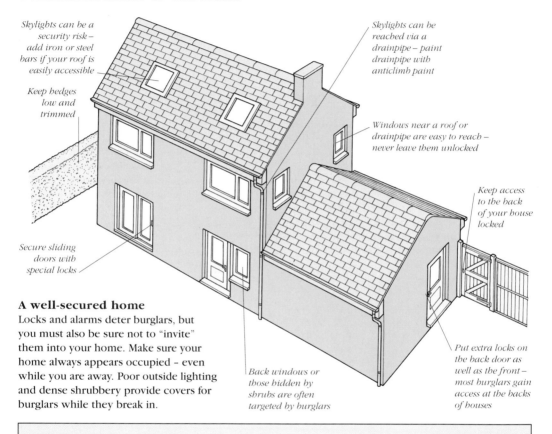

Skylights can be a security risk – add iron or steel bars if your roof is easily accessible

Keep hedges low and trimmed

Secure sliding doors with special locks

Skylights can be reached via a drainpipe – paint drainpipe with anticlimb paint

Windows near a roof or drainpipe are easy to reach – never leave them unlocked

Keep access to the back of your house locked

Put extra locks on the back door as well as the front – most burglars gain access at the backs of houses

Back windows or those hidden by shrubs are often targeted by burglars

A well-secured home

Locks and alarms deter burglars, but you must also be sure not to "invite" them into your home. Make sure your home always appears occupied – even while you are away. Poor outside lighting and dense shrubbery provide covers for burglars while they break in.

MAKING YOUR HOME MORE SECURE

● **Alarms** Install a house alarm system, and make sure it is clearly visible in order to deter any casual intruders.
● **Doors** Use good-quality, solid wood exterior doors. Flimsy doors can easily be kicked in. Put secure locks on exterior doors, and a chain or peephole so that you can inspect visitors.
● **Windows** Put locks on every window, especially windows close to drainpipes, ground-floor windows, and French windows. Lock them each time you go out.

● **Rear entrances** Make the back of your home as inaccessible as possible. Most burglars break in at the backs of houses.
● **Garage** Secure the door leading from the garage to the house, as well as the garage doors. A burglar could work unseen in the garage.
● **Hedges** Keep hedges trimmed as low as possible so that anyone trying to break in can be easily seen. Prickly hedges and shrubs will also act as a deterrent to intruders.

● **Cars** Always lock your car when you leave it, even if you are coming right back. Burglars can use tools they find in cars to break into the house.
● **Sheds** Lock sheds so that your tools cannot be used to break into the house. Put shed door hinges on the inside so that they cannot be removed by burglars to take the door off.
● **Ladders** Keep ladders locked up so that burglars cannot use them to break into the house through the upper floors.

INSIDE YOUR HOME

Locks, bolts, and alarms are only as good as the fabric of the home they are protecting. Make it more difficult for thieves to get in by having good-quality doors and windows that are always kept locked. Always change the locks when you move into a new house.

SECURING DOORS AND WINDOWS

● **Internal doors** Do not lock internal doors. Burglars will think you are hiding valuables and may break them down.

● **Exterior doors** Put special bolts into the hinge sides of exterior doors to make them harder to break through.

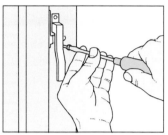

Casement windows
Sink a long screw into a casement window beside the handle to prevent it from being opened. Put permanent locks on windows as soon as possible.

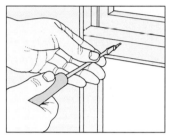

Sash windows
Install locks on sash windows, or put a long wood screw through the meeting rails. Do not permanently screw down windows, in case of a fire.

DRAWING CURTAINS

● **Daytime** Open curtains during the day. Drawn curtains show you are out, and enable burglars to work inside without being seen.
● **Evening** Draw your curtains at night when you have lights on, so that no one can see any valuable possessions.

POSSESSIONS

● **Marking** Print your name and zipcode on valuables in invisible ink so you can prove ownership to the police. Record all serial numbers.
● **Photographing** Take a picture of all your valuable objects so you can prove they are yours if they are stolen.

IN A BURGLARY

● **Confronting a burglar** If you interrupt a burglary, do not fight the burglar. Cooperate, then call the police. If you suspect that a burglar is in your home, call the police from a neighbor's and report a "burglary in progress."

VACATION SECURITY PRECAUTIONS

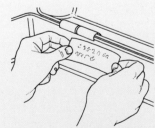

● **Luggage labels** Labeling your luggage by sticking the address to the outside announces that your house is unoccupied. Place labels inside suitcases instead.

● **Deliveries** Cancel deliveries such as newspapers.
● **Mail** Arrange with a neighbor or the post office to hold your mail and packages while you are away. Even if you have a mail slot, be sure the delivered mail cannot be seen from the outside.
● **Timer switches** Install several timer switches in different rooms to turn on lights, the radio, and the television at night.
● **Garage door** Close the garage door so that no one can see if your car is there or not.

● **Car** On a short vacation, leave your car outside your home. Ask a neighbor to brush snow or ice off the car if you are going to be away for a long time.
● **Indicate occupation** Ask a neighbor to mow the lawn, rake leaves, and leave signs of occupation, such as footprints in snow on the porch.
● **Protection** Put any valuables in a bank before you go away. Tell the police that your house will be empty so that they can keep an eye on it for you.

FOOD & DRINK

GOOD FOOD DEPENDS *more on choosing the best ingredients and preparing them well than it does on using fancy recipes and complicated techniques. Assemble ingredients and equipment before you start cooking, and always allow yourself ample time and space in the kitchen – this will help prevent such accidents as burns and fires, as well as avoiding ruined food and frayed tempers.*

EQUIPMENT AND INGREDIENTS

Keep your kitchen well organized – it is difficult to work in a room cluttered with seldom used gadgets and items put back in the wrong places. See pages 26–30 for cleaning kitchens and equipment, and use the tips below to solve common kitchen problems.

SOLVING COMMON PROBLEMS

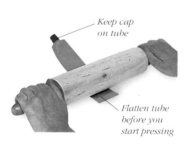

Keep cap on tube

Flatten tube before you start pressing

Cork has been screwed into position

Push straw to bottom of bottle

Introducing air through straw will release stuck sauce

Emptying paste tubes
To get the last bit of paste out of a tube, use a rolling pin to push the contents up to the top.

Replacing a pan knob
If a saucepan lid loses its knob, replace it with an ordinary cork, which will be heat-resistant.

Making sauce flow
If thick sauce is stuck in a bottle, insert a straw to introduce air into it, then remove the straw.

HOW TO UNSCREW A TIGHT JAR

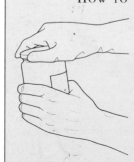

There are a number of ways to make unscrewing tight jars easier:

● **Finding a grip** Wear a rubber glove on one hand to grip the tight lid firmly, then twist. Use a nutcracker to grip small lids.
● **Using heat** Hold the lid under hot running water to expand the metal.
● **Loosening the lid** Tap all around the lid at an angle with a spoon.

BURNS AND FIRES

● **Avoiding burns** Turn saucepan handles inward during cooking; this prevents pans from being knocked over and causing scalds.
● **Oil fires** If you do not have a fire blanket, smother flames with a lid, or throw salt, dirt, washing soda, or bath salts on the flames. Do not use water on oil fires.

KITCHEN BASICS

When using an oven, bake as many items as possible to save energy – and remember that dishes on the top shelf will cook faster than those at the bottom. Cover saucepans when cooking – the food will heat more quickly with the lid on than with it off.

KITCHEN ITEMS

● **Kitchen containers** Measure the volumes of all your dishes and pans. Write the volume on the bottom of each one in nail polish. This will make it easy for you to locate the right item in a hurry.

● **Heating plates** Putting plates in the oven can cause discoloration or cracking. Heat plates by holding them under hot running water for several minutes instead.

● **Cookbooks** Keep a series of bound blank books for recipes, and index each one for ease of reference. Cover much-used cookbooks with aluminum foil so that you can wipe them clean easily.

SEASONING FOOD

When to add salt

Add salt to soups or stews early to enhance flavor. Add salt to roasted meat near the end – the meat becomes tough otherwise. Cook vegetables in salted water.

BRIGHT IDEA

Clean cookbooks

To prevent a cookbook from being soiled when you refer to it during cooking, open it to the required page and slip it into a clear plastic bag before you start cooking. The book will remain clean, no matter how messy the task.

RECTIFYING MISTAKES

If food does not turn out as intended, do not panic. Lumpy sauces can be liquidized to a smooth consistency. Add potato or yogurt to dishes with too many hot peppers. Use potato to thicken thin soups; add a little flour made into a paste with milk to thicken thin sauces.

EXCESS FAT

● **In cooked dishes** Cool the dish in the refrigerator until the fat hardens on the top. Lift all the fat off with a spoon.

Ice cubes will cause fat around them to congeal

During preparation

Drop ice cubes into the food – fat will cling to them. Remove at once. Alternatively, brush a lettuce leaf over the surface.

BURNED FOOD

● **Stews** Pour the stew into a new saucepan – the burned stew will stay behind. Add water to the unburned stew, and chili powder or pepper to disguise any burned taste.

● **Meat** Grill vegetables such as tomatoes and mushrooms, cut up the burned meat, and serve on skewers as kebabs.

BOIL OVERS

● **Preventing** Stop milk from boiling over by rinsing the pan in cold water first. Grease the rims of pans to prevent other liquids from boiling over.

● **Rescuing** If milk is about to boil over, remove it from the heat and bump the saucepan sharply as you put it down.

OVERSALTED FOOD

● **Vegetables** Pour boiling water on boiled vegetables. Mash boiled potatoes with milk and a beaten egg.

Soups and stews

Add raw potato to soup or stew, boil, then throw out the potato. Alternatively, make a new batch without salt, and mix the two.

FRUIT AND VEGETABLES

Buy fruit and vegetables fresh in small quantities, so that you do not have to store them for too long. Check fruit bowls and vegetable containers regularly, and throw out damaged items so that any rot does not spread.

STORAGE

Store highly perishable salad vegetables and soft fruit in the refrigerator. You can buy bags containing a gas that makes them last longer. If fruit such as bananas are becoming overripe, liquidize them, and store in the freezer for use in baking cakes or bread.

FRUIT STORAGE
● **Apples** Store unblemished apples on trays or racks, not touching each other. Remove any that are not perfect.
● **Lemons and limes** Store small citrus fruits in an egg carton in the refrigerator.

VEGETABLE STORAGE
● **Fresh mushrooms** Cover mushrooms with damp paper towels and refrigerate. They will keep for several days.
● **Tomatoes and cucumbers** These taste best when stored at room temperature, rather than being refrigerated.

POTATOES

Preserving a glut
If you have too many potatoes, stop them from sprouting by storing a few apples with them. If you have peeled too many potatoes, cover them with water and store in the refrigerator.

WATER STORAGE

Make sure stems are covered in water

Keeping food crisp
Certain vegetables are best stored in water. Stand scallions and celery upright in a glass of water in the refrigerator. Store watercress and olives in a bowl of water in the refrigerator.

RIPENING FRUIT

Many fruits will continue to ripen after they have been picked, but it is still useful to know the best methods for ripening different varieties. Refrigerating fruit will slow the ripening process, while storing already-ripe fruit in a dark place tends to hasten ripening.

TOMATOES

Avoiding sunlight
Ripen tomatoes by storing them out of direct sunlight – a drawer is ideal. Exposure to sunlight merely softens tomatoes; it does not ripen them more quickly.

APPLES AND PEARS

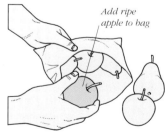

Add ripe apple to bag

Hastening ripening
Ripen apples and pears by placing them in a brown paper bag with an already-ripe apple. Pierce a few holes in the bag, and store in a cool, dark place.

RIPENING TIPS
● **Green fruit** Ripen green fruit in a perforated plastic bag. The holes let in air but retain ethylene – the odorless gas that promotes ripening.
● **Avocados** Ripen avocados by placing them in a warm cabinet, or in a plastic bag with a piece of banana peel, or by burying them in a bowl of flour. Refrigeration will stop avocados from ripening.
● **Bananas** To stop bananas from ripening, refrigerate them – the skins may darken but the flesh will stay firm.

SALAD VEGETABLES

Keep a small, dry sponge in the vegetable compartment of your refrigerator – it will absorb moisture and help prevent mildew and food spoilage. To give salad a mild flavor of garlic, rub half a peeled garlic clove around the salad bowl before you put the salad into it.

PREPARING MIXED SALADS

Push food with back of knife to avoid dulling blade

Saucer creates a false bottom – water collects underneath

Draining a salad
Place a saucer upside down in a salad bowl before adding the salad. Water from the washed lettuce leaves will then collect beneath the saucer, and not make the salad soggy.

REVIVING LETTUCE
● **Soggy lettuce** Soak soggy lettuce for an hour in a bowl of water plus 2 tsp (10 ml) of lemon juice in the refrigerator. To keep a head of lettuce crisp, store it wrapped in a plastic bag in the refrigerator.
● **Wilted lettuce** Sprinkle the lettuce with cool water, wrap it in a dish towel, then refrigerate it for an hour.

PREPARING LETTUCE
● **Cutting leaves** Cut crisp-headed lettuces and Chinese cabbages across the root into strips. Hold the root end and chop from the top, discarding any brown bits.

Tearing lettuce
To prepare soft-leaf lettuces, tear with your fingers – cutting will make the edges turn brown. For buffets, make sure you tear the lettuce into bite-sized pieces that do not need more cutting.

PREPARING VEGETABLES

To prevent vitamin loss and reduce the risk of spoiling, prepare vegetables as near to their cooking time as possible. Peel vegetables with a sharp knife or vegetable peeler to avoid removing too much skin. Alternatively, scrub vegetables clean, using a scouring pad.

EGGPLANT

Sprinkle salt over cut slices

Drawing out juices
Slice eggplant, sprinkle both sides with salt, and let drain for 30 minutes, turning once to release the bitter juices. Rinse and dry with paper towels.

OTHER VEGETABLES
● **Peeling peppers** To skin a pepper, hold it on a skewer over an open flame until it is charred all over. Rub the skin off with a paper towel.
● **Peeling tomatoes** Plunge tomatoes into boiling water, leave for one or two minutes, then immerse them in cold water. The skins will split so that you can peel them easily.
● **Preparing corn** To remove silk from corn cobs, remove the husks, then rub the ears with a damp paper towel.
● **Slicing onion** Grate onion if a recipe calls for it to be finely chopped. Leave the stem on to hold the onion together.

TRADITIONAL TIP

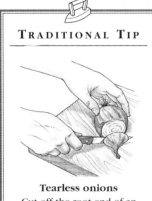

Tearless onions
Cut off the root end of an onion last to prevent tears. Peeling under cold, running water also helps. Breathe through your mouth.

COOKING VEGETABLES

Cook vegetables for as short a time as possible. Cut them into small pieces for cooking, and use the minimum amount of water. Reserve the water in which vegetables have been boiled, and use it for making soups, stocks, and sauces – it is full of vitamins.

BOILED VEGETABLES

● **Frozen vegetables** Restore freshness to frozen vegetables by pouring boiling water over them before cooking.
● **Cabbage** A pinch of baking soda added to boiling cabbage will help to eliminate odor and keep the cabbage green. Alternatively, place a heel of bread on top of the cabbage while it is being cooked. Remove before serving.
● **Cauliflower** To keep boiled cauliflower from becoming yellow, add 2 tbsp (30 ml) of milk to the cooking water.

ROASTING PEPPERS

Apply oil with a pastry brush

Protecting the skins
Coat peppers with olive oil before stuffing and baking them. They will keep their color, and the skins will not split.

BOILING CORN

Add fresh or bottled lemon juice

Perfect corn
Add 1 tsp (5 ml) of lemon juice to cooking water to keep corn yellow. Do not add any salt – it will toughen the corn.

PREPARING BROCCOLI

Cutting the stems
Make cross-shaped incisions in the ends of broccoli stems, so that the stems cook in the same amount of time as the florets.

CARROT SWEETENER

In tomato sauce
If your tomato-based sauce is acidic, add some grated carrot to sweeten it. The carrot will also help thicken the sauce.

OTHER VEGETABLES

● **Beans** Adding a pinch of baking soda to the cooking water will prevent beans from getting mushy.
● **Mushrooms** To prevent mushrooms from getting hard, saute them over high heat.
● **Spinach** After cooking fresh spinach, drain it well and press it between two plates to remove excess moisture. Toss in hot, seasoned butter.
● **Beet** Cook whole to retain juices. Simmer them for two hours – the skins will slip off.

PREPARING POTATOES

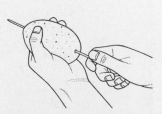

Putting a metal skewer through a potato speeds up the baking time. Alternatively, parboil potatoes for 15 minutes – this cuts the baking time in half.

● **Mashed potatoes** Add a pinch of baking powder to mashed potatoes to create a light, fluffy texture. If mashed potatoes become soggy after you have added milk (this usually occurs if the potatoes have been overcooked), make them fluffy by adding powdered milk.
● **Leftover baked potatoes** These can be rebaked if you dip them in water and bake in a 300°F (150°C) oven for 20 minutes.

● **Crisp roast potatoes** After scrubbing potatoes, rub the surfaces with a little salt – this will help to produce crisp skin. Scratch a criss-cross pattern on potatoes with a fork, and roast in hot fat in a high oven.
● **Old potatoes** To improve the flavor of old potatoes, add a little sugar to the water in which they are boiled. Add 1 tsp (5 ml) of white vinegar to prevent the potatoes from darkening.

PREPARING FRUIT

If you need to delay cooking peeled apples, put them in salted water to stop them from turning brown; rinse the apples before use.

A pinch of salt adds flavor to cooked apples. To reduce the amount of sugar used in stewing fruit, add the sugar after the fruit is cooked.

STONING AND SKINNING

● **Seeds and pits** Remove seeds from grapes with the small end of a paper clip. Use the tip of a vegetable peeler to remove stones from cherries.

Pour enough water to cover the fruit

Skinning fruit

Place thin-skinned fruits such as peaches in a bowl, and pour boiling water over them. After one minute, pour away the water, then peel the fruit.

PRESERVING FRESHNESS

● **Strawberries** Rinse and drain fresh strawberries well before hulling. Washing them after hulling lets water into the fruit, so that they become soggy.

Keeping bananas yellow

Add a little sherry to sliced bananas to prevent them from turning brown. Alternatively, sprinkle pineapple or lemon juice onto the banana slices.

MELONS

● **Storing** Wrap melons that are stored in the refrigerator – the flavor and scent will stay inside the fruit and not be transferred to other foods.

Cut a small slice from each side

Serving melon

To serve a melon on a plate, cut a slice off the side so that the fruit will sit flat. This is useful if you want to use the melon itself as a bowl to hold a fruit salad.

CITRUS FRUIT

Storing citrus fruit at room temperature will double the amount of juice you can extract from it. Alternatively, submerge the fruit in hot water for 15 minutes before squeezing. Use dried citrus peel for a pleasant scent in rooms, or scatter it in drawers to keep clothes fresh.

EXTRACTING JUICE

Piercing a hole

Extract a small amount of lemon juice through a hole made with a skewer. Then wrap the lemon in aluminum foil, and refrigerate.

ORANGES AND LEMONS

● **Citrus juice** Oranges and lemons will yield maximum juice if you heat them in a microwave before squeezing.
● **Peeling oranges** Before you peel an orange, place it in a bowl of boiling water for about five minutes. The peel will then lift off easily.
● **Storing lemons** A cut lemon will not dry out if you smear the surface with egg white. Lemons freeze well, so you can store any unused portions in the freezer. If you use only small pieces of lemon (or lime) at a time, cut the fruit in quarters and keep in the freezer in a plastic bag.

MONEY-SAVING TIP

Homemade citrus peel
Grate leftover citrus peel, add a little sugar, and store this homemade peel in an airtight jar in the refrigerator.

MEAT, DAIRY, AND EGGS

THESE ARE THE PROTEIN STAPLES of most people's diets and can be prepared in hundreds of ways to suit all tastes. Meat and fish are expensive and should not be wasted – add leftovers to stews, and use bones to make soup stock.

ROASTING, GRILLING, AND FRYING MEAT

Cook meat over high heat initially to seal in the juices. Turn meat with tongs rather than a fork, to avoid making holes that let juices out. Do not sprinkle salt on meat before cooking – this encourages juices to escape. Add salt just before you serve the meat.

SAUSAGES

● **Strings** To prevent meat from spilling out of a string of sausages, separate them only when they are nearly cooked.

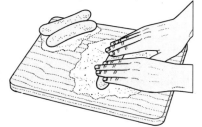

Shrinkless sausages
Roll sausages in flour before you fry them. This will prevent them from shrinking and breaking up in the pan. Alternatively, boil them first for eight minutes.

TECHNIQUES FOR FRYING MEAT

● **Oil-free frying** When frying hamburgers, sprinkle the pan lightly with salt instead of using cooking oil. The patties will fry in their juices, without sticking to the pan.

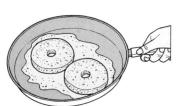

Quick-frying technique
To cook hamburgers quickly and evenly all over, make holes in the centers when shaping the patties. The holes will disappear as the meat cooks and swells.

SEASONING MEAT

Coat one piece of meat at a time

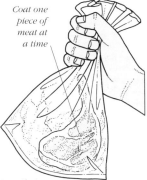

Applying a coating
To coat meat quickly and with a minimum of mess, put seasoned flour in a plastic bag and add the meat. Shake the bag until the meat is thoroughly coated.

● **Bacon** To stop bacon from curling, prick the frying pieces with a fork, or dip the strips in cold water before frying them.

Preventing spattering
Inverting a metal colander over a frying pan prevents fat from spattering the surrounding area, while allowing steam to escape. Use oven mitts to remove it.

GRILLING MEAT

● **Quick grilling** Speed up grilling by preheating the grill and its rack for 10 minutes.

Reducing fire risk
Put slices of bread under the rack in a grill pan to soak up dripping fat and prevent it from smoking. This will reduce the chance of the fat catching fire.

LAMB, PORK, AND HAM

● **Serving lamb** To prevent lamb's fat from congealing unattractively, use very hot plates for serving the meat.
● **Pork crackling** Score the rind of a pork roast deeply in a criss-cross pattern. Rub with oil, then with salt, and roast.
● **Ham** Soak too-salty ham in milk for half an hour. For juicy boiled ham, allow the ham to cool in the cooking water.

TOUGH MEAT

● **Marinading** Use vinegar to tenderize tough meat. Mix vinegar with equal parts of warm stock or cooking oil, and marinate meat in this for one hour before cooking.

POULTRY AND FISH

Poultry must be thawed and thoroughly cooked; otherwise, it may cause food poisoning. If you need to skin a fresh fish, the job will be easiest if you freeze the fish first. After using a pan for cooking fish, wash it with vinegar to remove the fishy odor.

POULTRY
● **Roasting chicken** When roasting an unstuffed chicken, season the cavity as well as the skin. Place half a lemon in the cavity to flavor the meat.
● **Roasting duck and goose** Prick duck flesh before roasting so that fat escapes. Do not prick goose – losing fat will make the flesh dry.

FISH
● **Slippery fish** To handle slippery fish, wet your hands, then dip them in salt, or rub vinegar onto the fish.
● **Poached fish** Adding 1 tbsp (15 ml) of vinegar to the cooking water will prevent poached fish from crumbling.

SOAKING FISH

Reserve liquid from thawing fish for sauce

Using milk
Thaw frozen fish in milk to give the fish a fresh taste; use the milk to make a sauce if you like. Soak anchovies for half an hour in milk to reduce saltiness.

REDUCING FISH SMELLS
● **Fried fish** Adding lemon juice to the fat used to fry fish reduces the smoke and odor.

Fish smells on hands
Rub your hands with vinegar, lemon juice, or salt, then rinse them in tepid water before washing them. You will prevent the fishy smell from setting.

SOUPS, STEWS, AND CASSEROLES

Soups and stews are best made in advance, so that the flavors have time to mingle. Add tea, beer, or wine to stews to tenderize any tough meat. Add a little instant potato to thicken thin soups. See page 121 for removing excess fat from soups and stews.

CLARIFYING STOCK

Add eggshells

Using eggshells
Add eggshells to cloudy stock – any impurities will cling to the insides of the shells. Remove the shells when the stock is clear.

SOUP STOCK
● **Fish stock** Use the bones and clean heads from filleted fish to make fish stock. Do not simmer fish stock for longer than 20 minutes; otherwise it tends to become bitter.
● **Storing stock** Freeze soup stock in ice-cube trays, then store the cubes in a plastic bag in the freezer until needed.

STEWS AND CASSEROLES
● **Broken casserole dishes** Use a piece of aluminum foil to cover a casserole dish if you have broken the lid.
● **Bouquet garni** Make your own bouquet garni for stews by tying two sprigs of parsley, one bay leaf, and a sprig of thyme in a piece of muslin.

TIMESAVING TIP

Opening soup cans
Before opening a can of soup, shake it well, then open it at the bottom end. All the soup will pour out neatly, without sticking to the can.

DAIRY FOODS

Dairy products perish quickly and should be kept refrigerated. Take butter out of the refrigerator about half an hour before you intend to use it – softened butter spreads easily. When cooking with cream, be careful not to let it boil, which will make it curdle.

FRYING WITH BUTTER

Add oil as butter begins to melt

Adding cooking oil

Before sautéeing vegetables or meat in butter, add a little olive or vegetable oil to the pan. This will lower the point at which butter would burn, and leave the food a rich, golden color.

SOFTENING BUTTER

Place warm bowl over butter

Quick solution

To soften butter for spreading, invert a small, heated bowl over the butter. Heat the bowl by rinsing it with hot water, or by filling it with cold water and heating it in a microwave.

USING DAIRY FOODS

● **Butter stretcher** Beat a little milk into butter to soften it and make it go further when making lots of sandwiches.
● **Yogurt** Use yogurt as a low-fat substitute for sour cream. Buy plain yogurt and flavor it yourself instead of buying flavored yogurt.
● **Ice cream** Prevent crystals from forming on opened ice cream by placing waxed paper over the ice cream before you replace the lid.
● **Milk** Prevent milk from boiling over by adding a clean marble to the pan – this stirs the contents. Alternatively, use the method on page 121.

TECHNIQUES FOR WHIPPING CREAM

● **Perfect whipped cream** When whipping cream, use half light and half heavy, with a little superfine sugar. If you overwhip cream, add a little milk or yogurt to restore the correct consistency.

Foil prevents splashing

Preventing splashes

Avoid splattering cream when whipping it with an electric mixer by covering the bowl with foil so that no cream splashes out. Push the beater shafts through the circle of foil.

● **Cream substitute** Should you run out of cream for whipping, you can substitute evaporated milk instead. If you add the juice of half a lemon to a small can of milk, the milk will whip stiff.

Cream that will not whip

If you have difficulty getting cream to whip, add one egg white, chill thoroughly, then whip the cream again. A few drops of lemon juice added to cream will also help.

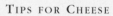

TIPS FOR CHEESE

● **Storing cheese** Butter the cut edge of a block of cheese to prevent it from drying out. Wrap cheese in a moist paper towel, then in plastic wrap, and store in the refrigerator.
● **Grating cheese** Put cheese in the freezer for 15 minutes to make it grate easily.
● **Stale cheese** Grate stale cheese and mix it with onion to make a sandwich filling.
● **Cottage cheese** Make a sour cream substitute by running cottage cheese through a blender. Always store cottage cheese containers upside down.

EGGS

Brown and white eggs are no different in quality. Eggs will keep longest if stored thin end down. If they are to be beaten, store them at room temperature. To test whether an egg is fresh, put it in a bowl of cold water – if the egg rises to the top, it is not fresh.

SEPARATING EGGS
● **Removing yolk** Use a piece of eggshell to remove any bits of yolk from egg whites. The thin end of the shell is ideal for picking up the yolk.

Glass keeps yolk separate from white

Separating an egg
To separate an egg easily, break it onto a saucer and place a small tumbler over the yolk. Holding the glass and saucer together firmly, pour the egg white off into a container.

BOILED EGGS
● **Cutting hardcooked eggs** To slice hardcooked eggs cleanly, first dip your knife in boiling water. For chopped eggs, cut first along the length, then along the width.

Preventing cracking
Pierce the end of an egg before boiling it, using a pin. This will allow air to escape from the shell, and will prevent the shell from cracking. Add vinegar to the water to seal cracked eggs.

BEATING EGGS
● **Clean bowls** Rinse a bowl with cold water before you beat egg yolks in it – the yolks will slide out without sticking to the sides of the bowl.

Small quantities of salt and vinegar will stiffen whites

Beating egg whites
Add 1 tsp (5 ml) white vinegar and a pinch of salt to egg whites if they will not stiffen when you are beating them. (Any traces of yolk present in the whites will make them difficult to beat.)

EGGS FOR GARNISH

Stir gently to avoid breaking eggs

Centering the yolks
When cooking eggs for garnish, stir them gently but continually with a wooden spoon, so that the yolks do not settle on one side. Immerse them in cold water after boiling, then peel.

TRADITIONAL TIP

Preventing tarnish
Egg yolk tarnishes silver. Use plastic or stainless steel cutlery when eating boiled eggs to save polishing silver.

COOKING TIPS
● **Poached eggs** Add a few drops of white vinegar to the pan to stop poached eggs from losing their shape. For perfect poached eggs, stir the water as it boils, and drop each egg into the well created by the movement of the water.
● **Scrambled eggs** To make scrambled eggs go further, add 1 tbsp (15 g) of bread-crumbs to every three eggs.

STORING EGGS
● **Yolks** Egg yolks will remain fresh for several days if they are submerged in cold water and stored in the refrigerator.
● **Freezing** Egg whites can be frozen. Store them in a clearly labeled plastic container.

MAYONNAISE
● **Homemade** When making mayonnaise, add the oil one drop at a time to prevent curdling. Try not to pause during the making process.

BREAD, PASTA, AND RICE

THESE ARE DIETARY ESSENTIALS that provide fiber and energy. Bread lasts only a few days if stored at room temperature – but stale bread has its uses. Store dry pasta and rice in airtight containers. Fresh pasta should be refrigerated.

BREAD

Keep sliced bread in the refrigerator. Bread and breadcrumbs freeze well, but should not be kept in the freezer for any longer than a couple of months. When slicing fresh bread, dip the bread knife into boiling water first – it will then cut through the bread easily.

TOAST
● **Thin bread slices** When making toast with thin slices of bread, place two pieces in each side of the toaster – this will prevent the bread from curling or breaking.

BREADCRUMBS
● **Stale bread** When making breadcrumbs from stale bread, put the bread in a plastic bag and roll with a rolling pin.
● **Breadcrumb substitute** If you run out of breadcrumbs, use cornflakes or any other dry cereal instead, crushed in a food processor or blender.

FRESH BREAD

Keeping bread fresh
Put a slice of apple or potato in a bread bin to prevent bread from drying out. Clean bread bins weekly to prevent mildew from forming (see p. 29).

Grating for breadcrumbs
Fresh bread does not crumble into breadcrumbs easily. If you must make crumbs using fresh bread, freeze the loaf first, then grate it to make it into crumbs.

STORING AND MAKING SANDWICHES
● **Freezing** Make sandwiches in advance and freeze them. Remove them from the freezer several hours before serving.

Cut loaf into sandwiches after fillings have been added

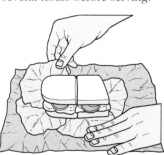

Preserving sandwiches
If you have to make sandwiches the night before but want to keep them moist and fresh, wrap them up in a few lettuce leaves, then in aluminum foil, and refrigerate them overnight.

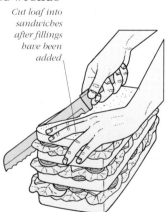

Layered sandwiches
Make layered sandwiches quickly and easily by slicing a loaf of bread horizontally, and applying the filling to each layer. Reassemble the loaf, then cut into individual vertical slices.

HOMEMADE BREAD
● **Adding salt** Make sure you use exactly the right amount of salt in bread making – too much salt will kill the yeast; too little salt will cause the dough to rise too fast.
● **Covering dough** Bread dough must be covered in order to rise well. A damp cloth is the traditional way, but plastic wrap works just as well, and can be discarded.
● **Quick bread** Warm the flour used in bread making in a low oven for a few minutes before you mix the dough – this will help the bread bake quickly.
● **Crisp bread** For a crisp crust on homemade bread, brush the loaf with oil before you put it in the oven.

LEFTOVER BREAD

Stale bread need not be thrown away – it can be freshened up as shown below, or made into breadcrumbs (see opposite). Use leftover toast to make French toast. Sandwiches that are left over from a party can be dipped in egg, then fried and served as a breakfast dish.

REVIVING BREAD, BUNS, AND CRACKERS

Moistening bread
To freshen stale bread, brush water over the bread, then wrap it in a sheet of aluminum foil. Heat the bread in a medium oven for around 10 minutes, or until the bread feels springy.

Use a pastry brush

Dipping buns in milk
Buns can become stale quickly, but if you have some left over, dip them into a bowl of milk, then put them in a hot oven for a few minutes. They will freshen up and the tops will crisp.

Crisping crackers
Soggy crackers can be crisped up on a baking sheet in the oven for a few minutes. Alternatively, place them in a microwave on high for 30 seconds. These methods also revive stale cereal.

PASTA AND RICE

Pasta can be added to soup to make the soup go further. If pasta sticks together, toss it in a clean pan with a little olive oil to separate the strands. To keep cooked rice hot, stand the container over a pan of simmering water, and cover it with a kitchen towel.

BASIC TECHNIQUES FOR COOKING PASTA

● **Fresh pasta** To cook fresh pasta, drop it into a large pan of rapidly boiling, salted water. Cook for five minutes, or until the pasta rises to the surface. Serve very hot.

● **Preventing sticking** When pasta is just cooked, add 1 tbsp (15 ml) of cold water to the pan before draining.

PREPARING RICE

● **Overcooked rice** Rinse rice that has been overcooked in cold water, then drain it well. Spread the rice on waxed paper, and heat it in a warm oven for about 30 minutes.

Add oil before pasta starts to boil

Protect your hands from hot metal

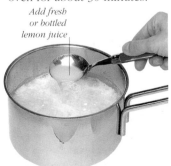

Add fresh or bottled lemon juice

Preventing boil overs
A small amount of oil or butter added to the water when cooking pasta prevents it from boiling over or sticking together.

Small portions
Cook a small portion of pasta in a metal colander set in a pan full of water. Lift out the colander when the pasta is cooked.

Perfect rice
Add a little lemon juice to white rice while it is cooking to keep it white and fluffy. Add butter to prevent it from boiling over.

ALL THE EXTRAS

ESSENTIAL INGREDIENTS IN every kitchen are those that – like spices, nuts, and oils – add flavor and interest to dishes. Preserving foods in season and making perfect sauces are skills that will stand every cook in good stead.

NUTS

Store nuts in a dark, dry, and cool place. Warmth turns the fat in nuts rancid, so that they shrivel in their shells. Heating nuts briefly in an oven or a microwave will make them easy to crack. To chop nut meats, put them in a plastic bag and crush with a rolling pin.

WALNUTS

Soaking in salted water
Soak walnuts in a bowl of salted water overnight. They will be easy to crack afterward, and the flesh will remain whole.

PEANUT BUTTER

Use liquid honey to moisten peanut butter

Preventing dryness
If peanut butter dries out, adding a spoonful of liquid honey will make the peanut butter moist again. Stir the honey in well.

USING NUTS

● **Chestnuts** To prepare, cut a slit in the flat side of each shell. Cover with water and boil for 10 minutes. Remove the shells with a paring knife.
● **Coconuts** Pierce the eyes of a coconut with an ice pick, and drain out the juice. Using a hammer, crack open the coconut to get at the flesh.
● **Brazil nuts** Store Brazil nuts in the freezer – they will shell easily and will not break up.
● **Walnuts** If walnuts taste old, cover with boiling water, drain, then heat on a shallow pan in a medium oven for 20 minutes.

OILS

Heating a frying pan before you add butter or oil will prevent foods from sticking. Sprinkle a pinch of salt into frying pans to stop oil from spattering. Adding 1 tbsp (15 ml) of vinegar to fat before deep frying will prevent food from absorbing too much fat.

REUSING OIL

Straining impurities
Clean oil that has been used for deep frying by straining it through a fine metal sieve. Store the oil in a sealed container.

CHOOSING OILS

● **Types of oil** Use oils that contain polyunsaturated fats for cooking: corn, sesame, olive, cottonseed, peanut, safflower, sunflower, and soy. Avoid coconut and palm oils, which contain saturated fat. Peanut oil is good for frying food at high temperatures.

DEEP FRYING

● **Removing flavors** Oil can be reused until it turns brown. If it takes on food flavors, fry sliced potato in the oil until crisp to remove the flavors.

TRADITIONAL TIP

"Nonstick" pan
To season a new frying pan, boil some vinegar in it. This will prevent food from sticking to the pan when frying in the future.

HERBS AND SEASONINGS

Dried herbs are stronger than fresh herbs – 1 tbsp (15 g) of dried herbs equals 2 tbsp (30 g) of fresh herbs. To make your own herb vinegar, steep a handful of fresh herbs in 2 cups (600 ml) of vinegar for two weeks. Shake daily. Strain into a lidded container.

PREPARING HERBS

Simple cutting

Instead of cutting fresh herbs on a chopping board with a knife, it is quicker and more efficient to use a pair of food scissors to snip the herbs directly into a bowl.

TIPS ON USE

● **Salt** Put a few grains of rice in a salt shaker to prevent salt from clogging. If you double a recipe, you only need to use one-and-a-half times as much salt. See page 121 for when to add salt to dishes.

● **Parsley** Add parsley to dishes just before they have finished cooking – cooked parsley has a bitter flavor. Chew parsley to get rid of garlic breath.

● **Tarragon** Before using, soak dried tarragon in warm water to bring out the flavor.

GARLIC

Immerse cloves completely in oil

Storing in oil

Peel garlic cloves and place them in a bottle of olive or vegetable oil to preserve them. You can use the flavored oil at a later date to make salad dressings.

SWEET FLAVORINGS

Put a few crackers in your sugar cannister to prevent sugar from caking. Store brown sugar in the freezer to stop it from hardening. If a recipe calls for superfine sugar and you do not have any, grind granulated sugar in a blender and use that as a substitute instead.

HARD BROWN SUGAR

● **Softening** Hardened brown sugar will soften in two days if you add a slice of bread or apple to the container.

Quick solution

If brown sugar has hardened and you need a little in a hurry, grate off the amount required, using the fine end of a grater.

SYRUP TIPS

● **Keeping bottles clean** To prevent syrup bottles from becoming sticky, grease the threads of the bottle so that syrup does not run down the sides.

Preventing sticking

Before measuring syrup, grease the measuring cup – the syrup will slide out. Heat measuring spoons in hot water before use.

QUICK RESCUES

● **Brown sugar substitute** Use white sugar and molasses in baking if you run out of brown sugar. Add 1 tbsp (15 ml) of molasses to each cup (225 g) of white sugar.

Restoring honey

If honey (or jam) crystallizes, stand the jar in a bowl of boiling water for a few minutes until it becomes runny again.

SAUCES AND SOUFFLÉS

Leftover sauces can be reheated and used as toppings for vegetables, added to pie fillings, or used in pasta sauces. If a sauce gets lumpy, beat it in an electric blender until it is smooth. A can of soup can be used as a substitute for sauce in an emergency.

PREVENTING PROBLEMS
- **Greasy sauces** Add a small amount of baking soda to greasy sauces to absorb fat. Alternatively, see page 120.
- **Lumpy sauces** If beating a sauce in a blender fails to remove lumps, strain the sauce through a sieve.

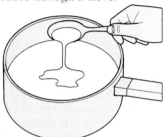

Preventing "skins"
Spread a thin layer of melted butter or cream over sauces after cooking to prevent a skin from forming. When you are ready to use the sauce, stir in the butter or cream to add flavor.

MAKING GRAVY
- **Quick recipe** To make gravy for roasted meat, skim, then sprinkle a little flour into the juices left in the roasting pan. Add water, stock, or wine for the required consistency.
- **Thickening gravy** Mix water and flour into a paste, then add gradually to the gravy while bringing it to boil. Alternatively, thicken gravy by adding instant potato flakes.

VARIOUS SAUCES
- **Cheese sauce** Use a pinch of cayenne pepper or a dash of lemon juice or mustard to add interest to a cheese sauce.
- **Apple sauce** A pinch of salt added to apple sauce will bring out the flavor and allow you to use less sugar.
- **Hollandaise sauce** If this begins to curdle, beat in a small amount of hot water.

MAKING AND RESCUING SOUFFLÉS
- **Light soufflés** Add a pinch of cream of tartar to egg whites during whisking – this makes soufflés light and fluffy.

WHITE SAUCE
- **Reheating** White sauce will keep in the refrigerator for a week. Reheat the sauce over a pan of simmering water, rather than using direct heat.

Combine all ingredients, then simmer together

Instant white sauce
There is no need to make white sauce in stages. Put the butter, flour, milk, and any seasonings in a pan. Heat them all up together, stirring all the time to prevent lumps from forming.

- **Collapsed soufflé** If a sweet soufflé collapses, spoon it into a glass dish and decorate with whipped cream or cookies.

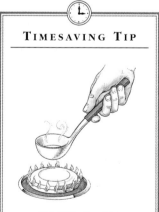

TIMESAVING TIP

Heating liquids
If you need a small amount of melted butter, boiling water, or hot milk, use a metal ladle to heat it directly over the burner. The long handle prevents burned fingers.

MAKING PANCAKES
- **Useful tips** When making pancakes, heat the frying pan before you add the oil or butter. This prevents pancakes from sticking.
- **Pouring batter** Make your pancake batter in a large measuring cup instead of in a bowl – the lip of the cup helps you pour the batter neatly into the frying pan.
- **Preventing burning** Rub raw potato over the griddle before frying pancakes to prevent them from sticking.
- **Pancake additions** A dash of soda water added to the batter for pancakes makes them light and fluffy. Adding 1 tsp (5 ml) of honey to the pancake batter will make pancakes moist.
- **Storing pancakes** Stack leftover pancakes on a plate with waxed paper between layers to prevent them from sticking. Wrap them in plastic wrap, and store in the refrigerator for a few days, or in the freezer. Reheat them in an oven or a microwave.

PRESERVING

Save used jars and their lids in a safe place, and recycle them when you make jams or other preserves. When making jam, stand the warmed jars on a cloth or wooden board. Always warm a thermometer in water before putting it in hot jam – otherwise, it may crack.

PREPARING JAM JARS

Nail polish provides protective coating

Tempering jars
Wash jars thoroughly, then place them upside down on a baking tray in a cold oven. Switch the oven on to low, and leave the jars for 10 minutes. They will now be tempered, and will not crack when you pour hot jam in.

Labeling and decorating
Paint clear nail polish over jam-jar labels to prevent the writing from smudging. Wait until jam has cooled before labeling jars; otherwise, the labels will not stick. Decorate jam to be given as a gift with fabric and ribbon.

REDUCING SCUM
● **Using butter** Reduce scum by stirring in a lump of butter when the jam is ready to set, or by rubbing butter inside a jam jar before you use it.
● **In jars** Prevent scum in jars by add 2 tbsp (30 ml) of vinegar to the water you use when sterilizing the jars.

SETTING JAM
● **If jam will not set** Add 1 tbsp (15 ml) of lemon juice to every 1 lb (450 g) of fruit. (Remove the pan from the heat while testing for setting.)
● **Jarred jam not setting** Stand the jars in a baking pan full of hot water and place in a low oven for a few minutes.

AVOIDING PROBLEMS
● **Timesaver** Heat the sugar used in jam making in a bowl in a moderate oven while you cook the fruit. This speeds up the dissolving process when you combine the ingredients.
● **Using jam jars** Do not fill jam jars more than halfway, since the jam may boil over.

HOME FREEZING

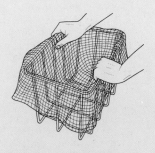

Line freezer baskets with net so that small items do not fall through. A full, tightly packed freezer runs economically.

● **Freezer log** Keep a log of what is stored in a deep freezer, along with the date that each item went in.
● **Ice cubes** Use styrofoam cartons to make extra ice cubes for parties.
● **Stock** Freeze excess stock in ice-cube trays for later use. There is no need to defrost stock before adding to stews and casseroles.
● **Nonstick storage** Freeze soft fruit, vegetables, and beans spread out on trays.

● **Soups and stews** Line a container with a plastic bag and pour soup or stew into it. Remove the plastic bag when the contents are frozen solid, to free the container for other uses.
● **Cake** Freeze odd pieces of cake until you have enough to make a trifle.
● **Herbs** Pack chopped parsley and mint in ice-cube trays, cover with water, and freeze. Reserve for adding to sauces.

BAKING AND CANDY

Homemade cakes and cookies are, in general, much better than store-bought ones. Many cake mixtures freeze well, and it is worth doubling recipes so that you can later bake treats quickly, with no time-consuming preparation.

CAKE MAKING

Place a shallow tray of water in the bottom of the oven while cakes are baking to prevent them from burning. Avoid opening the oven door during baking; if you have to in order to check a cake, close the door gently afterward – otherwise, the cake may collapse.

GENERAL TIPS
● **Greasing tins** Use waxed-paper butter wrappers to line cake pans. Save foil butter wrappers and use them to grease cake pans.
● **Unsticking cakes** If a cake sticks to the pan, stand the pan on a damp cloth for a few minutes, then try removing the cake from the pan again.
● **Dried fruit** Soak dried fruit such as raisins and currants in tea overnight to improve the flavor. Roll dried fruit in flour before stirring into cake batter; this prevents the fruit from sinking to the bottom.

MISSING INGREDIENTS

Useful substitutes
Replace a missing egg with 1 tsp (5 ml) of white vinegar. To make your own self-rising flour, add 2 tsp (10 g) of baking powder to 1 cup (225 g) plain flour.

PREVENTING STICKING

Pull foil to unstick cake

Using aluminum foil
Place a strip of foil across a cake pan before you put in the cake mixture. This keeps the center – the part most likely to stick – out of contact with the cake pan.

SLICING A LAYER CAKE IN HALF

Place thread around circumference

Cross ends of thread

Cotton thread produces perfect cut

1 Use strong cotton thread to cut a sponge cake into two layers. Line the thread up around the cake carefully, then cross the two ends.

2 Pull the two ends firmly so that the thread slices evenly through the cake, then lift off the top layer. This method produces a clean cut.

PREVENTING CAKE PANS FROM RUSTING
● **New pans** Grease new cake pans and heat in the oven for 15 minutes to prevent them from rusting in the future.

● **Used pans** To make sure that pans are thoroughly dry after washing, put them in a hot oven for a few minutes.

PROBLEM SOLVING

● **Sunken center** If the center of a cake sinks, cut out the middle with a glass tumbler, and discard it. Make a ring cake from the remainder.
● **Dry cake** If a fruit cake seems dry, prick the top all over with a darning needle and sprinkle with whisky or brandy. Let it soak in.
● **Burned cake** If a cake has burned, cut off the worst parts, turn the cake upside down, and ice the base.
● **Cracked cake** If a cake has cracked, you may have used too much rising agent. Cut off the top layer, reverse it, and sandwich with icing.
● **Leftover batter** Store excess batter in the refrigerator, and use it to make pancakes.

DECORATING CAKES

Improvise a piping bag for icing either by cutting off the corner of a strong plastic bag, or by rolling sheets of waxed paper into a cone shape. Use fancy-shaped cookie cutters to mark out patterns to ice on a cake, or mark out your own design with pinpricks.

ICING AND TOPPINGS

● **Before icing** To keep icing from running off a cake, dust a little confectioner's sugar onto the cake before icing it.

● **Royal icing** Adding ½ tsp (2.5 ml) glycerin to royal icing stops it from becoming too brittle when it hardens.

● **Colored sugar** To make colored sugar for decorating cakes, put a couple of drops of food coloring into a small plastic bag with 2 tsp (10 g) of granulated sugar. Tie the bag, and work the sugar and the coloring together with your fingers for a few minutes.

● **Confectioner's sugar** To stretch confectioner's sugar, add a little plain flour to it.

USING CHOCOLATE

Making shapes
Use a vegetable peeler to make chocolate curls and shavings. Chill the chocolate first in the refrigerator or freezer. For flat shapes, pour melted chocolate onto greaseproof paper. Chill, then cut out the shapes.

BRIGHT IDEA

Making candied flowers
To use real flowers as cake decorations, dip the flowers in beaten egg white, then in superfine sugar. Arrange them on the tops of cakes. Candied flowers will keep for a few days in an airtight container.

STORING AND SERVING

Fruit cakes have good keeping qualities, and the flavor improves if they are stored, well wrapped, for several months. Lighter cakes such as sponge cakes are best eaten fresh. Dust serving plates with granulated sugar to prevent cakes from sticking to them.

STORING CAKES IN TINS

Place apple half among cakes

Keeping cakes fresh
Put half an apple in the cake tin to keep cakes fresh and moist. Alternatively, cover the cut portion of a cake with a slice of bread, held in place with toothpicks – this will prevent the cake from drying out.

Lift tin away from lid

Upside-down storage
Store an iced cake on the lid of a cake tin – this makes it easy to remove the cake for serving without damaging the icing each time. Remember that the cake tin is supposed to be upside down before you open it.

PRESERVING FRESHNESS

● **Slicing cake** When slicing only a few pieces from a fresh cake, take the slices from the center, then slide the two halves together. The cake will stay fresh longer.

● **Cake mix** If you use cake mixes, do not keep them for longer than six months, since they will deteriorate.

FREEZING CAKES

● **Small portions** For packed lunches, cut a cake into slices and wrap and freeze the slices individually. Remove from the freezer in the morning.

● **Spice cake** Leave cloves out of a spice cake if you plan to freeze it. Cloves get stronger when they are frozen.

PREPARING PASTRY

The secret of successful pastry making is to keep everything cool – your hands, the fat, the water, and the rolling surface should all be as cold as possible. Chill pastry in the refrigerator for at least half an hour before rolling, so that it will not shrink while baking.

ROLLING PASTRY
● **Flouring equipment** Sprinkle flour onto the pastry board and the rolling pin – never directly onto the pastry.

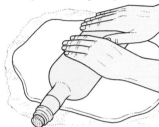

Improvised rolling pin
A straight-sided wine bottle filled with chilled water makes an ideal rolling pin because it keeps the pastry cool. Always roll pastry in the same direction.

ADDING FAT

Grating chilled fat
Small pieces of fat are easier to rub into flour than large ones. Cool fat for pastry making in the refrigerator, then grate it on the coarse end of a grater.

PERFECT PASTRY
● **Handle with care** Keep pastry light by using the tips of your fingers to rub the fat into the flour. Be careful not to overwork the pastry.
● **Crisp pastry** For extra crisp pie crusts, substitute 1 tbsp (15 ml) of white vinegar for the same amount of water.
● **Flaky pastry** Replace 1 tbsp (15 ml) of water with the same amount of orange or lemon juice for flaky pastry.
● **Storing pastry** Shortcrust pastry can be stored – without the water or salt added – for two weeks in the refrigerator. Add the missing ingredients before you use the pastry.

BAKING PASTRY

Glaze pies with egg or milk before baking. When reheating pies, place a small dish of water in the oven to keep the pastry moist. Two-crust pies should be baked on the bottom shelf of an oven so that the bottom crust bakes thoroughly, without the top crust burning.

PREVENTING SOGGINESS
● **Glass ovenware** If you bake pastry in a glass dish, place the dish on a metal baking tray in the oven – the bottom crust will cook thoroughly.

Applying coatings
Brush a pastry shell with egg white before adding the filling to prevent it from becoming soggy. Brush uncooked pastry with melted butter before freezing.

SPECIAL TECHNIQUES
● **Pie funnels** Insert long lengths of uncooked macaroni into pie centers as pie funnels.

Use dried beans as a substitute for pie weights

Baking pastry empty
Place dried beans or rice on foil inside a pastry case and bake for 15 minutes. Remove the foil and beans, then return the pastry to the oven for five minutes more.

PASTRY-MAKING PROBLEMS

● **Hard pastry** This is caused by adding too much water, and adding flour will not solve the problem. Always use exact measures – do not try to estimate quantities.
● **Crumbly pastry** This is caused by adding insufficient water, resulting in a pastry that will break and cause fillings to leak. Always check the consistency of the dough with your hands, and add more cold water if necessary.
● **Thin pastry** If pastry rises through a flan filling during baking, the pastry is not heavy enough to stay in place. Baking pastry empty before adding fillings will prevent this from happening.

COOKIES

Keep a batch of prepared cookie mix in the refrigerator so that you can make cookies in minutes. Store cookies in airtight containers, but do not mix different types, since their moisture contents may vary. A piece of bread in the container keeps cookies moist.

REMOVING COOKIES

Loosen cookies while hot

Preventing sticking
Placing a tray of cookies on a damp dish towel makes the cookies easy to remove. Lift them off the tray while they are still warm.

Damp dish towel

CUTTING COOKIES
● **Time-savers** Dip cookies cutters in flour to make them cut cleanly. To cut cookies quickly, roll the dough into a sausage shape and slice it.

BAKING COOKIES
● **Testing batches** Always test bake one cookie first, since the moisture content of flour varies. This saves ruining a whole tray of cookies.

ADDITIONAL TIPS
● **Preventing spreading** Chill baking trays before you place cookies on them – this will prevent the cookies from spreading during baking.
● **Fragile cookies** Line the baking pan with waxed paper when making cookies that are fragile. They are less likely to break when removing.
● **Cookie crumbs** To crush cookies for making cheese-cake bases, put them in a plastic bag and crush them with a rolling pin.
● **Sprinkling sugar** Use an empty salt or spice container to sprinkle sugar on cookies.

CANDY AND TREATS

When making boiled candy, add a small amount of vinegar or a pinch of salt to the ingredients before cooking to cut down on the sweetness. If you use gelatin in a dessert, be sure to dissolve the gelatin thoroughly in water before adding it to the other ingredients.

CHOCOLATE
● **Melting chocolate** Butter the pan before melting chocolate so that it will pour out easily. Alternatively, line a pan with foil when melting chocolate; discard the foil afterward.
● **Improvised chocolate** If you run out of cooking chocolate, add 4 tbsp (60 g) of cocoa powder to 1 tsp (5 g) of butter and use this as a substitute.

OTHER TREATS
● **Pie fillings** Add 1 tsp (5 ml) of vinegar to pecan or maple syrup pie filling to cut down on the sugary sweetness.
● **Gelatin molds** Wet the inside of the mold before pouring in the gelatin so that it will be easy to turn out. Alternatively, dip the mold briefly in hot water before unmolding.

MERINGUES
● **Handling** To lift meringues from an oven tray without breakage, place the tray on a wet dish towel as soon as it is taken from the oven.

Making crisp meringue
To make your meringue crisp every time, add 1 tsp (5 ml) of white vinegar to every three egg whites. Alternatively, add a pinch of cream of tartar.

BRIGHT IDEA

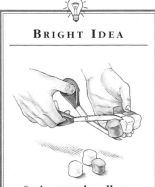

Saving marshmallows
Store marshmallows in the freezer to prevent them from drying out. When ready to use for decoration or grilling, cut them apart with sharp kitchen scissors. Dipping the scissors in hot water first will make the job easier.

BEVERAGES

Basic hot drinks such as coffee and tea can be much enhanced in flavor with the addition of extra ingredients. It is best to use purified water in hot and cold drinks, particularly in areas where the tap water has a distinctive taste.

HOT DRINKS

Keep ground coffee in a tightly covered container in the refrigerator. Using purified water in a coffee maker prolongs the life of the machine and improves the taste of the coffee. To enhance the flavor of tea, place a piece of dried orange peel inside your tea tin.

MAKING HOT DRINKS

- **Coffee makers** Place coins under the pot in drip coffee makers – this prevent a scum from forming and will keep the coffee from burning.
- **Best instant coffee** Add cold milk to the coffee powder or granules first, then add boiling water, and stir thoroughly.
- **Leftover coffee** Freeze in ice-cube trays and add cubes to iced or too-hot coffee.
- **Adding flavors** Dissolve lemon drops or mint candy in tea in place of sugar. Add flavor to coffee by putting vanilla or almond extract into the water as the coffee brews.

COFFEE

Perfect fresh coffee
Add a pinch of salt to coffee before brewing to help reduce bitterness. To preserve a fresh taste, remove the filter basket as soon as the coffee is brewed.

LEFTOVER TEA

Using leftover tea
Soaking dried fruit that will be used in baking – such as prunes, raisins, and apricots – in leftover tea will make the fruit plump and improve their flavor.

THERMOS FLASKS

Sugar cubes prevent mustiness

Storage and care
Put a couple of sugar cubes in thermos bottles to keep them fresh. Store with the lids off. To clean a thermos, fill it with hot water and baking soda, and leave overnight. Never immerse thermos bottles in water.

HOT CHOCOLATE

Beat hot chocolate with balloon whisk

Preventing problems
Whisk hot chocolate in a pan until frothy to prevent a scum from forming. Alternatively, put it in a blender and whisk at high speed before serving. Rinse the pan in cold water before adding the hot chocolate (see p. 121).

TRADITIONAL TIP

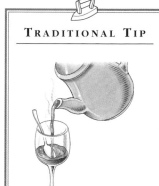

Heat-resistant glass
Put a metal spoon into a glass before pouring in any hot liquid – this will prevent the glass from cracking.

SOFT DRINKS

To be truly refreshing, soft drinks should be chilled. If your refrigerator is too full to chill drinks for a party, buy extra ice and chill the drinks in plastic buckets. Wrap adhesive tape around the caps of opened bottled drinks to prevent them from losing their fizz.

MAKING JUICE AND OTHER COLD DRINKS

● **Using fruit** Grate the peel from oranges, lemons, or limes, and mix the peel with a little sugar and enough boiling water to cover. When cool, strain and add the fruit juices, plus enough cold water to make a refreshing drink.

● **Powdered drinks** When making cool drinks using a flavored mix, dissolve the sugar first in a little hot water before adding it to the mix.

● **Decorative glasses** To make decorative drinking glasses for children's parties, dip the rims in a thick sugar solution, then in a dish of rainbow sprinkles or colored sugar (see p. 137).

● **Decorating punch** Freeze clusters of grapes and add them to punches as a garnish.

● **Iced tea** To prevent iced tea from becoming foamy, add the water to the pitcher or the glass before you add the tea.

Squeezing citrus fruit
To get the maximum amount of juice from citrus fruit, roll the fruit on a flat surface before squeezing. Vitamin C in citrus juice is destroyed by exposure to air, so cover juice when storing.

CHILLING PUNCH

● **Decorative ice cubes** Freeze twists of lemon, orange, or cucumber in ice cubes and add these to cocktails.

Serving cold punch
When serving a cold punch, freeze some of the punch in ice-cube trays beforehand. Add these cubes to chill the punch – when they melt they will not dilute the punch as ice would.

ALCOHOLIC DRINKS

Store spirits upright, but bottles of wine on their sides. If a wine cork has swollen and you cannot get it back in, soak it in boiling water to make it pliable. See page 161 for estimating drink quantities for parties; see pages 39–40 for removing alcohol stains.

STORING WINE

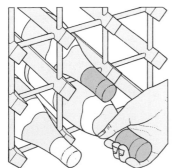

Ideal conditions
Store wine bottles on their sides so that the wine stays in contact with the cork – this prevents the cork from drying out. Ideally, wine should be stored at a cool, constant temperature.

LEFTOVER WINE

Freeze leftover wine in ice-cube trays

Saving wine for cooking
Pour leftover wine into ice-cube trays, and freeze it. The cubes can be added to gravy, soups, and stews. Add white wine that has become sour to vinegar, or use it for marinating meat.

SERVING WINE

● **Filling glasses** Wine glasses should only be half filled, to preserve the bouquet – but fill champagne glasses to the top to make the bubbles last.

● **Champagne** When opening a champagne bottle, hold it at a 45-degree angle, and turn the bottle, not the cork.

CIDER

● **Heating drinks** Serve hot hard or nonalcoholic cider from a pot on the stove on a low setting when entertaining. You can heat small quantities of cider in a microwave.

● **Using beer** Save leftover beer for fried food batters.

HOUSEKEEPING

RUNNING A HOME well does not mean that you should have to put all your effort into doing so. There are short cuts that you can take to make various household tasks quick and easy. If you organize your home, you will not have to spend time constantly cleaning or tidying up, and will have more time for relaxing and pleasant pursuits. Use your talents to create an environment that reflects your taste and suits your needs.

STORING AND SAVING

Keep things in the rooms in which they are used, and make sure everyone gets into the habit of returning them to their proper places. Organize your closets so that you can reach everyday objects easily. Reuse items as often as possible to save money and time.

USING SCREW-TOP JARS

Undershelf storage
Save screw-top jars, and attach their lids securely underneath shelves with screws. Use them to store sugar or dry beans; in a toolroom they can be used for storing nails and screws.

STORING MISCELLANEOUS ITEMS

● **Tablecloths** Sprinkle clean plastic tablecloths with a little talcum powder before putting them away. This will prevent stickiness and mildew.
● **Plastic wrap** Store this in the refrigerator – this makes it less likely to stick to itself.

EXTENSION CORDS

Tube holds cord together

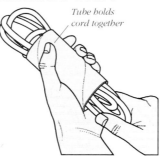

Storing extension cords
Use wide cardboard tubes from posters and toilet paper to keep extension cords in storage. Carefully coil the cords so that they will not tangle or trail over a drawer or cabinet door.

● **Newspapers** To stack newspapers tidily for recycling, lay two long pieces of twine in a cross across a cardboard box. Stack newspapers in the box, then tie the twine at the top to make a perfect stack.

SAVING AND PRESERVING

● **Boxes** Save small, lidded boxes and store buttons and pins in them. Use large boxes for storing postcards and family photographs. Label each box with the contents.
● **Hot-water bottles** Cut the top off an old hot-water bottle, stuff with old stockings, and seal the end with sturdy tape. Use as a kneeling pad for gardening.
● **Labels and stamps** Do not throw away postage stamps, or gummed labels that have stuck together. Place a piece of thin paper over them and press with a warm iron until they come apart again.
● **Newspaper clippings** To preserve a newspaper clipping, soak it in a solution of 4 cups (1 liter) of soda water and one milk of magnesia tablet for an hour. Remove the clipping, lay it on a towel, and pat dry.

WRAPPING AND PACKING

Many a package has gone astray in the mail because it has been inadequately wrapped. Wrapping materials such as brown paper and string can be reused several times, with a little care. Use foam coolers as gift boxes and old greeting cards as gift tags.

TIPS FOR GIFT-WRAPPING ITEMS

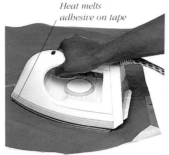

Heat melts adhesive on tape

TIMESAVING TIP

Tape-end finder
Stick a small button at the end of a roll of tape. When you use the tape, the end will be easy to find, and the button can be removed.

Reusing paper
Do not throw out old wrapping paper. A warm iron will smooth out creases and wrinkles and even remove adhesive tape so that you can use the paper again.

Measuring gifts
Cut wrapping paper to the correct length by measuring the gift first with a piece of string. Use the string to measure out enough paper to wrap the gift.

PROTECTING DELICATE OBJECTS

● **China** Wrap pieces of fine china to be sent in the mail in several layers of damp paper. When the paper dries, it will shrink to protect the china.

● **Fragile items** If you have no bubble wrap available for packing fragile items, use foam egg cartons or popped popcorn to line the box.

● **Documents** Wrap items you do not want to fold, such as documents or silk scarves, around a cardboard tube. Secure with masking tape.

SHIPPING ITEMS

Make sure that anything you have wrapped up is securely fastened and that it carries the recipient's name in large letters. Print your own name in small letters. It is a good idea to pack an extra addressed mailing label inside the package, too.

SHIPPING SAFELY
● **Make sure** Always call your shipping service to confirm size and packing requirements before wrapping your parcel.
● **Get-well cards** If you send a card to a hospital, write the patient's home address as the return address on the envelope. If the patient has been discharged, he or she will receive the card at home.
● **Postcards** When you go on vacation, make stick-on address labels for everyone you intend to send postcards to, so that you can leave your address book at home.

USING STRING

Pull end of string through lid

Storing string
To prevent string from tangling, store it in a screwtop jar. Punch a hole in the lid, and pull the end of the string through this.

Tying a parcel
Before tying up a parcel, wet the string. It will not slip when it is being tied, and when it dries it will shrink and stay in position.

HOUSEPLANTS AND FLOWERS

Plants and fresh flowers enhance a home. The secret to successful indoor plants is to match their native growing conditions to their positions in your house as closely as possible, and to feed and water them carefully.

CARING FOR PLANTS

Some houseplants thrive on neglect; others need a lot of care. Trial and error – or a good book – will tell you how often to water different types and what kind of shade or sun they like. If you have a yard, put them outside in summer, and they should do well.

PLANT-CARE BASICS
● **Choosing soil** Do not use garden soil for potting house- plants. It is not sterile and may harbor organisms that cause plant problems. Buy soil mix for indoor plants from a garden store.
● **Raising humidity** Central heating dries out the air. To raise the humidity for indoor plants, mist them with a fine spray of water daily.
● **Cleaning plants** Dust plants regularly. Clean shiny-leaved plants with glycerin – this creates a shine but does not attract dust. A solution of half milk and half water is also effective for shining leaves.

Mix plants of different shapes and sizes for best effects

Make sure plants are free of diseases before adding to groups

Grouping plants
Houseplants grow best when grouped together, especially in a dry room. Make sure that all the plants have similar temperature, light, and humidity needs.

FEEDING PLANTS

Place homemade fertilizer in plant pot

Using kitchen leftovers
Mix a little cold tea, used tea leaves, or coffee grounds with plant soil to aerate it and feed the plants. This mixture is good for ferns. The water from boiling eggs is also nutritious for plants.

POTTING PLANTS

Creating good drainage
Place a layer of broken clay pots or stones in the bottom of a pot before adding any soil, especially if the pot has no drainage hole. This helps keep the roots from becoming waterlogged.

PLANTS BY WINDOWS
● **Windowboxes** Cover the soil in windowboxes with gravel to prevent rain from splashing it onto windows.
● **Winter care** Move plants that are near windows into the room on winter nights to protect them from cold. Keep them away from hot radiators.

NEW PLANTS
● **Plant quarantine** Keep new plants away from others for a few weeks until you are sure that they are disease-free.
● **Repotted plants** Do not feed newly repotted plants for two or three months – if you do, the roots of the plants may not spread to the new soil.

WATERING PLANTS

Use room-temperature water on plants; water that is too cold or hot may damage plants. Allow the water to stand overnight before use to permit harmful chemicals to evaporate or settle. To test if a plant needs watering, check the soil with your fingers.

VACATION WATERING

● **Using a tub** When you go away on vacation, place your houseplants in the tub on thickly folded old towels in a few inches of water. The roots of the plants will take up the water they require without needing attention.

● **Using string** To water plants while you are away, place one end of a piece of string in a bucketful of water, and push the other into the soil of the plants. The bucket must be positioned higher than the plant. The string will soak up the water.

USING TEA

An occasional feeding
Water plants with cool, leftover tea occasionally to give them a boost. Do not do this too often, however – the acids in the tea may be too strong for them.

HANGING BASKETS

Ice-cube watering
To avoid drips when watering hanging baskets, use ice cubes, placing a few on the soil. Use them infrequently; they are too cold for regular use.

GROWING PROBLEMS

Watch your houseplants for any signs of infestation or failure to flourish. Houseplants thrive best if you rotate them regularly by a quarter of a turn – this evenly distributes their exposure to sunlight. Good ventilation is important to plants, but avoid drafts.

REMEDIAL ACTIONS

● **Pests** Treat disease by wrapping the plant in a plastic bag together with a pest strip. Leave it for a few days.

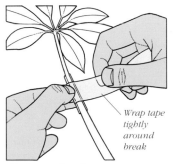

Wrap tape tightly around break

Fixing a broken stem
To support and mend a broken stem, make a splint using two toothpicks and a piece of adhesive tape. Inspect the join from time to time to make sure that the area is mending itself.

SPECIAL EFFECTS

● **Supports** Support tall plants with adjustable brass finish curtain rods. Use string to tie the plants to the rods.

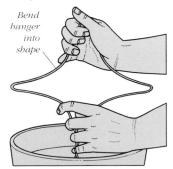

Bend hanger into shape

Making a trellis
Make your own trellis for ivy from a wire coat hanger. Snip off the hook, and bend the hanger into the desired shape – perhaps a diamond, a heart, or a star. Push the two ends into the pot.

SPECIAL CARE

● **African violets** Feed African violets with tomato fertilizer to encourage blooming. These plants are happiest in small pots, so do not be tempted to pot them on. Display them on a bright windowsill.

● **Bulbs** Always water bulbous plants from the saucer, so the soil absorbs the water. Be careful not to allow water to fall onto the leaves. Store dormant bulbs in plastic net bags and hang them up so that they are well ventilated.

● **Succulents** Cacti and some other succulent houseplants originate in the desert and need infrequent watering. Watch your fingers when handling spiky types. Use tongs if you need to repot cacti and succulents.

CUT FLOWERS

Cut flowers can be made to last much longer than usual if you take certain steps to preserve them – so do not rush home or in from the garden and expect to arrange them at once. Store-bought flowers will need greater attention than homegrown ones.

PREPARING CUT FLOWERS FOR ARRANGEMENTS

Cut at an angle

Asprin may help flowers last longer

1 Use a pair of pruning shears or a sharp knife to cut each flower stem at a slanted angle. Split the ends of thick stems before starting to arrange them in the vase, so that they have the best chance of taking up moisture.

2 Remove from the stem all the leaves that would be beneath the waterline in the vase. Otherwise, they will decay and poison the water, causing the flowers to die quickly, and the water to become brown and brackish.

3 Add two aspirins to the water – this may prolong the life of the flowers. If you are arranging them in a clear vase, add 1 tbsp (15 ml) of liquid bleach to each quart (1 liter) of water to stop the water from becoming cloudy.

ARRANGING FLOWERS

Some people have a greater knack for flower arranging than others. If your skills are limited, use straight-sided vases in which the flowers will virtually arrange themselves. Otherwise, make sure you have plenty of holding ballast in the base of the vase.

OVERCOMING COMMON PROBLEMS

Lengthening short stems
To make short-stemmed flowers appear longer, slip the stems into plastic drinking straws before you arrange them in the water. Make sure that there is enough water to reach up to the stems.

Reviving wilted flowers
Snip off the ends of the stems of wilting flowers, and stand the flowers in hot water. Allow the water to come to room temperature before arranging the flowers as you wish.

AIDS TO ARRANGING

● **Tall vase** If a vase is too deep for displaying your flowers, place crumpled paper, marbles, pebbles, or coarse sand in the base.

● **Positioning blooms** Plastic hair rollers stuck together with tape and placed in the bottom of the vase will help keep flowers in position.

● **Center flowers** Crumpled chicken wire and florist's foam are particularly good for use in containers where central flowers must be held securely in position.

● **Containers** You can use unconventional containers such as old teapots, wine goblets, and milk bottles for arranging cut flowers.

PREPARING SPECIFIC FLOWER TYPES

Find out which is the best treatment for preparing each different type of flower, and remember to vary it in a mixed arrangement.

Fill the hollow stems of dahlias with water and plug them with cotton before arranging them. Cut off any shrubby twigs with closed buds.

PREPARING ROSES

Petals and stems
Strip away any damaged petals and cut thorns from the stems with a sharp knife. Split the stems and peel off a little bark. Christmas roses will wilt quickly unless the stems are split all the way up, almost to the top.

TULIP STEMS

Treat fresh tulips to prevent them from drooping

Keeping stems straight
To prevent tulip stems from curving, wrap them tightly in wet newspaper and stand in 2 in (5 cm) of warm water for a few hours. Then push a short pin through each stem, just below the flower, to let in air.

PREPARING LILIES

Lily pollen stains badly

Anthers and stems
Cut off the anthers of flowers such as lilies to prevent the pollen from staining the petals, as well as wallcoverings and clothes. Cut the stems at an angle, and stand the flowers up to their necks in water.

DRIED AND ARTIFICIAL FLOWERS

Dried flowers can look just as attractive as fresh ones, particularly if they have been dried naturally after being picked. However, their colors fade in sunlight, and they therefore need to be replaced regularly. Silk flowers can look attractive for years with care.

DRIED FLOWERS
● **Choosing** Good blooms include statice, larkspur, and roses. Pick them when they are just open.

How to dry flowers
Tie small flower bunches with string, and hang them upside down in a dry, warm, dark place. Leave for several days until all the moisture has evaporated.

SILK FLOWERS
● **Cleaning** Put silk flowers in a plastic bag with 2 tbsp (30 g) salt. Shake it well so that the dust clings to the salt.

Dusting silk flowers
Remove dust from silk and dried flower arrangements using a hair dryer on a warm setting. Be careful where you do this – you may blow dust onto the wall.

TRADITIONAL TIP

Coloring flowers
Change the color of cut flowers by adding a little food coloring to warm water and placing stems in the solution. Use light-colored blooms and not too much coloring.

SEWING

Making your own repairs to clothing and upholstery can save you money as well as time. You do not need to be an expert to perform basic repairs – many techniques require no more than a little common sense.

SEWING BASICS

Keep an emergency sewing kit on hand in a workbox. This kit should contain several needles of different sizes, thread in various colors, buttons, straight pins, safety pins, and sharp scissors. This selection of items should enable you to do urgent repairs quickly.

THREAD

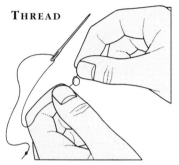

Trouble-free sewing
When using double thread, knot each strand separately, so that it does not become tangled. Spray hair spray on your fingers to make threading needles easy.

EXTRA TOOLS
● **Removing threads** Use a pair of eyebrow tweezers to remove tacking or stitching from a loose button.
● **Using thimbles** Wet your finger to create suction before putting on your thimble.

SEWING FABRICS
● **Thick material** To make sewing thick fabric seams easier, rub the material with a damp bar of hard soap.
● **Pile fabrics** When sewing pile fabric such as velvet on a sewing machine, put tissue paper over the pile to stop the fabric from sliding around.
● **Flimsy fabric** Before cutting a delicate fabric, wash the pair of scissors in hot water, then dry them thoroughly. They will cut the fabric cleanly.

PINCUSHIONS

Deterring rust
Make a pincushion from a fabric bag filled with dry, used coffee grounds. These prevent the pins from rusting. Alternatively, stick the pins in a bar of soap.

CARING FOR PINS
● **Picking up pins** Keep a magnet handy for picking up spilled pins. Use a flashlight to locate pins that drop on the floor.

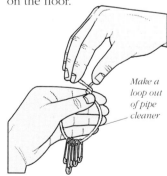

Make a loop out of pipe cleaner

Storing safety pins
Keep safety pins together by threading them onto a pipe cleaner. Twist the ends together, and store them in your workbox so that you can find them easily.

SEWING MACHINES
● **Sharpening needles** Stitch through a piece of canvas or fine sandpaper to sharpen sewing-machine needles.
● **Oiling machines** When oiling your machine or taking it apart, put a desk blotter underneath to stop it from soiling fabric, thread, and the surface underneath. When you have finished, stitch several rows on a piece of blotting paper to remove all traces of oil.
● **Steadying machines** If your sewing machine tends to slip around, stand it on a foam-backed carpet tile to grip.
● **Creeping foot** Glue a piece of foam rubber to the underside of the machine's foot control to stop it from creeping when pressed.
● **Removing lint** Use a small paintbrush or brush for an electric razor to remove lint from around the bobbin.

THREADS
● **Basic thread** Keep clear or neutral-colored thread in your sewing kit, and use this as a substitute when you do not have the right color.
● **Untangling** If thread tangles while you are hand sewing, rub it over a bar of hard soap.
● **Storing synthetic thread** Keep synthetic threads in the refrigerator – this will prevent static electricity when sewing.

ZIPPERS AND BUTTONS

The right buttons can make even cheap garments look expensive. Cut buttons off of worn-out garments and save them for later use. When buying specialty buttons, buy at least one extra button – this saves having to replace the whole set if one button falls off.

BUTTONS

● **Storing buttons** After you remove buttons from outfits, stitch the buttons together, or string them on a safety pin.

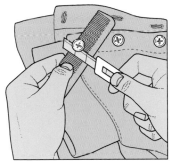

Removing tight buttons
If it is difficult to snip off a tight button, slide a comb underneath it to lift the button away from the fabric. Slice it off carefully with a sharp knife or razor blade. Be careful not to cut the fabric.

ZIPPERS

● **Recycling** Give new life to an old zipper by spraying it with starch. This will make the fabric stiff and easy to sew.

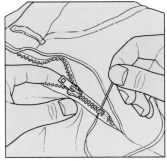

Repairing zippers
If a zipper is damaged near the base, pull the slide below the broken teeth and cut them off. Pull the slide over the missing teeth, and stitch directly above them for a new zipper base.

SEWING BUTTONS

● **Leaving a space** Place a bobby pin, match, or pin under a button when sewing it on, so that it is not held too tightly against the fabric and the buttonhole can fit over it.
● **Four-hole buttons** Sew four-hole buttons by stitching two holes at a time, then finish off the thread before doing the other two holes. This way, the buttons will not fall off, even if they become loose.

SPECIAL BUTTONS

● **Children's buttons** When sewing buttons on children's clothes, use unwaxed dental floss or fine elastic; the buttons will stay on longer.
● **Small buttons** Store extra-small buttons in plastic pill containers with snap-on lids.

SEWING TECHNIQUES

All your mending and sewing will be in vain if you do not start and finish off each job correctly, whether by hand or by machine. Make sure that thread is correctly anchored at both ends. Press seams with a hot iron over a damp cloth to keep them neat and flat.

BUTTONHOLES

Cutting thick fabric
To cut straight buttonholes in heavy fabric easily, place the area to be cut over a bar of household soap. Use a sharp craft knife or a safety razor blade to make the incisions.

TIMESAVERS

● **Sewing appliqués** Secure fabric appliqués on clothes with a dab of latex glue on the back; then sew the edges.
● **Replacement elastic** Pin new elastic to the end of the old piece. Pull the old elastic out to pull the new one in.

KNITTING

● **Knitted clothes** Place the torn part of a garment over a hairbrush to prevent it from stretching while you mend it.
● **Rescuing stitches** Keep a pipe cleaner in your knitting bag to hold dropped stitches until you can pick them up.

BRIGHT IDEA

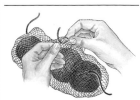

Keeping colors separate
When knitting with more than one color, place the balls of yarn in a net plastic vegetable bag. Pull each color through a different hole to prevent tangles.

CHILD AND PET CARE

KEEP CHILDREN SAFE in the home by taking basic precautions to prevent accidents and teaching them how to avoid possible dangers. Pets are also a serious responsibility, but they make rewarding and pleasant companions.

CHILD SAFETY

Take babies and very young children with you into stores and up and down stairs. Put them in a safe playpen when you answer the door or telephone or do housework. An older baby can be carried around in a backpack suitably padded to support the head.

PREVENTING ACCIDENTS
- **Glass doors** Stick colored labels at child's height on glass doors, so that there is no risk of children walking into them.
- **Pianos** Stick a cork at each end of the piano keyboard so that if the lid falls down, a child's fingers are not hurt.
- **Outlets** Plug electrical outlets with covers. This will prevent children from poking in fingers and other objects.
- **Appliances** Look for curly cords – they will not trail over counters for children to pull.

DOORS

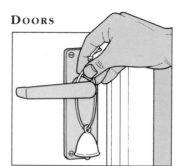

A warning bell
Fasten a small bell to a back-door handle, so that you will hear if a child has opened the door. Keep your front door securely locked.

FURNITURE

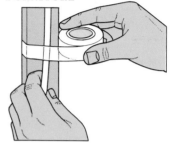

Securing trailing cords
Tape electrical cords firmly to furniture legs with adhesive tape; this prevents children from pulling items onto themselves.

CARING FOR BABIES

The mother of a baby must take care of her own health and make life as easy for herself as possible. When bringing a new baby home, try to put off any visitors for a week or two while you acquaint yourself with the new arrival and recover from the birth.

BABY BOTTLES

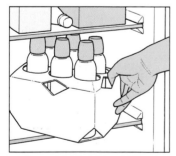

Refrigerator organizer
Use an empty cardboard beer carton to store a baby's bottles upright in the refrigerator. The bottles can easily be removed and will remain in one place, where you can find them easily.

DIAPERS

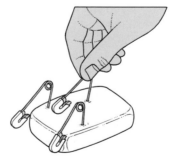

Using fastenings
If diaper pins become blunt, stick them into a bar of soap – this will also help prevent them from rusting. Use masking tape if the adhesive tape on a disposable diaper will not stick.

FEEDING AND COMFORT
- **Solid food** To make solid food for babies, purée fresh vegetables, store in ice-cube trays, and heat as needed.
- **Night feeding** When feeding a baby, put a hot-water bottle on the crib mattress so that it is still warm when you put the baby back to bed.
- **Powdering** Use a small powder puff to facilitate applying baby cornstarch during a diaper change.
- **Washing hair** Smear a line of petroleum jelly on a baby's forehead above the eyebrows to prevent shampoo from running into the eyes.

TODDLERS

Toddlers usually want to be independent faster than they are able. Make things as easy as possible for them, so that they do not have to learn the hard way – with bruises. Save yourself money by making toys from everyday household items, rather than buying them.

EATING AIDS
● **Securing plates** Use a soap saver with suction pads on both sides to help keep a child's plate steady on a table.

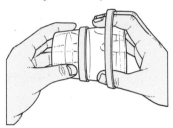

Drinking glasses
Place two rubber bands around a tumbler, about 1 in (2.5 cm) apart, to enable a child to grip it securely. Serve drinks to a child who is ill in bed in a jar with a straw through a hole in the lid.

ILLNESS AND FEAR
● **Taking pills** Get a reluctant child to take a pill by hiding it in a spoonful of jam or honey.
● **Splinters** Before removing a splinter in a child's skin, soak the area in cooking oil to soften the skin, then apply an ice cube to deaden the pain.
● **Removing bandages** Remove an adhesive bandage painlessly by rubbing a cotton ball saturated in baby oil over the surface of the bandage first.
● **Bedtime** When a child is old enough to move from a crib to a bed, place the crib mattress on the floor beside the bed – if the child falls out of the bed during the night, he or she will not be harmed.

BRIGHT IDEA

Long-lasting artworks
Apply a coating of hair spray to a child's drawing – this acts as a fixative and prevents the colors from fading and rubbing off. Hair spray also strengthens the paper.

CHILDREN'S CLOTHES

Unless you are aiming for designer perfection, secondhand clothes make sense for small children. These may be handed down from friends and relatives, or sought out in thrift shops and at rummage sales. Look for good brands or sturdily constructed garments.

KEEPING CLOTHES
● **Children's boots** To avoid losing boots at school, paint large spots of colored nail polish on the backs of the heels – the boots will stand out among others in a group.
● **Altering coats** To lengthen the life of a winter jacket, sew ready-made knitted cuffs to the sleeves.
● **Attaching gloves** To prevent a child's gloves from being lost, sew a string between them, and run the tape through the sleeves of the child's coat.
● **Girls' dresses** Turn dresses inside out if you dry them outdoors. When the hem is let down, the color will already have faded to match the dress.

SHOES AND BOOTS
● **Laces** Run shoelaces over beeswax or soap before lacing shoes or boots to make the knots last longer. Tie a knot in each end of the laces.

Children's shoes
To teach a child how to put shoes on correctly, put tape or a mark inside the right shoe so that it is clearly visible. Show the child that this shoe should always be put on the right foot.

PLAYCLOTHES
● **Protecting clothes** Spray knees, cuffs, and collars with fabric protector to keep playclothes cleaner.

Fixing cross straps
To stop cross straps on rompers and overalls from continually falling down, sew on a snap fastener at the point where the straps cross over at the back. The snap can easily be undone.

FEEDING PETS

Find out from a vet, or from a book on pet care, how to provide your pet with the nutrition it needs for good health. Feed your pet on a regular schedule, and remember that it too likes variety in its diet. Clean water should always be available for it to drink.

HEALTHY PETS
● **Teeth** Give dogs and cats marrow bones to keep their teeth in good shape. Never give chicken or fish bones.

Coat conditioner
Adding a raw egg or 2–3 tbsp (30–45 ml) of melted animal fat or cod liver oil to a dog's diet each day helps produce a shiny coat of fur. Vegetable oil does not have the same effect.

FEEDING CATS
● **Large cans** Keep a large can of cat food fresh by dividing it into separate small portions and placing each portion in a plastic sandwich bag. Seal the bag and freeze until needed.
● **The correct food** Do not feed cats with dog food – it does not have enough protein and vitamins for cats' needs.

FEEDING DOGS
● **Dog-food dishes** Keep disposable foam trays from supermarkets to use as dog-food dishes – simply throw them away after use.
● **Tuna oil** Save the oil from a can of tuna and pour it over a dog's dinner for extra taste.

GREEN TIP

Healthy food additions
Save the water from cooked vegetables to add extra flavor and vitamins to your pet's dry food. Allow the water to cool down before adding it to the food.

GROOMING AND CARE

Regular grooming and exercise are the main care elements needed by cats and dogs. They also need to eat grass occasionally, so grow some in a pot if you do not have a garden. Train a puppy to allow its teeth to be cleaned to prevent bad breath.

PREVENTING ODORS
● **Using vinegar** Place a small dish of vinegar near where a dog sleeps, or near a cat's litter box, to absorb odors.

Measure borax

Deodorizing litter boxes
Add one part of borax to six parts of cat litter, or 1 cup (225 g) of baking soda to a cat's litter box, to absorb odors.

TACKLING PARASITES
● **Flea deterrent** If you have no flea collar or powder, rub citrus oil from an orange on an animal's fur to discourage fleas and ticks. Pennyroyal oil under a collar also works.
● **Flea collar** A homemade flea collar for dogs can be made from a roll of strong fabric stuffed with tansy and catnip.
● **Tick removal** Remove ticks by dabbing them with turpentine so that they back out. Do not pull them – they may leave their heads in the pet's skin and cause infection.
● **Killing lice eggs** To kill lice eggs (called "nits"), wash your pet once every two weeks in a five percent solution of white vinegar and water.

CLEANING PETS
● **Bathing dogs** Put an old tea ball in the sink or bath drain to prevent it from becoming clogged with hair.
● **Rinsing soap** When bathing dogs, add vinegar or lemon juice to the rinse water to eliminate the soap smell.
● **Dry bath** Instead of bathing a dog in soap and water, rub baking soda into its coat, then brush it out. The baking soda acts as a deodorant and a dry cleaner.
● **Matted fur** Remove mats in fur by shampooing, then using conditioner. When the fur is dry, rub talcum powder into the mats and tease them apart. Large mats may have to be cut out by a vet.

PET PROBLEMS

Training your pet to obey house rules may take time and trouble but will pay off in the end. Ask the breeder or a vet for the best methods to use. Start training when the animal is young, before it has a chance to develop habits that may be difficult to correct later.

PROTECTING FURNITURE
● **Keeping pets off** Sprinkle pepper on upholstered surfaces to keep a pet off them. Vacuum it up later.

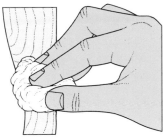

Preventing chewing
Wipe oil of cloves (from pharmacists) on furniture legs to prevent a new puppy from chewing them. Dogs dislike the smell and the bitter taste.

DOG BEHAVIOR
● **Acclimatizing a puppy** Help a puppy adjust to sleeping without its mother by putting a hot-water bottle wrapped up in a towel in its bed. A ticking clock in the bed will simulate its mother's heartbeat.
● **Wetting** If a puppy wets in the house, clean the spot with vinegar and water, then blot with plenty of ammonia. This will take away the smell and prevent it from happening in that particular area again.
● **Loneliness** If you have to leave a pet alone for a short period, give it something of yours for company, such as an old sweater. Soft radio music may provide comfort.

PETS AND SAFETY
● **Night safety** Stick reflective tape to your pet's collar to reduce the risk of it being struck by a car at night.
● **Balconies** Keep pets away from balconies and windows if you do not live on the ground floor. Even a cat can fall from a high-rise window.
● **Cords** Make sure that electric cords, cleaning substances, and valuable items are out of a puppy's reach until it has grown up beyond the chewing stage.
● **Car travel** Always restrain pets in a car. Use a pet carrier for cats; keep dogs behind a grille, or tie their leashes to a rear seatbelt.

SMALL ANIMALS

Small animals that live in hutches or cages, such as rabbits and guinea pigs, can make good pets. They grow up very quickly and are easy to handle. Small animals may be less expensive to feed than large pets, but they still require your commitment and care.

SMALL ANIMAL CARE
● **Choosing numbers** Find out from your vet whether your pet species likes company or prefers to be alone. Hamsters like to be solitary, and two male mice or rats may fight. Guinea pigs and rabbits like to have companions.
● **Pet toys** To stimulate small animals, give them household objects, such as thread spools, to play with. Make sure the objects do not have any sharp edges and are not toxic.
● **Chickens** To prevent free-range chickens from eating a favorite plant, cover it with a wire cage. Allow some shoots to push through the cage. The birds can eat these while the plant continues growing.

RABBITS
● **Safe cages** Suspend an outdoor rabbit hutch from a beam to prevent rodents from entering the cage at night.

Natural bedding
Save dry autumn leaves and dried grass cuttings to provide free bedding for rabbits and other small pets. Store the surplus away from dampness to keep the supply fresh.

WILD BIRDS
● **Bird cake** Mix a winter cake for wild birds from seeds and bacon rinds in melted fat. Put outside in a coconut shell.

Attracting birds
A bird feeder or bird-feeding net outside the window of anyone housebound or ill will provide entertainment. Replace the food as it is eaten or the birds will find a food source elsewhere.

HEALTH AND BEAUTY

WHILE YOU CAN PAY A FORTUNE for cosmetics that claim to do all kinds of things for your skin, hair, and body, the foundations for feeling and looking good can be laid with a balanced diet and a few home treatments.

COSMETICS

There is no need to throw out cosmetics just because they have dried up – they are usually too expensive to waste. Most bottles and jars can be recycled, while their contents can often be mixed with water or oil to rehydrate them and prolong their use.

NAIL POLISH

Softening nail polish
Stand hardened nail polish in a bowl of hot water to return it to its original consistency. Repeat as often as necessary. Keep your nail polish in the refrigerator to prevent it from thickening.

LIPSTICK
● **Empty tubes** Use a lip brush to get at the ends of a lipstick. Clean empty lipstick tubes out with hot water, and use them for storing bobby pins.

Hold broken end over flame

Repairs to lipstick
To mend a broken lipstick, heat the two ends over a flame until they melt enough to be stuck together again, then cool the lipstick in the refrigerator.

MASCARA

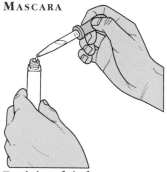

Reviving dried mascara
Use a cocktail straw to drip a couple of drops of hot water into a tube of mascara that is almost finished. Swivel the brush to mix. This will soften dried-out mascara; it can then be used.

PERFUME
● **Buying** Buy a trial size of new perfume to see if it suits you before purchasing a standard-sized bottle.
● **Storage** Store perfume in a dark, cool place. Constant exposure to light and heat will cause it to deteriorate.
● **Applying perfume** Oily skin holds perfume better than dry skin, so rub a little petroleum jelly into your skin before applying perfume.
● **Scenting drawers** Cut an old chamois into small pieces, sprinkle each piece with perfume, and put in your lingerie drawer. The chamois leather will hold the scent of the perfume longer than pieces of cotton would.

COSMETIC CARE
● **Storage** To stop bottles from falling over in drawers, cut circles in the lids of small cardboard boxes and place the bottles in the holes.
● **Stuck stoppers** If a stopper on a glass bottle is stuck, pour a little vegetable oil onto it. Hold the bottle near warm heat, and tap gently all around the stopper until it loosens.
● **Brushes** To keep makeup brushes soft, wash them in hair conditioner occasionally.
● **Pencils** Put eyebrow pencils in the refrigerator for a while before sharpening them. They will be less likely to break.

TRADITIONAL TIP

Cool cosmetics
Keep cosmetics such as face toner and moisturizing cream in the refrigerator if the weather is hot. They will be refreshing to use, and those that contain natural ingredients will remain fresh for as long as possible.

NATURAL BEAUTY

You can create natural beauty treatments yourself using fruit and vegetables. These homemade mixtures will be cheaper than manufactured products, contain no artificial additives, and are often kinder on your skin than store-bought cosmetics with chemicals.

SCENTING A BATH

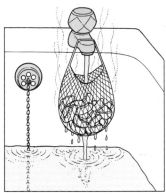

Lemon fresh
Fill a net bag with fresh lemon skins and let water run through it as you fill the bath. The oils in the lemons will be good for your skin, and the fragrance will give the water a delightful scent.

NATURAL INGREDIENTS

● **Puffy eyes** Treat tired, puffy eyes by holding peeled, grated raw potato against them in a clean handkerchief. Alternatively, use cucumber slices or cold, wet tea bags.
● **Dry shampoo** Mix 1 tbsp (15 g) salt and ½ cup (50 g) of cornmeal to make a dry shampoo. Sprinkle on your hair and brush out.
● **White teeth** Instead of toothpaste, brush with baking soda for whiter teeth.
● **Fresh breath** To sweeten breath, chew parsley.
● **Eliminating foot odor** Baking soda helps get rid of unpleasant odors from shoes and feet. Dust it over feet and sprinkle inside shoes.

GREEN TIP

Cleaning teeth
Remove stubborn stains from teeth – such as those from tobacco – by dipping your toothbrush in mashed strawberries. Brush your teeth thoroughly, then rinse your mouth with a little salt dissolved in warm water.

HANDS AND NAILS

Wear rubber gloves for rough household tasks – they will help protect your hands and nails from becoming dry and damaged. When applying nail polish, place your fingers in a bowl of iced water between applications to make each layer of polish dry quickly.

NAIL CARE

● **Strong nails** Strengthen nails by soaking fingertips in warm water and baking soda for 10 minutes once a week.

Softening cuticles
Soak cuticles in a bowl of warm olive oil to soften them. Push them gently back with a cotton swab. Use a little vitamin-E cream to coat cuticles regularly.

CLEANING HANDS

● **Grimy hands** Hands that are very grimy can be cleaned by massaging in a thick paste of oatmeal and water.

Removing stains on skin
Use the cut half of a lemon, or lemon juice, for removing stains from hands and then whitening them. Use vinegar to remove strong food odors, such as fish.

SOFT SKIN

● **Hand lotion** Make your own hand lotion from two parts glycerin to one part lemon juice. Massage a little into the hands after washing them.
● **Soft skin** Soften rough feet and hands by rubbing them in equal proportions of cooking oil and granulated sugar.

POLISHING NAILS

● **Making polish stick** Wipe nails with vinegar before you apply nail polish – this will help the varnish adhere.
● **Loosening bottle caps** To prevent a nail-polish bottle cap from sticking to the bottle, rub a little petroleum jelly in the grooves of the cap.

SKIN CARE

Keep your skin scrupulously clean if you want to avoid pimples and blemishes. To remove blackheads, steam your face over a bowl of warm water. Clean skin often if you live or work in a highly polluted area. Best of all, take care of your skin from the inside out.

SUNBURN

● **Reducing heat** Pat skin that has been sunburned with a cold, wet teabag, or dab the area with cider vinegar.

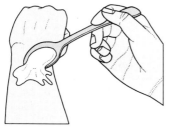

Natural remedy
Apply a thin coating of plain, natural yogurt to sunburned areas to take away the pain. Adding 1 cup (300 ml) cider vinegar to a tepid bath will also soothe sunburned skin.

CLEANSING

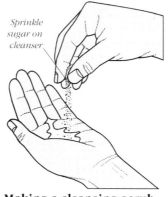

Sprinkle sugar on cleanser

Making a cleansing scrub
Add 1 tsp (5 g) of granulated sugar to your regular cream cleanser or to lather from soap. This makes an economical homemade scrub that will exfoliate rough areas of skin.

GENERAL SKINCARE

● **Body lotion** Make up a body lotion of equal proportions of glycerin and rosewater and smooth over the skin in the evening before going to bed.
● **Skin softener** Mix ¼ cup (50 ml) of milk with 1 tbsp (15 ml) of baby oil and add to your bath water to smooth and soften your skin.
● **Elbows** Rest your elbows in the skin of an avocado for a few minutes to soften them. The avocado pit will also lubricate dry skin. Rest your elbows in lemon skins for a few minutes to whiten them.
● **Milk bath** Sprinkle some powdered milk into running bath water for a relaxing bath that will soften the skin.

HOME FACIALS

Treat yourself to a home facial when you have time to enjoy it. Lie down and relax, perhaps listening to soothing music. You can make your own face masks and lotions from natural ingredients found in the kitchen. They are inexpensive and beneficial to your skin.

CARING FOR YOUR SKIN

● **Facial scrub** Make your own exfoliating scrub for your face by mixing cornmeal, honey, and ground walnuts. Rub it on your face with your fingertips and leave for five minutes before rinsing the scrub off.
● **Foundation** Wipe a wet sponge over your face before putting on liquid makeup. This will prevent the makeup from dragging on your skin.
● **Skin freshener** Make your own skin freshener from equal parts of rosewater and witch hazel, and apply it to your face with a cotton ball. Because it contains no alcohol, this mixture will not leave your skin feeling taut.

HOMEMADE FACE TREATMENTS

FOR DRY SKIN

● **Cucumber and yogurt** Cut up an unpeeled cucumber and liquidize with a small container of natural yogurt. Spread this on your face, then rinse off.
● **Egg yolk, oil, and lemon** Mix one egg yolk with ½ tsp (2.5 ml) each of olive oil and lemon juice. Wash your face and spread on well, avoiding the eyes. Leave for 10 minutes, then rinse off.

FOR OILY SKIN

● **Egg white and cornstarch** Mix one egg white with 2 tbsp (30 g) of cornstarch. Spread the mixture over your clean face and leave for several minutes until it feels dry and tight. Brush off what you can of the face pack with a dry cloth, and rinse thoroughly with cold water. Apply beaten egg white on its own to tone the skin and tighten the pores.

HEALTHY HAIR

There are all sorts of natural treatments for healthy, shiny hair, so you should be able to find one that suits your hair type. Regular cutting is essential for getting rid of split ends. Diet can also affect the way your hair looks, as can stress, mood, smoking, and air pollution.

FINAL RINSING
● **Adding shine** Shine up brunette or red hair by rinsing in coffee or cider vinegar before the final water rinse.

Blond hair
Pour 1 cup (300 ml) of boiling water over 2 tsp (10 g) of dried chamomile leaves or a handful of fresh ones. Let infuse, then strain. Use the liquid as a rinse for shining blond hair.

CARING FOR HAIR
● **Conditioner** Mayonnaise is a good conditioner for dry hair. Apply ½ cup (100 ml) to unwashed hair, cover with foil or plastic wrap, and let sit for 15 minutes. Rinse off the mayonnaise, then shampoo.
● **Hot oil** For a professional-style hot-oil treatment, run very hot water over two bath towels, then spin them in the washing machine. Saturate hair with olive or corn oil, and cover your head in foil or plastic wrap. Put the towels around this covering, so that they will not get dirty. Wait for 20 minutes before shampooing and rinsing.
● **Fine hair** Rinse very fine hair with beer to give it body.

RECIPE FOR NATURAL HAIR CONDITIONER

● **Almond and rosemary** Heat chopped rosemary and 1 tbsp (15 ml) each of almond oil, glycerin, and lanolin. Remove the mixture from the heat, cool, and beat in an egg (do not allow it to cook). Shampoo your hair, then massage in the head. Leave for 10 minutes, then rinse hair thoroughly.

MONEY-SAVING TREATMENTS

Economize where you can so that you can splurge occasionally on treatments such as facials, manicures, or even a visit to a health spa. Buy large sizes of products you use frequently, and make sure you use the last bits in containers and jars before you discard them.

UNUSED PERFUME

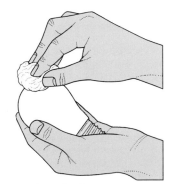

Scenting the home
If you do not like a particular perfume enough to wear it, wipe a small amount over lightbulbs. They will produce scent when heated up. Do not put on too much if the scent is strong.

LEFTOVER SOAP

Add boiling water to soap ends

Saving old soap
Save soap pieces in a screw-top jar. Add the juice of a lemon and fill up the jar with boiling water. Stir to dissolve, then add 1 tsp (5 ml) of glycerin. Let cool, and use for washing hands.

OTHER ECONOMIES
● **Shampoo** Put a few drops of water in an almost-empty shampoo bottle, and shake it well. Stand the bottle upside down for a few minutes. Use in showers as liquid soap.
● **Cotton** Buy surgical cotton, which is less expensive than other types. Break into pieces and store it in a plastic bag in an airing cupboard. The pieces will then swell and puff up, ready to be used.
● **Lip gloss** Use petroleum jelly as a lip gloss, or rub a little over your lipstick.
● **Talcum powder** Make talcum powder last longer by taping over all but three holes. This also saves mess.

CARS AND GARAGES

Your car is a valuable asset, so keep it clean and well maintained. Check it regularly for faults and dirt, especially before setting out on long journeys. Have the car serviced at regular intervals. Keep your garage orderly, too.

CLEANING YOUR CAR AND GARAGE

If you do not have time to clean your car yourself, use a valeting service, or take it through a do-it-yourself car wash at a garage. Do not forget to clean the interior. Bear in mind that keeping your car clean will prolong its useful life and help to maintain its value.

CLEAN SCREEN

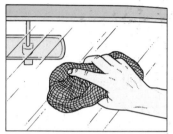

Wiping off insects
Use plastic net bags to wipe windshields on which insects have accumulated. Tie a few bags into one and rub well until the insects are gone. Then wash the windshield thoroughly. Wipe with white vinegar.

CLEANING TIPS
- **Washing** Use dishwashing liquid in your bucket when you wash the car – it is easier on the finish. Add a cup of ammonia for sparkle.
- **Windshield wipers** If your wipers are doing more smearing than cleaning, wash the windshield, and clean the wipers with rubbing alcohol. Or replace wipers.
- **Carpet** If salt from roads leaves marks on the carpet, wash with equal amounts of warm water and vinegar. Let dry, then vacuum.
- **Stickers** Use nail-polish remover to take off stickers.

GREEN TIP

Removing tar
Wipe tar spots on cars with a little linseed oil or eucalyptus oil. Let the oil soak until the tar softens, then wipe it off with a paper towel moistened in some fresh oil.

CLEANING GARAGES

Provided you keep the garage swept clear of leaves and debris, there will be little else to do except remove grease and oil stains from the floor.

- **Fresh stains** Sprinkle fresh oil stains on garage floors with plenty of cat litter, then grind the litter in with your foot. Sweep the litter up when it has absorbed the oil, and discard it.

- **Using TSP** First scrape off as much of the stain deposit as you can, using a putty knife. Wet the remaining oil stains, then sprinkle on TSP (available from hardware stores). As these dissolve, use a bristle brush to rub at the stains for 15–20 minutes. Add more TSP and continue to scrub. Rinse off the stains with clean water.
- **Old stains** For old stains, apply a spray-and-wash product and leave it for five minutes. Sprinkle with laundry detergent, scrub with a stiff broom, and hose the area down.
- **Tough stains** For really tough stains, use oven cleaner. Let it stand, then rinse it off. Keep children and pets away.

OTHER CARE TIPS
- **Scenting cars** Keep a sheet of fabric softener underneath your car seat to keep the whole car smelling fresh.
- **Stain guard** Before long trips, spray the front of your car with cooking oil to stop bugs from sticking to the grill.
- **Air conditioners** Run the air conditioner for five minutes each week during winter to keep it functioning smoothly.
- **Keeping oil clean** Keep open cans of motor oil clean by sealing them with the plastic lids from used cans of coffee.
- **Chrome** Clean car chrome with damp aluminum foil.
- **Windshield** Add a splash of white vinegar to a wet, lint-free rag to clean windshields.

WEATHER-RELATED PROBLEMS

Be prepared for when things go wrong with your car, particularly in cold weather. Carry an emergency kit consisting of a blanket, water, a chocolate bar, a flashlight, and a book. A cellular telephone is useful if you break down far from a public telephone.

FROZEN LOCKS
● **Heating locks** If your car is in a garage, use a hair dryer on the lock at a low setting to thaw it out. Alternatively, spray the lock with deicer.

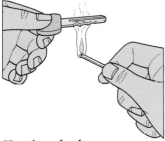

Heating the key
Heat the key (not the lock) with a match or lighter until it is warm. Insert it in the lock and leave for a couple of minutes before turning it. Repeat.

STUCK IN SNOW
● **Using cat litter** Keep a bag of cat litter in your trunk during the winter. If your car gets stuck on ice or in snow, sprinkle it to provide traction.

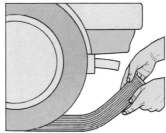

Using floor mats
Remove the rubber mats from your car and place them behind the rear wheels. They might just provide enough traction to get you moving again.

PRECAUTIONS
● **Washer** Check the level of windshield-washer water, particularly in hot weather, when it tends to evaporate.
● **Preventing frozen doors** Wipe the rubber gaskets of your car doors with vegetable oil to prevent them from freezing up in winter.
● **Morning starts** Back your car into the garage at night – it is easier to drive forward than to reverse when the engine has not warmed up.
● **Cold engine** If the car will not start on a cold morning, try blowing hot air from a hair dryer on the carburetor.
● **Full tank** A full fuel tank will give extra weight and traction when driving on icy roads.

GENERAL MAINTENANCE

The smallest problem with your car can become an enormous one when you break down or get a ticket as a result. Regular checks on items such as lights will help you avoid minor problems and may save you from needing to call out the emergency services.

REGULAR MAINTENANCE
● **Spare fuel** Keep the spare gas can full, especially when going on long journeys.
● **Spare tire** When checking tire pressure, always check the pressure on the spare tire. Inflate the spare each time you put air in the other tires.
● **Lights** Enlist the help of a second party to check that all lights are working. Always carry spare lightbulbs.
● **Tires** Regularly inspect the tires and remove any stones or nails lodged in the treads.
● **Wipers** Carry a set of spare wiper blades in the car.
● **Jumper cables** If your battery tends to fail, keep jumper cables in the car.

CAR ANTENNAES
● **Retractable antennaes** If your anntenna is retractable, put it in when you leave the car. This will prevent damage.

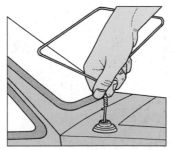

Temporary antenna
Use a coat hanger as a substitute for an antenna. Cut off the hook, shape into a diamond, and wedge into the antenna socket.

BRIGHT IDEA

Safe garage parking
When you are parked in your garage, measure the distance from the rear wall to your windscreen. Suspend a ball from the ceiling at this point; it will touch the windscreen, warning you to stop the next time you park in the garage.

ENTERTAINING

H AVING FRIENDS OVER to your home for food and friendship requires good planning. The guests will not enjoy themselves if the hosts are run ragged trying to serve drinks, get food on the table, and make conversation.

DINNER PARTIES

This type of entertaining is usually more formal than a supper or buffet party, or asking people around to take pot luck. Make sure everything is prepared well in advance to avoid a last-minute rush and to give yourself plenty of time to greet your guests.

THE GUESTS

● **Choosing** Select guests carefully so that they are all compatible. Do not invite more people than you can seat, and avoid people who may argue or dominate the conversation. Indicate both an arrival time and a dinner time when you invite guests.

THE FOOD

● **Planning a menu** Do not aim to have all the courses hot, otherwise you will never get out of the kitchen. Give yourself plenty of time to get all the ingredients you will require. Be careful not to experiment with dishes that you have never tried before.

PREPARATIONS

● **Lists** Make a full list of everything required for the event – this includes not only food and drink, but also table linen, candles, and flowers.
● **Timetable** Make a timetable of what to do. Do not leave everything for the last minute.

LAYING A DINNER TABLE

Correct place settings

Lay the dinner table according to what you are going to eat, starting from the outside. This setting is laid for a four-course meal that will include soup, fish, a main course, and a dessert. Place all the glasses you are going to use to the right of the place setting.

Place bread knife on bread plate, or with other knives

White wine glass

Red wine glass

Dessert utensils sit at top of plate

Fish fork sits on outside, since it will be used first

Tumbler for water

Use a special knife if serving fish

Place soup spoon with knives, to right of plate

SEATING

● **Predinner** If you are sitting down for predinner drinks, make sure there are enough chairs – if necessary, move some from the dining area.
● **Table plan** Work out the seating plan in advance and put place cards around the table to avoid embarrassment.

CLOTHES

● **Dress code** Decide what you will be wearing for the occasion, in case any guests telephone and want to know in advance how to dress.
● **Coats** Make sure you have somewhere to put guests' coats where they will not be squashed or creased.

ETIQUETTE

● **Timing** Be ready on time. It is embarrassing for guests if their hostess is in the bath or getting dressed.
● **Avoid cliques** Try to keep people who will be sitting next to each other at dinner from talking to each other during predinner drinks.

CHILDREN'S PARTIES

These can be hard on parents, but are usually much enjoyed by children. With younger children, do not invite too many guests, or they may be overwhelmed and unhappy. Try to keep children from overeating, or from becoming overly excited.

PARTY GAMES

● **Planning ahead** Decide what the activities will be – games, magic, songs, or swimming – and make a rough timetable.
● **Games helpers** Enlist a helper (teenagers are good) to supervise activities while you deal with food, visits to the toilet, accidents, and so on.
● **Prizes** Buy prizes for games and sports and try to make sure everyone wins one.

PARTY FOOD

● **Kid's treats** Choose simple foods that can be eaten with the fingers. It does not matter if it is not particularly healthy. That can be remedied at other meals taken with the family.

PROTECTING FURNITURE

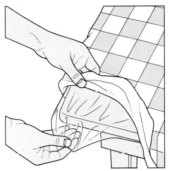

Lining food tables
Protect table surfaces by putting plastic wrap under the tablecloths. Do the same for anywhere else that food and drinks are likely to be placed or spilled. Ideally, eat in the kitchen, where spills can be mopped up.

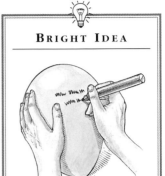

BRIGHT IDEA

Party invitations
Inflate large, brightly colored balloons, and write the invitation details on them with a felt-tip pen. Deflate the balloons, put them in envelopes, and deliver them.

OTHER SOCIAL OCCASIONS

Most social occasions are less formal than dinner parties – apart from weddings, christenings, and other life events. Planning is the key to everyone enjoying themselves. If you plan ahead, you will have time to prepare properly and to enjoy the occasion as well.

DRINKS PARTIES

● **Seating** If you want to invite a lot of people, provide food that can be eaten standing up. Allow a few chairs and tables for those who prefer to sit down, such as the elderly.
● **Serving buffet food** Spread serving dishes out and put beverages in a separate area to avoid crowding. Do not use paper plates – they bend and cannot take hot food.
● **Drinks** Provide plenty of soft drinks for drivers and those who prefer not to drink.
● **Food preparation** Prepare as much hot food in advance as possible, and keep it warm. Keep cold desserts and salads in the refrigerator, ready to receive dressings and sauces.

PICNICS

● **Food** Wrap sandwiches and portions individually, then label them with each person's name to make serving easy.
● **Picnic dressings** Empty pill bottles, thoroughly washed, make ideal containers for salad dressings at a picnic.

SPECIAL EVENTS

● **Christmas** Buy wrapping paper and cards at sales after Christmas, and gifts when you see them during the year. This prevents a huge hole in your budget at Christmas time.
● **Weddings** Use any leftover fabric from the wedding dress to make a large bow. Hang on the entrance to the reception to welcome your guests.

ESTIMATING DRINKS QUANTITIES

Use the guidelines below to work out how much drink to buy for a party. People drink more at small parties than they do at large ones.

● **Wine** A 24 fl oz (750 ml) bottle of wine or champagne gives six glasses. If serving wine at a party, allow about one-half bottle per person.
● **Sherry and port** A standard bottle will yield 16 glasses.
● **Spirits** A standard bottle of spirits gives 30 measures.
● **Soft drinks** Drunk alone, a 1 quart (1 liter) bottle gives six servings; mixed with spirits, it gives 10 servings.

MOVING

OVING IS A TRAUMATIC EXPERIENCE for most people, especially if they have a lot of possessions to be packed and transported. Whether you are going just around the corner or across the country, there is a lot to think about.

BEFORE YOU MOVE

Plan the move carefully. There are things to do in both your old and new homes. Time spent in organization will reduce the chaos, particularly where children and pets are concerned. Hire a reputable moving company so that you benefit from their experience.

PACKING UP

● **Thinning** Go through your possessions, discarding those you do not want or never use. Give them away to charity, or hold a garage sale.

● **Insurance** You will be insured for damage only if the movers, rather than you, have packed everything. They are professionals, so trust them with delicate items.

● **Children** Arrange for young children who would get in the way to stay with friends. Put pets in a kennel for a few days while you get the new home sorted out.

MOVING PLANTS

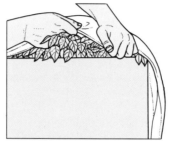

Plant carrier
Transport plants yourself instead of leaving them for the movers. Water them well two days in advance. Put in wood crates, wedge the pots with newspaper, and cover with heavy plastic.

MOVING PICTURES

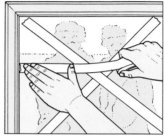

Protecting picture glass
Reinforce picture glass with criss-crossed masking tape – this also prevents the glass from splintering if broken. When you remove the tape, clean the glass with denatured alcohol.

CHANGE OF ADDRESS

People will need to be informed of your change of address. Local services will also need to be told if you are moving far away.

● **Utilities** Arrange for the utility meters to be read at a specific time, and make sure the bills are sent to your new address. Arrange for utilities to be supplied at your new home, checking well in advance whether a deposit is required.

● **Doctors** Tell your doctor, dentist, and any other medical advisers where you are moving to, and ask them to recommend local practitioners.

● **Banks** Inform your banks and brokers, as well as any professional financial advisers, of your new address.

● **Schools** Give notice to your children's schools, and check out where you will send your children in the new area – ask about registration requirements. In addition, check how they can get to the new school.

● **Local commitments** Cancel library cards and memberships to local clubs. Resign from local commitments such as the school board or neighborhood watch.

● **Insurance** Tell all your insurance companies your new address, and check if premiums increase or decrease according to the new area.

● **Investments** Inform your tax preparer of your new address, and also any companies in which you hold shares and any government investments.

● **Mail order** Change your address with any mail-order suppliers with whom you wish to stay in touch. (They will probably find you anyway.)

● **Post office** Arrange with the post office for your mail to be forwarded for a year, after which everyone who needs it should have your new address.

● **Companies** Inform any companies with whom you have local contracts – burglar-alarm or mobile-phone companies, for example.

● **Credit cards** Make sure you send your new address to your credit-card companies.

● **Telephone** Tell the telephone company of your move several weeks in advance, so that a final bill can be sent to you.

MOVING DAY

It helps if one person can go to the new home and await the moving truck, while another stays in the old place to check on the packing. With you are moving yourself, make a similar arrangement to facilitate the move, enlisting the help of friends if necessary.

SURVIVAL KIT

Make up a kit of what you will need when you arrive at your new home. You do not want to wait for the moving truck to arrive to have a cup of coffee.

● **Bedding** Take enough sheets and blankets for all family members so that when the beds arrive they can be made immediately. Making the beds is a priority, since you will be tired after moving into the new house and will not feel like doing it later on.
● **Food and equipment** Take tea or coffee, milk, sugar, something to eat, cups, plates, a toaster oven, a can opener, a saucepan, and cutlery.

● **Emergency supplies** Do not forget to take toilet paper, dishwashing liquid and a dish cloth, and soap. Detergent is also a useful item.
● **Tool kit** Take a basic tool kit in case things need fixing. This kit could include an adjustable wrench, a hammer, a pair of pliers, and a screwdriver. Take a flashlight and candles in case the electricity is not turned on.
● **Clothes** Take enough clothes for the following day in case you are too tired to unpack.
● **Keys** Of course, do not forget the keys to your new home.
● **Alarm clock** An alarm clock (preferably battery operated) is useful for the first morning.

ON ARRIVAL
● **New home** Check your new home, making sure that the previous owners have not removed anything they indicated they would leave behind, or left their unwanted furniture or belongings. If there is a problem, call your lawyer immediately.
● **Make signs** Post signs outside each room giving the name ("Bedroom 1") and a list of major furniture that goes there. Your floor plan and packed boxes should be labeled in the same way.
● **Damages** Check for any damage and make any necessary insurance claim as soon as you possibly can.

YOUR NEW HOME

Do not imagine that you will be able to put your feet up until everything is unpacked and the movers have left. You need to be constantly vigilant to ensure that everything is under control. Check that all your belongings have arrived, and that there is no breakage.

ACTION PLAN
● **Protect carpets** Protect carpets from muddy boots by putting newspapers over the carpets. Give the movers a plan of the house and tell them how you have labeled the boxes for each area.
● **Drinks** Be prepared to make endless supplies of drinks for the movers – but no alcohol. Moving furniture is physically demanding and thirsty work.
● **Children** If there are small children with you, keep them well out of the way of the movers. Take toys with you to keep the children amused.
● **Pets** If pets have traveled with you, shut them in one room and ask the movers to deal with that one last.

MOVING BY YOURSELF
● **Renting a truck** Consider renting a truck to move house by yourself. It will be cheaper than hiring movers.

Labeling boxes
Put different-colored pieces of tape on boxes and items of furniture to indicate in which room they should go. Stick the relevant color tape on the door of the room when you arrive.

MOVERS
● **Tipping** Expect to tip the movers in addition to paying the amount agreed when you signed the contract for the job.

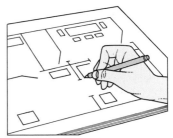

Using a floor plan
Give the foreman a floor plan of the house, showing where you want the major pieces of furniture to go. This way you will not have to move heavy items around afterward.

HEALTH & SAFETY

Health and safety should take top priority in a home, especially one that has small children, or elderly or disabled people. Try to look at your home as a stranger would to spot possible danger areas. Bear in mind that learning first-aid techniques from a book, although useful, is not a substitute for the hands-on training of a first-aid course.

FIRST-AID KIT

Keep all first-aid items together in a box that is accessible for adults but out of reach of small children. Replace items as you use them, and dispose of any that are past their prime. Your pharmacist can help you with this. Supplement the first-aid kit with a supply of painkillers such as aspirin or acetaminophen. Do not, however, keep medicines in the first-aid box; they should be locked in a medicine cabinet. The items shown here comprise a basic first-aid kit for the home.

● **Creams and lotions** Keep antihistamine cream for insect bites and stings, and calamine lotion for sunburn.
● **Dressings** Your kit should contain two sterile pads, one sterile dressing with bandage, two sterile eye pads with bandages, and gauze swabs. Keep a selection of adhesive bandages for minor wounds.
● **Bandages** Keep two folded, triangular bandages, small and large bandages (crêpe or conforming), and a finger bandage with an applicator.
● **Fastenings and tools** Keep hypoallergenic tape or safety pins for holding dressings, tweezers for removing splinters, and blunt scissors for cutting dressings and bandages.

Folded triangular bandage

Large conforming bandage

Small conforming bandage

Sterile eye pad with bandage

Hypoallergenic tape

Finger bandage with applicator

Sterile nonadhesive pad

Sterile dressing with bandage

Scissors

Gauze swabs

Adhesive bandages

Tweezers

SAFETY IN THE HOME

Simple precautions can prevent accidents and even save lives. The kitchen is the most dangerous room in the home, followed by the bathroom. Always mop up spills that could cause people to slip, especially on tiled floors. Put a safety rail on the bath if necessary.

KITCHEN SAFETY

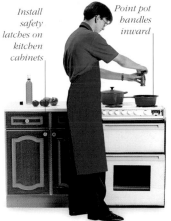

Install safety latches on kitchen cabinets

Point pot handles inward

Preventing accidents
Turn pan handles away from the stove edge, and keep children away from hot oven doors. Put safety latches on cabinets, and store matches out of reach. Teach children about safety.

GENERAL SAFETY
● **Glass doors** Replace the ordinary glass panels used in doors with safety or laminated glass, which does not splinter dangerously when broken.
● **Firescreen** Always use a firescreen when you leave an open fire unattended. This also applies to gas-flame fires, which get very hot.
● **Rugs** Secure all loose rugs or mats into position with antislip pads or tape.
● **Lighting** Ensure hazardous areas of the house, such as stairways and landings, are well lit at all times.
● **Irons** Always switch off an electric iron if you have to answer the door or telephone.
● **Outlets** Unused electrical outlets should be covered with plastic safety covers.

FIRE PRECAUTIONS

● **Smoke alarms** Install a smoke alarm on each floor of your home. Change batteries when you change the clocks in spring and fall.
● **Fire blankets** Keep a fire blanket in the kitchen.
● **Ashtrays** Keep ashtrays on hand for smokers.
● **Hinges** Install self-closing hinges on doors if your home has a high fire risk.
● **Fire drills** Conduct regular family fire drills so that everyone knows the escape routes. Make sure that children know never to return to a burning building.
● **Furniture** Avoid buying old furniture that is stuffed with polyurethane foam. This can burst into flames in a fire and release poisonous fumes.

CALLING EMERGENCY SERVICES

Make a list of important telephone numbers, and keep the master in your home log book and a copy near each telephone. Stick the copies where they will not be moved – for example, inside cabinet doors. Add written instructions to the list in case the caller panics.

EMERGENCY NUMBERS

Keep the telephone numbers of the following services and people on your list:

● Emergency services (fire, police, and ambulance).
● Doctor and dentist (include their office hours).
● The nearest hospital with emergency services.
● Immediate family members (include workplace numbers).
● All-night pharmacy.
● Emergency numbers for the electricity, gas, and water companies.
● Taxi service.
● Veterinarian.

MAKING THE CALL
● **Relevant information** When making an emergency call, give your telephone number, the precise location, the nature and severity of the emergency, the age, sex, and condition of any persons involved, and details of any hazards, such as a gas leak.
● **Teaching children** Drill your children in the basics of calling emergency services so that if you are injured they will know what to do.
● **Fires** If your house is on fire, call the emergency services from a neighbor's house or a public telephone.

STAYING IN CONTROL

Keeping calm
In an emergency, it is important to stay calm. When calling emergency services, try to answer questions and give details precisely. Stay on the line until the dispatcher hangs up.

ACTION IN EMERGENCIES

Knowing what to do in an emergency can contribute greatly to preventing and limiting casualties and damage to property. See pages 108 and 111 for what to do in the event of flooding in the home or a gas leak, respectively.

ACTION IN CASE OF FIRE

Fire is frightening and moves very quickly. If you cannot put out a small fire yourself, the most important thing to do is to evacuate the entire building. If you live in an apartment building, pull the fire alarm, then save yourself and your family. Try to keep everyone calm.

SMALL FIRES

● **Chimney fires** If an open fire is out of control, douse it with water. If the chimney is on fire, call the fire department. Pull furniture and carpets away from the fire.

● **Electrical fires** Do not use water on electrical fires. If an appliance such as a television or computer is on fire, turn off the electricity at the fuse box, and smother the flames with a heavy blanket or coat.

● **Kitchen fires** If a frying pan catches fire, immediately turn off the heat at the burner. Cover the pan with a fire blanket, a damp dish towel, or a large saucepan lid.

● **Controlling small fires** Shut doors and windows to isolate the fire in one room. Air will cause fire to spread.

BUILDINGS ON FIRE

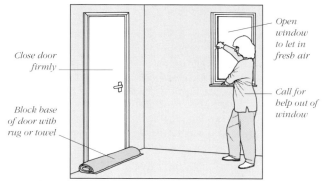

Close door firmly

Block base of door with rug or towel

Open window to let in fresh air

Call for help out of window

Escaping a fire

If you are unable to get out of a burning building, shut yourself as far away from the fire as possible. Block the door with a roll of fabric, dampened if possible. Do not jump out of a window unless there is no other way of saving your life. Open a window and call for help.

> ### WARNING
> When evacuating a building, carry any babies and small children out with you. Never, for any reason, go back into a blazing building. Alert the fire department if you know that someone is trapped.

CLOTHES ON FIRE

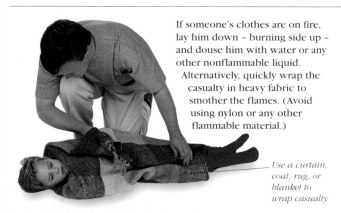

If someone's clothes are on fire, lay him down – burning side up – and douse him with water or any other nonflammable liquid. Alternatively, quickly wrap the casualty in heavy fabric to smother the flames. (Avoid using nylon or any other flammable material.)

Use a curtain, coat, rug, or blanket to wrap casualty

ACTIONS TO AVOID

● **Feeding flames** Do not let the casualty panic. Movement will fan the flames.

● **Spreading burns** Roll the casualty on the ground only if you have no alternative. The burns may spread to other parts of his body.

TREATING YOURSELF

● **Extinguishing flames** Wrap yourself in heavy fabric and lie down. Try to remain calm.

ELECTRICAL INJURIES

Many electrical injuries in the home result from faulty switches, frayed cords, and defective appliances. Handling appliances with wet hands, or when standing on a wet floor, can greatly increase the risk of shock. See page 111 for Safety with Electricity.

BREAKING THE CONTACT

1 If someone has been injured by electricity, the casualty may be conscious or unconscious. First break the current by switching off power at the circuit breaker.

Use a wooden broom handle – not a metallic or plastic one

Do not touch casualty's skin with your hands

Push source of current away from casualty

Stand on telephone books, newspapers, or a wooden chair

2 If you cannot switch off the power, stand on dry insulating material, and use a wooden broom handle or a chair to push the limbs away from the source.

3 Wrap a dry towel around the casualty's feet, and drag him away from the appliance. Avoid touching his skin.

4 Check for breathing and pulse if the casualty is unconscious. Resuscitate if necessary (see p. 168). If the casualty seems unharmed, make him rest, and call a doctor. Treat for shock and burns if necessary (see p. 170).

DROWNING

Never let young children play in or near water without an attentive adult watching. Encourage all the family to learn to swim as early as possible. Do not leave young children or babies alone in the tub. Remember: a child can drown in as little as 1 in (2.5 cm) of water.

RESCUING A CASUALTY FROM DROWNING

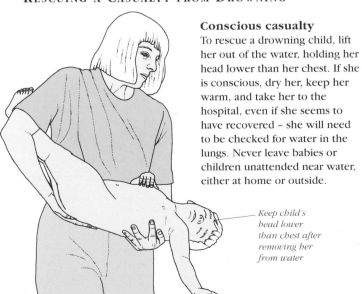

Conscious casualty
To rescue a drowning child, lift her out of the water, holding her head lower than her chest. If she is conscious, dry her, keep her warm, and take her to the hospital, even if she seems to have recovered – she will need to be checked for water in the lungs. Never leave babies or children unattended near water, either at home or outside.

Keep child's head lower than chest after removing her from water

UNCONSCIOUSNESS
● Administering CPR If a casualty is unconscious after being rescued from drowning, check for breathing and pulse. Restart breathing with artificial respiration; use chest compressions only if there is no pulse present (see p. 169). Proceed with caution.

RELATED PROBLEMS
● Hypothermia A victim of drowning may develop hypothermia. Remove wet clothes, dry the casualty, and keep him or her warm.
● Water in the lungs Take the casualty to the hospital to check that water has not been inhaled – this could cause secondary drowning later on.

RESUSCITATION

W HEN TREATING AN UNCONSCIOUS CASUALTY, the priority is to check whether the lungs and heart are working. Open the airway, then check for breathing and a pulse. If you suspect back or neck injury, do not move the casualty.

ABC OF RESUSCITATION

T hese letters stand for Airway, Breathing, and Circulation – three areas that you must immediately assess in an unconscious casualty.

If an unconscious casualty is breathing and has a pulse, place him or her in the recovery position (see below) and call an ambulance.

ASSESSING THE CASUALTY

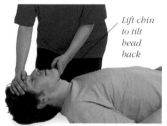

Lift chin to tilt head back

Look and listen for breathing

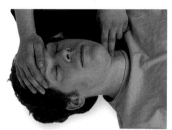

Opening the airway
Open the casualty's mouth, and sweep out anything anything that could obstruct the airway. Open the airway by placing one hand on the casualty's forehead and two fingers of the other hand under the casualty's chin to tilt his head back slightly.

Checking for breathing
Keeping the airway open, place your cheek beside the casualty's mouth and nose for five seconds, and listen and feel for any breath being exhaled. At the same time, carefully look along the casualty's chest to see if there is any sign of movement of the lungs.

Checking for pulse
Keeping the head tilted, feel for the large muscle at the side of the neck. Slide two fingers into the groove in front of this muscle. If there is a pulse but no breathing, begin artificial respiration. If there is no pulse or breathing, start CPR.

THE RECOVERY POSITION

T he position shown below is the safest for someone who is unconscious, because the tongue cannot block the throat, and liquids can drain from the mouth. This greatly reduces the risk of the casualty inhaling stomach contents, then choking on vomit as a result.

PLACING A CASUALTY IN THE RECOVERY POSITION

1 Bend the casualty's near arm at a right angle to the body. Place the back of her far hand to her near cheek. With her near leg straight, bend the other leg so that the knee is at a right angle.

2 Holding the casualty's hand against her cheek, pull the thigh of the bent leg toward you, and roll her onto her side. Working in this way, you should even be able to roll someone heavy.

3 Guide the casualty's head as you turn her. Tilt her head back, and pull the jaw forward to open the airway. Continue to check the ABC of resuscitation (see above) until an ambulance arrives.

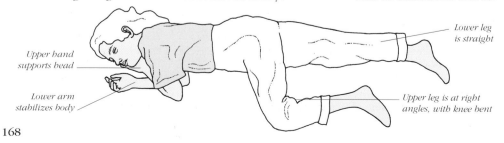

Upper hand supports head

Lower arm stabilizes body

Lower leg is straight

Upper leg is at right angles, with knee bent

ARTIFICIAL RESPIRATION

If an unconscious casualty is not breathing, you will need to blow air into his or her lungs. Give 12 breaths per minute, and check for a pulse after every 12 breaths. Continue for as long as you can – until the casualty starts to breathe again, or until help arrives.

ADMINISTERING MOUTH-TO-MOUTH RESUSCITATION

Cover casualty's mouth completely, so that no air escapes

Look to see that chest is rising and falling

1 Lay the casualty on his back. Remove obstructions from his mouth. Place your hand on his forehead, and pinch his nose while placing two fingers under his chin and tilting his head back.

2 Place your mouth over the casualty's, sealing it. Give two slow breaths, breathing until casualty's chest rises. Check for a pulse. If present but person is not breathing, give 12 breaths per minute.

3 Continue Step 2 until the casualty is breathing unaided or professional help arrives. Stop every 12 breaths and check for a pulse. Start cardiopulmonary resuscitation if the casualty's pulse fails.

CARDIOPULMONARY RESUSCITATION (CPR)

CPR is a combination of artifical respiration and chest compressions. If there is no breathing or pulse, give 15 chest compressions, then two slow breaths of artificial respiration. Repeat three more times, then check for pulse. Continue until you feel a pulse or help arrives.

ADMINISTERING CHEST COMPRESSIONS

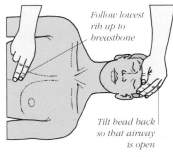

Follow lowest rib up to breastbone

Tilt head back so that airway is open

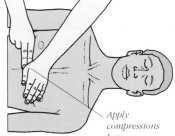

Apply compressions here

1 Lay the casualty on a firm surface. To locate the area for applying compressions, feel for the casualty's lowest rib with your first and middle fingers. Slide your fingers upward until your middle finger reaches where the rib meets the breastbone – there may be a slight hollow here.

2 Your first finger should now be lying on the casualty's breastbone. Slide the heel of your other hand down the breastbone until it reaches the point where your first finger is. The heel of your hand is now sitting in the area to which the compressions will be applied.

3 Keep the heel of your hand in position. Place the other hand on top, then interlock your fingers. Lean over the casualty, keeping your arms straight. Press down 2 in (5 cm) and release, without removing your hands. Stop and check if you suspect pulse and breathing have returned.

TREATING INJURIES

E VEN IF YOU KNOW THAT A CASUALTY needs medical or hospital treatment, you can keep him or her comfortable, reduce the risk of shock, and prevent any injuries from getting worse. Prompt, efficient action may save a life.

BLEEDING

I t is important to stop all bleeding as quickly as possible. Remove clothing from around the wound, and wash away blood and dirt.

You may need to apply pressure to control the bleeding. Reassure the casualty, and be aware that you may have to treat for shock.

TREATING MAJOR WOUNDS

Raise wound above level of heart

Lay casualty down so that wound can be easily elevated

1 Make a pad from a piece of clean cloth, and hold it over the wound, pressing firmly with your hand. Raise the wound above the level of the casualty's heart to reduce bleeding. Do not try to remove anything that is embedded in the wound.

2 Lay the casualty down, taking care to keep the wound above the level of the heart. Keep him as flat as possible, using only a thin pad under the head for comfort. Continue to press the wound firmly, until the bleeding begins to lessen.

3 Leave the pad in place, and cover the wound with a sterile dressing. Bandage this into place, keeping the wound above heart level. The bandage should be tight but should not cut off the blood supply. If blood starts to seep through the dressing, place another pad on top.

4 When the bleeding seems under control, keep the injured part elevated, and take the casualty to the hospital. If there is an object embedded in the wound, place rolls of gauze around the wound – this will stop the bandage from pressing on the object.

RECOGNIZING AND TREATING SHOCK

Shock occurs when not enough oxygen circulates around the body. This may occur as a result of failure of the circulatory system, as in the case of heart attack, or loss of fluid through bleeding, burns, vomiting, or diarrhea. As the body responds by diverting the blood supply from the surface to the core of the body, the casualty's skin may become gray, and the pulse may race. To treat a casualty for shock, help her lie down. Raise the legs about 12 in (30 cm) unless you suspect head, neck, back, hip, or leg injuries. Keep the casualty warm. Call an ambulance, and be prepared to resuscitate (see p. 168). Do not give food or drink.

Raise legs to improve circulation

Elevate any wounded limb to minimize loss of blood

CUTS AND SCRAPES

Minor cuts and abrasions can be treated without medical help, unless there is a foreign body or a risk of infection.

1 Wash dirt out of a cut gently, using soap and water on a gauze pad. Avoid fluffy cloths, since they may stick to the wound.

2 Press firmly on the wound with a clean gauze pad to stop the flow of bleeding.

3 Cover the wound with a dressing that is large enough to cover the entire area. (If necessary, apply antiseptic cream first.)

BURNS AND SCALDS

Cool burns and scalds at once to prevent further tissue damage and reduce pain. If a fire is the cause of the casualty's burn injury, make sure that both you and the casualty are safe before attempting treatment. See page 167 for rescuing a casualty from electric shock.

TREATING MAJOR BURNS AND SCALDS

1 Remove the casualty from the source of the burn. Pour cool water onto the burn for at least 10 minutes.

2 Carefully remove clothing and jewelry from the burn area, cutting around any cloth sticking to the wound.

3 Continue to cool the burn if necessary, by immersing it in cool water or any other cool liquid, such as milk.

4 Cover the burn with a clean, sterile dressing. If the burn is large, use a clean sheet or pillowcase. Do not apply lotions, fat, or ointment.

5 Get medical attention as quickly as possible. Treat the casualty for shock if necessary (see opposite). Do not offer her food or drink. Continue to reassure her.

Cool burn with cool water

Do not remove clothing until burn has been cooled

Avoid touching burn

MINOR BURNS
● **Treating** Cool the burn for at least 10 minutes, as above. Remove any jewelry and clothing from around the burn before the area starts to swell.
● **Dressing** Cover minor burns with any clean, lint-free material. Clean, dry sheets or pillowcases make good temporary coverings. Burns are susceptible to infection.

CHEMICAL BURNS
● **Detection** These can be caused by toxic household substances. They are less obvious than heat burns, and may take time to develop.

Removing chemicals
Hold the burned area under cool, running water at once, and wash away all traces of the chemical. Wear rubber gloves to prevent the chemical from splashing onto your own hands. Treat the affected area as for major burns (see above).

ELECTRICAL BURNS
● **Causes** Electrical burns are caused by lightning or high- or low-voltage current. In the home, low-voltage current can cause scorching to the skin.

Treating the injury
Make sure the current is off (see p. 167). Cover burn with a dry, sterile dressing – do not cool the burn. Seek medical help, since electrical current can cause internal injury. Be prepared to administer CPR or treat for shock if necessary.

BURNS TO THE AIRWAY

Administering water
Burns to the mouth or throat are dangerous, since they can cause the airway to become blocked by swelling. Loosen the casualty's clothing around the neck, and administer sips of cold water. Go immediately to the hospital. Reassure the casualty.

POISONING

Household chemicals can be poisonous if ingested, as can certain plants and drugs. Seek medical attention as soon as possible. Try to identify the type of poison involved. Keep a sample of the substance ingested, any vomit, or containers or pill bottles found nearby.

TREATING CHEMICAL POISONING

Empty containers are clues to what type of poison has been swallowed

1 Wipe away any chemical residue from around the casualty's mouth and face, taking care not to contaminate yourself. Wash the area gently with cold water. Remove any contaminated clothing.

2 Call your Poison Control Center. If they advise, give the casualty sips of cool water or milk if lips are burned. Do not try to make her vomit, since this can cause more damage.

3 Take the casualty to the hospital. Make sure you take the chemical container, so that doctors can give the correct treatment. See below for the appropriate action if the casualty is unconscious.

TREATING DRUG POISONING

Tell Poison Control what drug has been taken, and how much

Save container to give to emergency services

Keep a conscious casualty close to you until help arrives

1 If the casualty is conscious, try to find out which drug has been taken, how much, and when it was ingested. Do not induce vomiting, since this may cause further injury. If he has vomited, keep a sample for the doctor.

2 Take the casualty to hospital, talking to him calmly to keep him conscious. Take the drug bottle with you. Be prepared to treat for shock (see p. 170). See below for the appropriate action if the casualty is unconscious.

> **WARNING**
> Do not give the casualty food or drink. This will dilute the drug, causing it to be more readily absorbed.

IF THE CASUALTY IS UNCONSCIOUS

BREATHING AND PULSE PRESENT

1 If breathing and pulse are present, place the casualty in the recovery position (see p. 168) to keep the airway open, and call Poison Control or 911.

2 Treat any related injuries such as chemical burns (see p. 171) if necessary.

NO BREATHING, BUT PULSE PRESENT

1 Give artificial respiration (see p. 169). Call for an ambulance, and repeat.

2 Continue to give artificial respiration until help arrives or breathing restarts. Check the pulse for five full seconds every minute (after every 12 breaths).

NO BREATHING, NO PULSE

1 Administer CPR. Check for pulse after every four sets of 15 compressions and two breaths (see p. 169).

2 Continue administering CPR until the pulse restarts. Continue artificial respiration until breathing restarts.

COMMON INJURIES

T HE HOME IS A DANGEROUS PLACE. Accidents can happen even if every safety precaution has been taken. Children in particular arc at risk because they have less of a sense of danger than adults. Be prepared for any emergency.

ANIMAL BITES

A ll animals, including humans, have germs in their mouths, and bites can not only break the skin but can also cause infection. Always treat animal bites immediately – start by cleaning the wound thoroughly. Take every precaution to avoid being bitten yourself.

TETANUS AND RABIES

● **Tetanus** This produces poisons in the nervous system and is a serious illness. It can be caused by organisms in the soil infecting cuts and bites. Regular immunization is part of a baby's vaccination program. Adults should have boosters every 10 years.

● **Rabies** This is a potentially fatal disease that is spread to humans through the bites of infected animals. If you are bitten, seek medical help, even it appears that the animal has not been infected.

TREATING MINOR ANIMAL BITES

Run wound under water

1 Wash a minor bite wound in soap and water. Then hold it under running water for at least five minutes to rinse away any dirt and reduce the risk of germs.

2 Pat the wound dry with a clean gauze pad or tissues. Do not apply an ointment or tincture. Cover with an adhesive bandage or sterile dressing. Visit a doctor to explain what has happened, in case there is any infection.

WARNING

Rabies can be fatal. Treat all animal bites as potentially dangerous, and seek professional medical attention immediately.

TREATING SERIOUS ANIMAL BITES

1 Wash the wound in soap and water. Hold it under running water for five minutes to remove as much dirt and as many germs as possible.

2 Press a clean dressing or pad firmly on the wound. Raise the affected part above the level of the heart. If the bleeding is severe, follow the treatment for major wounds shown on page 170.

3 When the bleeding stops, cover the wound with a sterile dressing or with a pad bandaged firmly in place. Take the casualty to the hospital. Do not assume that the wound will heal on its own – it may have been infected by germs from the animal.

Cover wound with dressing and bandage

Keep casualty calm as you work

SNAKE BITES

Wash bite wound

Indications of a snake bite include a pair of puncture marks, severe pain, redness and swelling around the wound, vomiting, and breathing difficulties. Seek medical help immediately.

● **Treating snake bite** Wash the wound clean. Bandage it firmly, and hold it still and below the level of the heart. Keep the casualty calm. Do not cut the wound or try to suck out the venom.

INSECT STINGS

For some people, insect stings can be dangerous and require immediate medical attention or treatment for anaphylactic shock (see below). For other people, the treatments described below are sufficient. Treat stings immediately. Do not let the casualty panic.

INSECT STINGS

1 If the stinger is still present, carefully remove it with a pair of tweezers, grasping the stinger at the base. Take care that the stinger does not break while you are extracting it. Do not squeeze the poison sac at the top of the stinger.

2 Apply a cold compress to the area to reduce pain and swelling. Use a cloth wrung out in cold water, or a bag of frozen peas or ice cubes, wrapped in a cloth. Leave the compress on the wound for 10 minutes.

MOUTH AND THROAT

1 If a casualty has been stung in the mouth or throat, reduce the swelling by giving him or her an ice cube or an ice pop to suck, or some cold water to drink.

2 Take the casualty to a doctor. Call an ambulance if the casualty's breathing becomes difficult because of swelling. If the casualty loses consciousness, treat immediately for anaphylactic shock (see below).

TICK BITES

● **Treatment** Ticks burrow underneath the skin to feed on blood, and can cause disease. Grasp a tick with a pair of tweezers, taking care not to leave any part of the tick in the skin. Keep the tick to show a doctor in case the victim begins to feel sick.

HIVES

● **Description** This is a rash of raised red spots that both itches and hurts. Hives may be caused by exposure to many allergy-inducing substances, including cold, dust, pets, and a wide variety of foods.

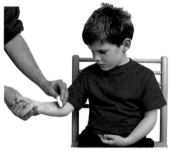

Treating hives
The pain and itching of hives can be relieved by applying calamine lotion. Reapply until the itching and pain have ceased. If extensive, call a doctor; antihistamines are a common treatment.

RECOGNIZING ANAPHYLACTIC SHOCK

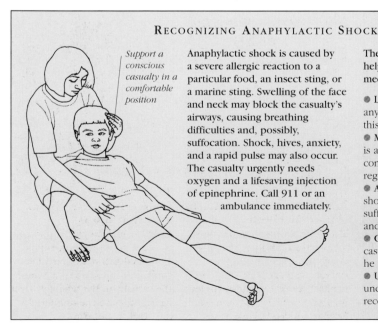

Support a conscious casualty in a comfortable position

Anaphylactic shock is caused by a severe allergic reaction to a particular food, an insect sting, or a marine sting. Swelling of the face and neck may block the casualty's airways, causing breathing difficulties and, possibly, suffocation. Shock, hives, anxiety, and a rapid pulse may also occur. The casualty urgently needs oxygen and a lifesaving injection of epinephrine. Call 911 or an ambulance immediately.

The following measures will help minimize shock until medical help arrives.

● **Loosen clothing** Ensure that any tight clothing is loosened – this will aid breathing.
● **Medication** If the casualty is a known sufferer from this condition, administer any regular medication.
● **Avoiding panic** Anaphylactic shock can cause panic in the sufferer. Try to keep him calm and warm until help arrives.
● **Conscious casualty** Help the casualty sit up in a position that he finds comfortable.
● **Unconsciousness** Place an unconscious casualty in the recovery position (see p. 168).

BRUISES AND SWELLING

Bruising may be caused by a blunt blow rupturing blood capillaries beneath the skin, and blood leaking into the tissues. Severe bruising may indicate deep injury, such as a fracture. Likewise, swellings should always be examined, in case they indicate serious injury.

TREATING BRUISES

1 Sit the casualty down, with the injured limb supported. Elevate the injured area on a cushion in order to rest it.

2 Apply a cold compress to the injury. Hold the compress against the injury for 10 minutes to reduce the swelling.

Make sure casualty is comfortable

Elevate injured limb

COLD COMPRESSES

● **Making a cold compress** Wring out a clean cloth in very cold water, or wrap it around ice cubes. Keep it pressed on the swelling for about 10 minutes.

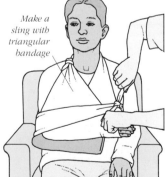

TIMESAVING TIP

Instant compress
If you need a cold compress in a hurry, a package of frozen peas is an excellent alternative to ice cubes. Wrap it in a light towel and lay it on the injury. Remove when the swelling has gone down.

BONE AND MUSCLE INJURIES

Treat all bone and muscle injuries as serious until you have discovered the extent of the damage. Look for bruises and swelling, and if you think there may be a fracture, take the casualty to the hospital for an X ray. Prevent movements that may aggravate the problem.

COMMON BONE AND MUSCLE INJURIES

● **Sprain** Elevate the injured area, and apply a cold compress. Wrap with cotton and bandage firmly. Take the casualty to the hospital as soon as possible.
● **Dislocated shoulder** This occurs when the head of the arm comes out of the shoulder-joint socket. Support the arm in a sling with the hand across the chest. Get the casualty to the hospital as soon as possible. Do not give the casualty any food or drink.
● **Broken collarbone** Put the arm on the side of the collarbone in a sling, and take the casualty to the hospital.

IMMOBILIZING BONE INJURIES

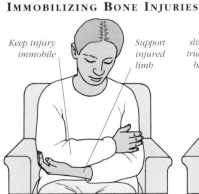

Keep injury immobile

Support injured limb

Make a sling with triangular bandage

Supporting limbs
The immediate action for bone injuries is to support the injury. For an injured arm, seat the casualty, and ask her to support her arm across her chest. For leg injuries, lay the casualty down. Support the leg in your hands.

Securing limbs
Keep the injured part supported by securing it properly. Support an injured arm in a sling, then bandage it to the chest and take the casualty to the hospital. Tie a damaged leg to the uninjured one. Call an ambulance.

CHOKING

A blocked airway can be frightening for the person who is choking and those around him or her. Action must be quick; otherwise, the casualty may suffocate. Choking is often caused by eating too fast, or by young children putting small objects in their mouths.

RECOGNIZING AND AVOIDING CHOKING

● **Symptoms** The casualty may have difficulty speaking and breathing, and the skin may be blue. The casualty may clutch the throat or neck.

● **Prevention** Encourage family members to chew their food thoroughly. Make sure children do not put foreign objects in their mouths.

TREATING CHOKING IN CONSCIOUS ADULTS

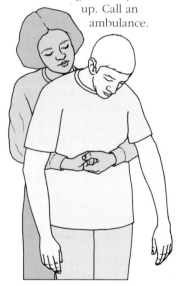

1 If the casualty is coughing forcefully, encourage him or her to cough the object up. Call an ambulance.

2 If the casualty cannot speak, cough forcefully, or breathe, the airway is blocked completely. Stand behind him, and place your arms around his abdomen just above the navel. Center your fist, thumb side in, cover with the other hand, and thrust inward and upward several times (the Heimlich maneuver).

3 Continue abdominal thrusts until you dislodge the object. (If this fails and the casualty becomes unconscious, follow the treatment below.)

4 Once the object has been dislodged, encourage the casualty to sit down. Help him calm down.

CHOKING IN INFANTS

The treatment for infants differs from the treatment for adults and children. The following steps are a quick outline; if your household includes an infant, a first-aid course is recommended.

1 Determine if the airway is completely blocked. The infant's face may turn blue, and he may make strange noises or no sound at all

2 Lay the infant face down along your forearm, with the head low. Give five sharp blows to his back.

3 Turn the infant face up. Place two fingers on the breastbone just below the nipple line, and give five sharp downward thrusts.

4 If you can see an object in his mouth, remove it.

5 For unconscious infants, try to give breaths. Call 911. Repeat back blows and chest thrusts until the airway is cleared or help arrives.

TREATING CHOKING IN UNCONSCIOUS ADULTS

1 If choking has caused loss of consciousness, call for help as you lie the casualty on his back. Give two breaths of artificial respiration. If chest does not rise, retilt head and try the two breaths again.

2 If the casualty's chest still does not rise, straddle his body and place the heel of one hand against the middle of the abdomen above the navel. Give up to five abdominal thrusts. Lift tongue and sweep out the mouth if you can see an object.

3 Retilt the head and give artifical respiration. Continue these steps until breath goes in, breathing resumes, or professional help arrives. Once breathing resumes, place the casualty in the recovery position (see p. 168). Get the casualty to the hospital.

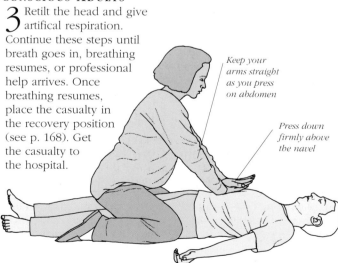

Keep your arms straight as you press on abdomen

Press down firmly above the navel

FOREIGN BODIES

Foreign bodies in the eyes, ears, nose, or throat are uncomfortable, even frightening, and may be dangerous. Use the appropriate technique below to deal with the obstruction, taking care not to cause harm to the casualty. Get medical help as soon as possible.

IN THE EYE

1 Hold the eyelids apart with two fingers and get the casualty to look up, down, left, then right. Do not touch a foreign body that is embedded in the eye – take the casualty to a doctor.

2 Pour clean water into the inner corner of the eye to try to wash out the object. If this fails, provided the object is not embedded, lift it out with a moist gauze pad or the corner of a handkerchief.

IN THE EAR

● **Looking for objects** With a flashlight, try to see what is in the ear. If it is embedded, do not try to remove it – you may damage the eardrum. Ask adults and older children what the object is. Keep the casualty calm, and take him or her to the hospital.

INSECT IN THE EAR

1 Place the casualty in a chair with the affected ear facing up. Flood the ear with tepid water so that the insect floats out. Use a towel to catch any overflow.

2 If the insect does not come out, or if it is a stinging insect, keep the casualty calm, and take him or her to the hospital. Never put anything in the ear to remove a foreign body.

IN THE NOSE

● **Recognition and treatment** A foreign object inside the nose may cause difficult breathing, bloody discharge, or swelling. Encourage the casualty to breathe through the mouth. Keep the casualty calm, and take him or her to hospital. Do not attempt to remove the object yourself.

SWALLOWED OBJECTS

● **Identifying objects** Ask the casualty what has been swallowed. Small or smooth objects will work through the system. Large or sharp items must be removed by a doctor.

> **WARNING**
> Do not allow the casualty to eat or drink if the swallowed object is large or sharp. Take the casualty to the hospital.

SPLINTERS AND BLISTERS

Splinters and burst blisters must be treated properly, or they may be the cause of an infection. Remove splinters as soon as possible, but do not try to treat deeply embedded objects. Seat the casualty while removing splinters and keep the affected area steady.

REMOVING SPLINTERS

Hold ends of tweezers over flame

1 Wash your hands, then clean the area around the splinter with soap and warm water. Sterilize a pair of tweezers by passing them through a flame. Alternatively, boil them in water for about 10 minutes. Let the tweezers cool before you use them.

Pull splinter out in direction it went in

2 Grasp the splinter with the pair of tweezers, as close to the skin as possible. Draw the splinter out at the angle at which it went in. Squeeze the wound so that it bleeds a little to flush out any dirt. Wash the area again, pat dry, and cover with an adhesive bandage.

TREATING BLISTERS

● **Cleaning blisters** Wash the blistered area with soap and warm water. Rinse with clear water. Pat gently with tissues or a clean gauze pad to dry. Cover the area with an adhesive bandage.
● **Burn blisters** Burns often cause fluid to collect under the skin. Never break a blister caused by a burn – the burn may become infected, causing more damage. See page 171 for treating burns and scalds.

NOSEBLEEDS

Nosebleeds often occur unexpectedly, and can be frightening if the blood flow is copious. Use a towel to mop up blood and protect the casualty's clothes. Frequent, serious nosebleeds may indicate a deeper problem, and cauterization may be necessary.

TREATING NOSEBLEEDS

1 Seat the casualty with the head tilted forward. Tell her to breathe through her mouth. Meanwhile, pinch the fleshy part of the nose so that the nostrils stay tightly together for 10 minutes.

Tilt casualty's head forward

Pinch nostrils together

Lean casualty over bowl to catch any fluid

2 Holding the head tilted over a bowl, encourage the casualty to spit out excess fluid in the mouth. Pinch the nostrils for 10 more minutes, then another 10 minutes if necessary. If the bleeding persists, go to the hospital.

3 Once the bleeding has stopped, clean around the nose and mouth with a damp towel or cotton balls and tepid water. Instruct her not to blow her nose, since this may cause the nosebleed to start again.

WARNING

If there is a watery discharge from the nose or if the bleeding lasts for more than 30 minutes, take the casualty to the hospital at once.

BLEEDING MOUTH AND EAR

Cuts to the tongue, lips, or lining of the mouth may bleed profusely and cause concern. A knocked-out tooth can sometimes be replanted; always take the tooth and the victim to a dentist. Bleeding from inside an ear usually follows a rupture to the eardrum.

MOUTH WOUNDS

Make casualty lean forwards over bowl

Applying pressure
Lean the casualty over a bowl to catch the blood. Press the mouth wound with a gauze pad, and pinch it between your thumb and forefinger for about 10 minutes. Do not wash out the casualty's mouth – this may disturb a blood clot.

TOOTH LOSS

Saving teeth
In many cases a knocked-out tooth can be replanted in its socket. Store the tooth in milk, and place a pad over the socket, making sure it is higher than surrounding teeth so that the casualty can bite on it. Take him and the tooth to a dentist.

EAR INJURIES

● **Ear wounds** Place a gauze pad over the wound. Pinch the wound for about 10 minutes. When the bleeding stops, cover the wound with a sterile dressing lightly held in place with a bandage.

● **Bleeding from inside the ear** Seat the casualty in a semi-upright position with the head turned toward the injured side so that blood drains off. Put an absorbent pad over the ear, and bandage it in place. Do not plug the ear. Take the casualty to a doctor.

● **Danger signs** If bleeding from inside an ear follows a head injury, and the blood is watery, fluid may be leaking from around the brain. Take the casualty to the hospital.

COMMON AILMENTS

COLDS AND FEVERS MAY not seem like serious complaints, because they occur to people fairly frequently. However, they can have dangerous consequences if not treated correctly, especially for small children and elderly people.

FEVER AND COLDS

The common cold can often become more serious and produce a high temperature and fever because of infection. If someone develops a fever, you should try to bring his or her temperature down as quickly as possible, particularly if it rises above 102°F (39°C).

FEBRILE CONVULSIONS

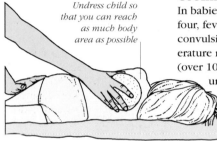

Undress child so that you can reach as much body area as possible

Cooling a child
In babies and children under four, fever can produce febrile convulsions. If a child's temperature rises above 102°F (39°C) (over 100°F, 38°C in babies under three months) call a doctor. Undress the child and cool her by sponging with tepid water.

TREATING FEVER IN ADULTS AND CHILDREN

1 Take the temperature of the casualty. It should be approximately 98.6°F (37°C); anything above 100°F (38°C) indicates a fever. Make the casualty comfortable – let him or her rest in bed in a room that is comfortably warm.

2 Give the casualty plenty of water to drink to help bring down the temperature. Give an adult two acetaminophen tablets; a child may be given a dose of children's acetaminophen. Sponge with water if the fever is high.

TREATING COLDS

● **Avoiding overheating** Colds usually result in a raised temperature, so be careful not to become overheated in excess clothes or blankets.
● **Humidity** Grow green plants and boil water on the stove periodically to increase the humidity in your home. This can soothe irritated membranes. Use humidifiers, but keep them very clean.
● **Clearing breathing** Clear a congested nose by inhaling a few drops of eucalyptus oil sprinkled on a handkerchief at regular intervals. Fresh air may also help clear breathing.

● **Easing a sore throat** If you have a sore throat, gargle with warm water mixed with a little cider vinegar and cayenne or hot pepper. The vinegar creates a mild acidic environment to kill bacteria, and the heat from the warm water and pepper helps speed extra blood to the irritated tissues. A warm water and salt gargle may also help to relieve a sore throat.
● **Getting exercise** Some light exercise may help clear a congested head through producing sweat. You should also drink plenty of fluids.

TREATING MENINGITIS

This is an inflammation of the tissues surrounding the brain. It usually occurs in children and must be treated promptly, since it can be fatal.

● **Recognition** Symptoms are: sensitivity to light, fever, loss of appetite, listlessness, vomiting, stiffness and pain in the neck, a rash of red or purple spots, and convulsions. A change for the worse in a child who has recently had an infection may indicate meningitis.
● **Medical attention** Make the casualty comfortable, and call a doctor or 911 immediately. Immediate admission to the hospital is likely.

GREEN TIP

Natural soothers
Infuse honey, cloves, and lemon in hot water as a natural remedy for coughs and sore throats. Sucking a whole clove will quiet tickles in the throat.

STOMACHACHE

Pain in the stomach can be relatively trivial indigestion, or it can indicate a damaged intestine – particularly if the pain fluctuates in intensity and is accompanied by vomiting. Stomach pain may also indicate inflammation of the appendix, particularly in older children.

TREATING STOMACH ACHES

1 Ensure that the casualty is comfortable in a bed or on a sofa, propped up on pillows. Leave a bowl nearby in case she has to vomit.

2 Give her a covered hot-water bottle, or wrap one in a towel, to hold against her stomach. Do not give her medication or anything to eat.

3 If this fails to alleviate the pain after 30 minutes, or if the pain is severe, call a doctor. Severe pain could indicate a serious condition.

WARNING

Do not wait more than 30 minutes before calling a doctor if the pain continues. It could indicate appendicitis.

APPENDICITIS

● **Symptoms** Appendicitis tends to affect older children, particularly teenagers. The symptoms include pains in the middle of the abdomen, acute pain in the right lower abdomen, loss of appetite, raised temperature, nausea, vomiting, and diarrhea.
● **Medical help** Do not give food or drink to a casualty with appendicitis symptoms. Call a doctor at once.

VOMITING

Adults can usually cope with their own vomiting, but children will need assistance and care. Vomiting can cause children to panic, so reassurance is important. If vomiting occurs together with diarrhea, call a doctor – this may indicate a serious illness or cause dehydration.

TREATING VOMITING IN CHILDREN

1 Hold the casualty's head over a bowl and support her upper body with your free hand while she vomits. Constantly reassure her.

2 When she has finished vomiting, wipe her face and around her mouth with a sponge or cloth wrung out in tepid water.

3 Give her plenty of water to drink. This will replace lost fluids and remove any unpleasant taste. Encourage her to sip it slowly.

4 Encourage the casualty to rest on a sofa or in bed. If the vomiting persists, call a doctor. Do not give her milk to drink, since this may make the vomiting worse.

Let casualty vomit into a bowl

Hold casualty and continue to reassure her

WARNING

A baby or small child can easily become dehydrated. Give him or her sips of cool water – do not give milk. Call a doctor if vomiting persists.

EARACHE AND TOOTHACHE

Earaches may be caused by an infection, a cold, a boil in the ear canal, or a foreign body in the ear. Toothaches may be the result of a cavity, an abscess, or a mouth infection. Children may need a lot of attention while the pain of an earache or toothache is present.

TREATING TOOTHACHE

1 Give the casualty the recommended dose of acetaminophen to ease the pain and make him or her more comfortable. If the pain persists, call the dentist.

2 Lay the casualty down, or prop him or her up with pillows. Place a covered, warm hot-water bottle under the affected cheek. Give an adult a small measure of spirits to hold in the mouth – this eases the pain.

TREATING EARACHE

1 Encourage the casualty to lie down, or seat him or her in a propped up position. Give the recommended dose of acetaminophen to ease the pain and discomfort in the ear.

2 Cover a hot-water bottle, and give it to the casualty to lean the painful ear against. Advise the casualty to see a doctor. If you are worried about the casualty's condition, or if the earache does not subside, call a doctor.

> ## WARNING
> When treating a toothache, if the jaw is affected or swollen, call a doctor. When treating an earache, call a doctor if there is discharge from the ear, fever, or hearing loss.

TRADITIONAL TIP

Temporary filling
If you need a tooth filled but cannot get to a dentist immediately, soak a small piece of cotton in oil of cloves. Pack it into the cavity to relieve the discomfort.

TREATING A PRESSURE-CHANGE EARACHE

Clearing the ears
Blocked ears may occur on flights during takeoff and landing, or when traveling through tunnels, particularly in trains. Tell the casualty to make the ears "pop" by closing the mouth, pinching the nostrils, and blowing out hard through the nose. Yawning widely or sucking a candy will also help.

Ask casualty to pinch her nose and blow out

HICCUPS

Hiccups are contractions of the diaphragm against a partially closed windpipe. They occur unexpectedly and can be frightening for children, particularly if they will not go away. Contact a doctor for advice if the hiccups persist more than a few hours.

VARIOUS CURES FOR HICCUPS

● **Drinking water** To cure hiccups, try drinking water from the wrong side of a cup. This awkward task should change your breathing pattern and stop the hiccups.

● **Breath holding** Try holding your breath for as long as possible. Repeat until the hiccups have stopped and you can breathe properly.

● **Relaxation** It is best to stand or sit quietly while trying to cure hiccups – moving around may only make the hiccups worse.

Breathing exhaled air
Hold a paper bag over the mouth and nose and rebreathe your exhaled air for one minute. Never use a plastic bag.

INDEX

ACKNOWLEDGMENTS

AUTHOR'S ACKNOWLEDGMENTS
I would like to thank my husband Michael Taylor for his
unfailing patience and support while I have been writing this
book, and my son Damian and daughter Flavia for, over the
years, providing a fair number of the problems it aims to solve.

I would also like to thank my editor Victoria Sorzano for her
continued charm and calmness in the face of missed deadlines
and writer's block. Thanks, too, to art editor Jayne Carter and
her assistant Darren Hill, and to the management by
Stephanie Jackson and Nigel Duffield.

PUBLISHER'S ACKNOWLEDGMENTS
Dorling Kindersley would like to thank the following:

Prop loan Elizabeth David Cookshop, Covent Garden, for props
used in the Food & Drink chapter. Thanks also to Churches
Shoes and Hugo Boss at Moss Bros., Covent Garden.

Reference Rentokil Ltd. (for mildew reference).

Editorial and design Adèle Hayward and Lynn Parr for
editorial assistance; Chacasta Pritlove for data entry;
Chris Bernstein for the index.
Jackie Dollar and Jan Richter for design assistance.
Raúl López Cabello for DTP design and
Harvey De Roemer for DTP assistance.

ILLUSTRATIONS
Illustrators All illustrations by Kuo Kang Chen and
John Woodcock. Additional illustrations on pages 106–119
and 165–181 by David Ashby.

PHOTOGRAPHY
Photographer Andy Crawford.
Assistant Gary Ombler.
Additional photography Steve Gorton, Tim Ridley,
Colin Keates, Steve Shott, and Harry Taylor.

Hand models Linda Birungy, Lisa Broomhead,
Duncan Horastead, Helen Oyo, Victoria Sorzano,
and Nick Turpin.